# Collins
# French
Phrasebook
and Dictionary

French Phrasebook and Dictionary

Other languages in the
*Collins Phrasebook and Dictionary* series:
German, Greek, Italian, Japanese, Mandarin, Polish, Portuguese,
Spanish, Turkish.

HarperCollins Publishers
Westerhill Road, Bishopbriggs,
Glasgow G64 2QT

www.collinslanguage.com

First published 2004
This edition published 2008

Reprint 10 9 8 7 6 5

© HarperCollins Publishers 2004, 2008

ISBN 978-0-00-726453-7

Typeset by Davidson Pre-Press Graphics Ltd, Glasgow

Printed in Malaysia for Imago

Contents

3

Your *Collins French Phrasebook and Dictionary* is a handy, quick-reference guide that will help make the most of your stay abroad. Its clear layout will save valuable time when you need that crucial word or phrase. Download free all the essential words and phrases you need to get by from www.collinslanguage.com/talk60. These hour long audio files are ideal for practising listening comprehension and pronunciation. The main sections in this book are:

### Everyday France – photoguide
Packed full of photos, this section allows you to see all the practical visual information that will help with using cash machines, driving on motorways, reading signs, etc.

### Phrases
Practical topics are arranged thematically with an opening section, Key talk containing vital phrases that should stand you in good stead in most situations. Phrases are short, useful and each one has a pronunciation guide so that there is no problem saying them.

### Eating out
This section contains phrases for ordering food and drink (and special requirements) plus a photoguide showing different places to eat, menus and practical information to help choose the best options. The menu reader allows you to work out what to choose.

### Grammar
There is a short Grammar section explaining how the language works.

### Dictionary
And finally, the practical 5000-word English-French and French-English Dictionary means that you won't be stuck for words.

So, just flick through the pages to find the information you need and listen to the free audio download to improve your pronunciation.

## Useful websites

### Accommodation

www.europeanhostels.com
www.francehotelreservation.com
www.hotels-france.com
www.hotel-restaurant-fr.com

### Culture & Activities

www.chateaux-france.com
www.culture.fr (cultural events)
www.culture.gouv.fr (cultural info)
www.lesrestos.com (French restaur.)
www.louvre.fr
www.operabase.com
www.opera-de-paris.fr (Paris opera)
www.qualite-tourisme.gouv.fr
   (hotels and restaurants)
www.ski-nordic-france.com

### Currency Converter

www.x-rates.com

### Driving

www.autoroutes.fr
   (Traffic/road conditions)
www.bison-fute.equipement.gouv.fr
   (Traffic info)
www.drivingabroad.co.uk
www.parisrhinrhone.com
   (Motorway info)

### Facts

www.cia.gov/library/publications/
   the-world-factbook

### Foreign Office Advice

www.fco.gov.uk/travel
www.dfat.gov.au (Australia)
www.voyage.gc.ca (Canada)

### Health advice

www.dh.gov.uk/travellers
www.thetraveldoctor.com
www.smartraveller.gov.au (Australia)
www.phac-aspc.gc.ca (Canada)

### Internet Cafés

www.cybercafes.com

### Passport Office

www.ukpa.gov.uk
www.passports.gov.au (Australia)
www.pptc.gc.ca (Canada)

### Pets

www.defra.gov.uk/animalh/
   quarantine

### Sightseeing

www.cybevasion.com/france
   (Info on France)
www.franceguide.com
   (French Tourist Office)
www.handicap.gouv.fr
   (Info for disabled)
www.intermusees.com (Museums)
www.paris-tours-guides.com
www.paris.org (Paris site)
www.parismuseumpass.com

### Transport

www.aeroport.fr
www.batobus.com
   (Boat trips along Seine)
www.raileurope.com
www.sncf.com (French railways)

### Weather

www.bbc.co.uk/weather

We've tried to make the pronunciation under the phrases as clear as possible by breaking the words up with hyphens, but remember not to pause between syllables.

The consonants are not difficult, and are mostly pronounced as in English: **b**, **d**, **f**, **k**, **l**, **m**, **n**, **p**, **s**, **t**, **v**, **x** and **z**. The letter **h** is always silent, and **r** should be pronounced at the back of the throat in the well-known French way, although an English 'r' will be understood. When **c** comes before the vowels **e** or **i** it is pronounced like 's'; otherwise it is a hard 'k'. Likewise, **g** before **e** or **i** is 'zh' like 's' in 'pleasure', not hard 'g'. The letter **ç** is pronounced the same as 's'; **q** is always like 'k' in 'kick' (not the 'kw' sound in 'quick'); **ch** is 'sh'; **gn** is 'ny', something like the sound in 'onion'; and **w** is either 'v' or 'w'. Final consonants, especially **s** and **n**, are often silent, but sometimes not, for example when the following word begins with a vowel. Don't worry, just follow the pronunciation guide.

The sound spelt **ou** in French is something like 'oo' in English. To pronounce the sound written **u**, start by pronouncing 'ee' but pucker up and round your lips as if to say 'oo' – careful to keep your tongue in the 'ee' position! We use the symbol '<u>oo</u>' in the pronunciation guide. There are two **o** sounds in French; one is something like the 'o' in English 'hope' and one something like 'hop'. We've represented the first by 'oh' and the second by 'o' in the transcriptions. Meanwhile 'uh' represents both the rounded sounds of **peu** and **peur**, and also the sound (like 'a' in English 'ago' or 'sofa') found in **je** and **se** and the first syllables of **retard** and **demain**. Look out for the following letter combinations: **au** and **eau** are 'oh'; **oi** is 'wa'; and **ui** is something like 'wee'.

There are various 'nasalised' vowels in French. When you see a 'ñ' you should nasalise the vowel before it rather than pronouncing an **n**. For example '**mañ**' in the pronunciation guide represents 'm' plus the vowel in the well-known French words **fin** or **rien**, rather than the sounds in English 'man'. The others are '**uñ**' (as in **brun**) and '**oñ**', which we use to cover the similar vowel sounds in **dans** or **en** or **blanc** and **mon** or **blond**.

# Everyday photoguide

## Everyday France

**OUVERT 24H / 24H**

**Open 24 Hours** Small shops tend to close between 12 and 2pm, but stay open later till about 7pm.

**ENTREE ↓**

**Entrance** Look out for the words **entrée libre** which means 'free entry' (for museums, etc).

**sortie**

Exit **Sortie** is also used for exit on motorways.

**FERME**

Closed

Push | Pull

HORS SERVICE
machine en panne

**Out Of Order** If something is working, you will see the words **en service**. The words **en panne** mean 'broken down'.

*Horaires d'ouverture*

| MARDI | 9" - 12" |
| MERCREDI | 14"30 - 19" |
| JEUDI | |

**Opening Hours**

**CAISSE ↓**

**Pay Here** The word **caisse** actually means till or cash box.

*Hôtel de Ville*

**Town Hall** don't be fooled by the word **hôtel**.

*Musée*

Museum

Cash machines (ATMs) are known as **distributeurs de billets** and are widely available. You can carry out the transaction in English and it saves time queuing in banks to change money.

**Euro** Symbol for the euro. France is in the euro zone.

PRIX FOUS

**Price** Pronounced pree. The word stays the same in the plural **les prix**.

**Banque** (boñk). You will also see words such as **crédit** (**Crédit Agricole**) and **société** (**Société Générale**).

PIÈCES ACCEPTEES:

(0,10€) (0,20€) (0,50€) (1€)

Ne rend pas la monnaie

**Pièces acceptées** = coins accepted
**Ne rend pas la monnaie** = no change given.

The euro is the currency of France. It breaks down into 100 euro cents. Notes: 5, 10, 20, 50, 100, 200, 500. Coins: 1 and 2 euros, 1, 2, 5, 10, 20 and 50 cents. Although coins are officially **cents**, French people call them **centimes** (soñ-teem), a more familiar French term. Euro is pronounced un-roh. Euro notes are the same throughout Europe. The backs of coins carry different designs from each of the member European countries.

Tipping in France is not compulsory and should be simply an appreciation of good service. If you are dining in a restaurant, you might consider tipping the waiter 5–10% of the bill. In cafés it is customary to leave any loose change from the bill.

When friends or family meet up, they kiss each other on the cheeks (usually one on each cheek, but it depends on the region – 3 kisses in Paris, 4 in Normandy). It can be quite time consuming when 2 families meet up at the market in Normandy: 4 kisses to everyone, a quick chat, then 4 kisses again to say goodbye!

# GENDARMERIE

**Police** In small towns and villages you find **gendarmerie**, and in larger towns, **police**. You must report any crimes to them. The emergency no is **17**.

Forbidden = **interdit** or **défense de…**

The red lozenge sign of the **tabac**. An extremely useful place, often it sells cigarettes, stamps, envelopes, transport tickets and lottery tickets. You can also have a flutter on the horses. If it is just a shop it is open till 7pm. If a bar is attached, it is open till late.

**Tourist Information**
The tourist office is also known as the **Syndicat d'Initiative**.

A **Chambre d'Hôte** is a bed and breakfast.

**CHAMBRES DISPONIBLES**

Rooms Available

**A VENDRE**
IMMO - BOIS
10 Rue du 8 Mai 1945  CHAUFFAILLES
03 85.84.65.49
04 77.72.95.38 (Le Soir)

Most towns have a guide to the area. It is full of useful information such as emergency numbers for police, doctor, dentist, etc, as well as details of hotels, restaurants, shops, sporting activities, etc.

**A LOUER MEUBLES TOUT CONFORT**

À Louer = to rent

**For Sale** 'Sold' in French is **Vendu** (voñ-<u>doo</u>).

**Town Names** are displayed on signs as you enter the area – with a line through them as you leave.

**VACANCES**
DU
04 - 08 - 03
AU
19 - 08 - 03

**On Holiday** The main French holiday is the first half of August. Roads are particularly busy every Saturday when France is on the move. Real-time information about traffic on French roads is provided by **Bison Fûté** at **www.bison-fute.equipement.gouv.fr**

**Unpatrolled Beach** Beaches without lifeguards generally have few facilities. Look out for the flag; green means that there is no danger and the beach is patrolled, orange that swimming is dangerous and red that swimming is forbidden.

**Drinking Water**

## LOCATION

**For Hire** Different from the English word! It's pronounced loh-ka-syoñ.

**Postbox** These are yellow, like the French post office logo. Collection times are shown on the box.

**Bottlebank** Recycling banks for glass (**verre**), paper (**papiers**) and plastic (**plastique**) can be found everywhere.

*Piscine*

**Swimming Pool** Most French towns have a municipal pool.

**DAMES**

**MESSIEURS**

← WC    WC →

**Ladies and Gents** Ladies and men's toilets are generally shown with a pictogram. WC is pronounced vay say.

**Toilets** Many public toilets (especially in shopping centres) aren't free. Make sure you have some small change on you.

# Timetables

| Les jours | | Days |
|---|---|---|
| lundi | luñ-dee | Monday |
| mardi | mar-dee | Tuesday |
| mercredi | mer-kruh-dee | Wednesday |
| jeudi | zhuh-dee | Thursday |
| vendredi | voñ-druh-dee | Friday |
| samedi | sam-dee | Saturday |
| dimanche | dee-moñsh | Sunday |

In French, neither months nor days start with a capital letter as they do in English.

**Timetable**
**à partir du 2 mai**
= with effect from 2 May

**HORAIRES**
Samedi, Dimanche
et jours fériés

**Horaires** = timetable
**Samedi, Dimanche et jours fériés** = weekend and public holidays

| Les mois | | Months |
|---|---|---|
| janvier | zhoñv-yay | January |
| février | fev-ree-yay | February |
| mars | mars | March |
| avril | av-reel | April |
| mai | may | May |
| juin | zhwañ | June |
| juillet | zhwee-yay | July |
| août | oot | August |
| septembre | sept-oñb-ruh | September |
| octobre | ok-tob-ruh | October |
| novembre | nov-oñb-ruh | November |
| décembre | day-soñb-ruh | December |

**Bus Timetable**
normal service

Saturday (**samedi**) service and reduced service in school holidays

| Service normal |
| Service du samedi et service réduit en vacances |
| Service des dimanches et fêtes |
| Pas de service |
| Service été |

Sundays (**dimanches**) and holidays (**fêtes**) service

No service

Summer (**été**) service

# Tickets

**Carnet** A book of 10 tickets or multiple-journey ticket is called **un carnet** (uñ kar-nay). Train ticket = **un billet** (uñ bee-yay) and bus ticket = **un ticket** (un tee-kay). Museum or art gallery ticket = **une entrée** (oon on-tray), i.e. entrance fee.

**Ticket à Oblitérer** Bus tickets have to be validated in the machine at the front of the bus, which stamps it and slices off the corner. If you are catching a connection you have to validate the ticket a second time (slicing off the opposite corner).

**Carte** (kart) = pass. **Carte musée et monuments** or the **Paris Museum Pass**, is for museums and monuments (go to www.parismuseum-pass.com). Buying **The Paris Pass** gives you free entry to over 60 attractions for a 2, 4 or 6 day duration.

**Ticket Validating Machine** Train tickets must be validated (**composté**) in the machines before boarding or you risk a fine.

**Paris Visite** is a special travel pass that entitles you to unlimited travel on metro, buses, RER trains and SNCF Ile-de-France trains. On sale at all main metro and RER stations.

# Getting around

Trains au départ *Train departures • Treni in partenza* ▬▬ = Voie ⑤ à ㉓ / Platform ⑤ to ㉓

| Train | n° | Heure | Destination | Particularités | Voie |
|---|---|---|---|---|---|
| TGV | 9249 | 15h50 | MILANO-CENTRALE | Retard probable150mn | ▬ |
| TGV | 6119 | 15h20 | MARSEILLE-ST-CHARLES | 1ERE ET 2ENE CLASSE 🍴 | L |
| | 800011 | 15h22 | TRAIN DE SERVICE | 2ENE CLASSE | |
| TGV | 6231 | 15h24 | MONTPELLIER | 1ERE ET 2ENE CLASSE 🍴 | X |
| TGV | 6659 | 15h30 | LYON-PERRACHE | 1ERE ET 2ENE CLASSE 🍴 | ▬ |
| TGV | 9205 | 15h44 | ZURICH-HB | 1ERE ET 2ENE CLASSE 🍴 | ▬ |
| TGV | 9273 | 15h44 | LAUSANNE | 1ERE ET 2ENE CLASSE 🍴 | ▬ |
| CORAIL | 5907 | 15h47 | NEVERS | CORAIL INTERCITES | ▬ |
| TGV | 6121 | 15h50 | MARSEILLE-ST-CHARLES | 1ERE ET 2ENE CLASSE 🍴 | ▬ |
| TGV | 6161 | 15h53 | NICE-VILLE | 1ERE ET 2ENE CLASSE 🍴 | ▬ |
| | 891047 | 15h57 | LAROCHE-MIGENNES | 2ENE CLASSE | ▬ |
| TGV | 6623 | 16h00 | LYON-PERRACHE | ACCUEIL A L'EMBARQUEMENT | ▬ |

| Train | n° | Heure | Destination |
|---|---|---|---|
| | 132951 | 16h00 | MONTEREAU VIA MORET |
| | 132951 | 16h07 | MONTEREAU VIA HERICY |
| TGV | 6769 | 16h14 | BESANCON-VIOTTE |
| TGV | 6123 | 16h20 | MARSEILLE-ST-CHARLES |
| TGV | 6235 | 16h24 | BEZIERS |
| TGV | 5985 | 16h27 | CLERMONT-FERRAND |
| TGV | 6125 | 16h30 | LYON-PERRACHE |
| | 6687 | 16h30 | ST-ETIENNE-CHATEAUCR |
| TGV | 6920 | 16h34 | GRENOBLE |
| TGV | 891159 | 16h37 | LAROCHE-MIGENNES |
| | 151955 | 16h37 | MONTARGIS |
| | 6561 | 16h40 | GENEVE |

**Departure Board** Some useful terms: **retard** = delay, **TER** = local train, **TGV** is the fast train (must be booked), **1re et 2è cl** = 1st and 2nd class, **voie** = track the train is leaving from.

French railway.
Station = **la gare**
(la gar).

**Bus Station**

**Bus Stops** often have a timetable. Routes are usually numbered and colour-coded. Bus stop = **l'arrêt de bus** (la-ray duh boos). Remember to validate your ticket at the machine near the driver. It's better to take change with you as some drivers won't accept notes.

The symbol for the **Métro** is **M**. Lines are numbered. Connecting lines are **Correspondance**. Public transport is generally integrated and you can use tickets on bus, tram and metro.

 Green roads are major French routes (E = European, N = National). Motorways are signposted with **A** for **Auto-route**. The yellow D-roads (**départementale**) are what we would term

b- or secondary roads. However, these can be

 good roads with little traffic. Many French roads have a solid white central line. You should not over-take or cross this line. In towns, local destinations are signposted in white. Motorways are in blue.

French towns are well sign-posted.
**gare routière** = bus station
**la poste** = post office

If you don't see your destination signposted, follow the **autres directions** (other routes) or **toutes directions** (all routes). To get to the town centre, follow **centre ville**.

 Local amenities, such as shops and supermarkets are signposted.

Vieux Port
Les Plages
Vieille Ville

**Vieux Port** (vee-uh por) = old harbour
**les Plages** (lay plazh) = beaches
**Vieille Ville** (vee-ay veel) = old town

**Rue**
**Place**
Impasse

**Rue** roo = road/street
**Place** plass = square
**Impasse** = cul de sac

# Driving

No parking on pavement.

No parking anywhere along road.

Parking 3 minutes only.

**Give Way** Indicates a roundabout and reminds drivers to give way.

**Bis**

If main roads are busy, look out for **Bis** signs – these indicate alternative (and less busy) routes to main towns.

**RAPPEL**

**Reminder** restriction still in force.

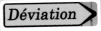

**Detour**

**Parking - Pay at Meter**

**Market** no parking Saturday 12–3.30pm.

**Priority Road**

RALENTIR

**Slow Down**

French speed limits

**50** – In built-up areas
**90** – on open roads
**130** – on motorways.
Remember speeds
are in kilometres per
hour. When it rains,
the speed limit is
reduced by 20 kph
on the motorway
and 10 kph on all
other roads.

**Road Toll** You pay a toll on most French motorways. Don't use the orange 't' lane. These are for drivers with a special device in their car, i.e. pre-paid and they can just drive through.

**Diesel** is spelt in a number of ways, **gazole**, **gaz oil** and **gasoil**. It is usually the black pump.

**Aire de...** Don't be fooled by word **aire**, it means area not air.

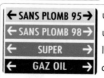

← SANS PLOMB 95→   unleaded 95 octane
← SANS PLOMB 98→   unleaded 98 octane
← SUPER →   leaded super
← GAZ OIL →   diesel

**Petrol** 95-octane petrol is usually fine for most cars, unless they have powerful engines or are towing a caravan.

# Shopping

**Supermarket** Welcomes you Monday to Saturday from 8.30am to 9pm. Late night shopping on Friday till 10pm. Sunday opening is not very common in France. Most small shops close between 12 and 2pm. **Intermarché** is one of the bigger supermarket chains. They are generally situated out of town and they have cheaper petrol for sale 24 hours a day.

**Baker's** A **baguette** (bag-et) = French stick, **une ficelle** (<u>oon</u> fee-sell) = thinner French stick, **un pain** (uñ pañ) = fat round country loaf. Some bakers specialise in different types of bread: **seigle** (say-gluh) – rye; **complet** (konñ-play) – wholemeal. Bakers often sell sandwiches and bake at least twice a day and some open Sunday mornings.

**Milk** Here, red is whole milk (**entier** oñt-yay), blue is semi-skimmed (**demi-écrémé** duh-mee ay-kray-may) and green is skimmed (**écréme** ay-kray-may).

**La Pièce** (la pyess) means per item, in this case per lettuce. Otherwise produce is generally sold by the weight.

## MARCHÉ

**Market** Larger towns have a daily market and smaller towns, a weekly market.

**Pharmacy** You can recognise a pharmacy by the green cross. If you are worried about a medical condition, ask the pharmacist for advice. They are medically trained and are often able to supply suitable medication. If you need over-the-counter medicine (for headaches, etc), buy them here. They aren't sold in supermarkets. If the address of the duty pharmacy is not posted, ask at the local police station. Details will also be printed in the local paper.

Pharmacie de Garde

M. ROUSSELON

48, rue Centrale - 71170 CHAUFFAILLES

Look out for offers – 3 for the price of 2.

**tranche** troñsh = slice, **gratuite** gra-tweet = free, **jambon cuit** hoñ-boñ kwee = cooked ham
Ham is sold by the slice.

Prices are generally written with a comma.

**Water** Look out for the colour-coding used for sparkling (**pétillante** pay-tee-yoñt) and still (**plate** plat). It can vary from brand to brand.

**Organic Eggs Biologique** (bee-o-loh-zheek) or **bio** means organic.

**Special Offer** Look out for these signs in the supermarkets.

# Keeping in touch

Some postboxes have 2 slots, one for local mail. **Autres destinations** = elsewhere.
**Heures des levées** = collection times.
**Jours ouvrables** = weekdays. **Samedi** = Sat.
**Bureau le plus proche** = nearest post office.

M. et Mme Bertillon
16, rue des Poissons
14290 Orbec
France

Addressing an envelope: house number, road, postcode, town and country.

## PRIORITAIRE
### PRIORITY

**Express Post**
For a slightly higher price you can get a quicker service.

**Phonecards** are sold in units: 50 (**cinquante unités** sañkoñt oo-nee-tay) or 120 (**cent vingt unités** soñ vañ oo-nee-tay).

Most pay phones take phone-cards and credit cards, not coins. **Décrochez** = lift handset.

You can access the internet from larger post offices. Smaller post offices will soon be replaced with '**points postes**'. Some of their services will be provided in local shops like the **boulanger** (bakers) or **épicier** (grocers).

| 01. | 44. | 79. | 04. | 57. |
|---|---|---|---|---|
| zéro un | quarante-quatre | soixante-dix-neuf | zéro quatre | cinquante-sept |

French phone numbers are given in 2 digits, sometimes written with full stops in between.

'at' = **arrobase** (ar-roh-baz)
www dot = **trois double-vay point** (trwa doo-bluh-vay pwañ)

# Key talk

## Key talk

• • • • • • • • • • • • • • • • • • • • • • • • • • • • • • • • • • • • • • • • • • •

• The French are quite formal, especially the older generation. Only use the familiar **tu** 'you' with children or someone you know as a friend. Otherwise stick with the more formal **vous**.
• **Salut** is more informal than **bonjour**.
• The easiest way to ask for something is to name it and add please, **s'il vous plaît**.

| yes | oui | wee |
| no | non | noñ |
| that's fine | très bien | tray byañ |
| don't mention it | de rien | duh ryañ |
| please | s'il vous plaît | seel voo play |
| thank you | merci | mehr-see |
| thanks very much | merci beaucoup | mehr-see boh-koo |
| hello/hi | bonjour/salut | boñ-zhoor/sa-loo |
| goodbye | au revoir | oh ruh-vwar |
| good evening | bonsoir | boñ-swar |
| goodnight | bonne nuit | bon nwee |
| excuse me | excusez-moi | eks-koo-zay mwa |
| sorry! | pardon! | par-doñ! |
| what? | comment? | ko-moñ? |
| | | |
| a... | un... ('le' words) | uñ... |
| a coffee | un café | uñ ka-fay |
| 2 coffees | deux cafés | duh ka-fay |
| a... | une... ('la' words) | oon... |
| a bottle | une bouteille | oon boo-tay |
| 2 bottles | deux bouteilles | duh boo-tay |

| a coffee and two beers, please | un café et deux bières, s'il vous plaît | uñ ka-fay ay duh byehr, seel voo play |
| I'd like... | je voudrais... | zhuh voo-dray... |
| we'd like... | nous voudrions... | noo voo-dree-oñ... |

• When someone offers you something, simply replying **merci** can be misleading. Depending on the tone of your voice, it can mean 'yes, please' or 'no, thank you'. Make sure you stress – **oui, merci** or **non, merci**. Otherwise you might not get that second helping you were offered!
• **Super** (<u>soo</u>-pehr) means 'great!'.

| I'd like an ice cream | je voudrais une glace |
| | zhuh voo-dray <u>oo</u>n glass |
| we'd like to visit Paris | nous voudrions visiter Paris |
| | noo voo-dree-oñ vee-zee-tay pa-ree |
| do you have...? | est-ce que vous avez...? [or simply] vous avez...? |
| | ess kuh vooz av-ay...? vooz av-ay...? |
| do you have any milk? | vous avez du lait? |
| | vooz av-ay d<u>oo</u> lay? |
| do you have stamps? | est-ce que vous avez des timbres? |
| | ess kuh vooz av-ay day tañb-ruh? |
| do you have a map? | vous avez une carte? |
| | vooz av-ay <u>oo</u>n kart? |
| do you have cheese? | est-ce que vous avez du fromage? |
| | ess kuh vooz av-ay d<u>oo</u> fro-mazh? |
| how much is it? | c'est combien? |
| | say koñ-byañ? |
| how much is...? | c'est combien...? |
| | say koñ-byañ...? |
| how much is the cheese? | c'est combien le fromage? |
| | say koñ-byañ luh fro-mazh? |
| how much is the ticket? | c'est combien le billet? |
| | say koñ-byañ luh bee-yay? |
| how much is a kilo? | c'est combien le kilo? |
| | say koñ-byañ luh kee-loh? |

| how much is each one? | c'est combien la pièce? |
|---|---|
| | say koñ-byañ la pyess? |
| where is...? | où est...? |
| | oo ay...? |
| where are...? | où sont...? |
| | oo soñ...? |

---

- In French you can turn a statement into a question, simply by changing your intonation and putting a question mark in your voice: **Vous avez une chambre?**
- You might find French spoken in rural areas more difficult to understand. The southern French accent is quite pronounced. People roll their 'r's and have a twang.

---

| where is the station? | où est la gare? |
|---|---|
| | oo ay la gar? |
| where are the toilets? | où sont les toilettes? |
| | oo soñ lay twa-let? |
| is there/are there...? | est-ce qu'il y a...? |
| | ess keel ee a...? |
| is there a restaurant? | est-ce qu'il y a un restaurant? |
| | ess keel ee a uñ res-toh-roñ? |
| where is there a chemist? | où est-ce qu'il y a une pharmacie? |
| | oo ess keel ee a <u>oo</u>n far-ma-see? |
| are there children? | est-ce qu'il y a des enfants? |
| | ess keel ee a dayz oñ-foñ? |
| is there a swimming pool? | est-ce qu'il y a une piscine? |
| | ess keel ee a <u>oo</u>n pee-seen? |
| there is no... | il n'y a pas de... |
| | eel nee a pa duh... |
| there is no hot water | il n'y a pas d'eau chaude |
| | eel nee a pa doh shohd |
| there are no towels | il n'y a pas de serviettes |
| | eel nee a pa de sehr-vyet |
| I need... | j'ai besoin de... |
| | zhay buhz-wañ duh... |

| | |
|---|---|
| I need a receipt | j'ai besoin d'un reçu |
| | zhay buhz-wañ duñ ruh-soo |
| I need to phone | j'ai besoin de téléphoner |
| | zhay buhz-wañ duh tay-lay-foh-nay |

- To catch someone's attention, begin your request with **pardon Monsieur/Madame** or **s'il vous plaît Monsieur/Madame**.
- A greeting you hear frequently is **à bientôt,** 'bye for now'.
- The word for 'welcome' is **bienvenue**.

| | |
|---|---|
| can I...? | est-ce que je peux...? |
| | ess kuh zhuh puh...? |
| can we...? | est-ce que nous pouvons...? |
| | ess kuh noo poo-voñ...? |
| can I pay? | est-ce que je peux payer? |
| | ess kuh zhuh puh pay-ay? |
| can we go in? | est-ce que nous pouvons entrer? |
| | ess kuh noo poo-voñ oñ-tray? |
| where can I...? | où est-ce que je peux...? |
| | oo ess kuh zhuh puh...? |
| where can I buy bread? | où est-ce que je peux acheter du pain? |
| | oo ess kuh zhuh puh ash-tay doo pañ? |
| when? | quand? |
| | koñ? |
| when (at what time)? | à quelle heure? |
| | a kel uhr? |
| when does the train leave? | quand part le train? |
| | koñ par luh trañ? |
| when does the film end? | à quelle heure finit le film? |
| | a kel uhr fee-nee luh feelm? |
| when does it open? | ça ouvre à quelle heure? |
| | sa oovr a kel uhr? |
| when does it close? | ça ferme à quelle heure? |
| | sa fehrm a kel uhr? |
| yesterday | hier |
| | yehr |

| | |
|---|---|
| today | **aujourd'hui** |
| | oh-zhoor-dwee |
| tomorrow | **demain** |
| | duh-mañ |
| this morning | **ce matin** |
| | suh ma-tañ |
| this afternoon | **cet après-midi** |
| | set ap-ray mee-dee |
| tonight | **ce soir** |
| | suh swar |
| is it open? | **est-ce que c'est ouvert?** |
| | ess kuh say oo-vehr? |
| is it closed? | **est-ce que c'est fermé?** |
| | ess kuh say fehr-may? |

- The equivalent to Mr is **Monsieur**, abbreviated to **M**.
- The equivalent to Mrs or Ms is **Madame**, abbreviated to **Mme**.
- The equivalent to Miss is **Mademoiselle**, abbreviated to **Mlle**.
- Use **bonjour Madame** and **bonjour Monsieur**, not just **bonjour**.

| | |
|---|---|
| hello | **bonjour monsieur/madame** |
| | boñ-zhoor muh-syuh/ma-dam |
| this is my husband/ my wife | **voici mon mari/ma femme** |
| | vwa-see moñ ma-ree/ma fam |
| how are you? | **comment ça va?** |
| | ko-mañ sa va? |
| fine, thanks, and you? | **très bien, merci, et vous?** |
| | tray byañ, mehr-see, ay voo? |
| my name is... | **je m'appelle...** |
| | zhuh ma-pel... |
| what is your name? | **comment vous appelez-vous?** |
| | ko-moñ vooz ap-lay voo? |
| I don't understand | **je ne comprends pas** |
| | zhuh nuh koñ-proñ pa |
| do you speak English? | **est-ce que vous parlez anglais?** |
| | ess kuh voo par-lay oñ-glay? |

| thank you very much for your kindness | merci beaucoup pour votre gentillesse |
| | mehr-see boh-koo poor votr zhoñ-tee-ess |
| the meal was delicious | le repas était délicieux |
| | luh ruh-pa ay-tay day-lees-yuh |
| I have enjoyed myself very much | je me suis très bien amusé(e) |
| | zhuh muh swee tray byañ a-moo-zay |
| we'd like to come back | nous voudrions revenir |
| | noo voo-dree-oñ ruh-vuh-neer |
| here is my address | voici mon adresse |
| | vwa-see mon ad-ress |

# Money

## Money

- France is in the eurozone. Euro is pronounced uh-roh; cent, known as **centime**, is pronounced soñ-teem.
- Banks are generally open Monday to Friday till about 5pm, closed Saturday pm and Sunday.
- Cash machines are widespread and you will be able to use English instructions. It avoids wasting time in bank queues.

| | |
|---|---|
| where can I change money? | **où est-ce que je peux changer de l'argent?** <br> oo ess kuh zhuh puh shoñ-zhay duh lar-zhoñ? |
| where is the bank? | **où est la banque?** <br> oo ay la boñk? |
| where is there a cash machine (ATM)? | **où est-ce qu'il y a un distributeur de billets?** <br> oo ess keel ee a uñ dees-tree-boo-tuhr duh bee-yay? |
| where is the bureau de change? | **où est le bureau de change?** <br> oo ay luh boo-roh duh shoñzh? |
| when does the bank open? | **la banque ouvre à quelle heure?** <br> la boñk oovr a kel uhr? |
| when does it close? | **elle ferme à quelle heure?** <br> el fehrm a kel uhr? |
| I want to cash these traveller's cheques | **je voudrais changer ces chèques de voyage** <br> zhuh voo-dray shoñ-zhay say shek duh vwa-yazh |
| what is the rate...? | **à combien est...?** <br> a koñ-byañ ay...? |
| for pounds/ for dollars | **la livre sterling/le dollar** <br> la leev-ruh stehr-leeng/luh do-lar |
| I want to change ... pounds/dollars | **je voudrais changer ... livres/dollars** <br> zhuh voo-dray shoñ-zhay ... leev-ruh/do-lar |

- Credit cards are widely accepted.
- You will be frequently asked 'key in your PIN', **veuillez composer/taper votre code** (vuh-yay koñ-poh-zay/ta-pay voh-truh kohd).
- Take your bank's phone number in case of problems.

| | |
|---|---|
| I'd like small notes | **je voudrais des petites coupures** |
| | zhuh voo-dray day puh-teet koo-poor |
| how much is it? | **c'est combien?** |
| | say koñ-byañ? |
| where do I pay? | **où est-ce qu'il faut payer?** |
| | oo ess keel foh pay-ay? |
| I want to pay | **je voudrais payer** |
| | zhuh voo-dray pay-ay |
| we want to pay separately | **nous voulons payer séparément** |
| | noo voo-loñ pay-ay say-pa-ray-moñ |
| can I pay by credit card? | **je peux payer avec ma carte de crédit?** |
| | zhuh puh pay-ay a-vek ma kart duh kray-dee? |
| how many euros is it? | **ça fait combien d'euros?** |
| | sa fay koñ-byañ duh-roh? |
| how much is that in pounds/dollars? | **ça fait combien en livres/dollars?** |
| | sa fay koñ-byañ oñ leev-ruh/do-lar? |
| do you accept traveller's cheques? | **vous acceptez les chèques de voyage?** |
| | vooz ak-sep-tay lay shek duh vwa-yazh? |
| how much is it...? | **c'est combien...?** |
| | say koñ-byañ...? |
| per person/ per night | **par personne/par nuit** |
| | par pehr-son/par nwee |
| per kilo | **le kilo** |
| | luh kee-loh |
| are service and VAT included? | **le service et la TVA sont compris?** |
| | luh sehr-veess ay la tay-vay-a soñ koñ-pree? |
| I need a receipt | **j'ai besoin d'un reçu** |
| | zhay buhz-wañ duñ ruh-soo |
| do you require a deposit? | **est-ce qu'il faut verser des arrhes?** |
| | ess keel foh vehr-say dayz ahr? |

# Getting around

## Airport

....................................................

- Signs are generally in French and English.
- Research the best way of getting to and from the airport using **www.aeroport.fr**. It will take you to any of France's 190 airports.
- A shuttle bus, **navette**, may be available. Ask at the local tourist office.

| | |
|---|---|
| to the airport, please | **à l'aéroport, s'il vous plaît**<br>a la-ehr-oh-por, seel voo play |
| how do I get into town? | **pour aller en ville, s'il vous plaît?**<br>poor al-ay oñ veel, seel voo play? |
| which bus goes to the town centre? | **quel bus va au centre-ville?**<br>kel <u>boos</u> va oh soñ-truh-veel? |
| how much is it...? | **c'est combien...?**<br>say koñ-byañ...? |
| to the town centre | **pour aller en ville**<br>poor al-ay oñ veel |
| to the airport | **pour aller à l'aéroport**<br>poor al-ay a la-ehr-o-por |
| where do I check in for...? | **où est l'enregistrement pour...?**<br>oo ay loñ-rezh-ees-truh-moñ poor...? |
| which gate is it for the flight to...? | **quelle est la porte d'embarquement pour le vol à destination de...?**<br>kel ay la port doñ-bar-kuh-moñ poor luh vol a des-tee-nass-yoñ duh...? |
| boarding will take place at gate number... | **l'embarquement a lieu porte numéro...**<br>loñ-bar-kuh-moñ a lyuh port <u>noo</u>-may-roh... |
| last call for passengers on flight... | **dernier appel pour les passagers du vol...**<br>dehrn-yay a-pel poor lay pa-sa-zhay <u>doo</u> vol... |

# Customs and passports

• EU citizens with nothing to declare can use the blue customs channels.
• There's no restriction by quantity or value on goods purchased by travellers in another EU country, provided they are for their own personal use (this covers gifts). Check guidelines on **www.ukpa.gov.uk**

| | |
|---|---|
| I have nothing to declare | **je n'ai rien à déclarer** |
| | zhuh nay ryañ a day-kla-ray |
| here is... | **voici...** |
| | vwa-see... |
| my passport | **mon passeport** |
| | moñ pass-por |
| do I have to pay duty on this? | **je dois payer des droits de douane sur ça?** |
| | zhuh dwa pay-ay day drwa duh dwan <u>soor</u> sa? |
| it's for my own personal use | **c'est pour mon usage personnel** |
| | say poor moñ <u>oo</u>z-azh pehr-son-el |
| we're going to... | **nous allons en à/au/à la...** |
| | nooz a-loñ oñ a/oh/ala... |
| here is the receipt | **voici le reçu** |
| | vwa-see luh ruh-<u>soo</u> |
| this is the baby's passport | **voici le passeport du bébé** |
| | vwa-see luh pass-pohr <u>doo</u> bay-bay |
| I'm... | **je suis...** |
| | zhuh swee... |
| British | **britannique** |
| | bree-ta-neek |
| Australian | **australien(ne)** *(m/f)* |
| | ohs-tral-yañ (-yen) |
| I bought them in France | **je les ai achetés en France** |
| | zhuh layz ay ash-tay oñ froñs |

# Asking the way – questions

- You can also ask the way simply by asking **le musée, s'il vous plaît**? Nothing more complicated is required.
- **Tabacs** sell maps. Get free transport maps at metro and bus stations.
- You can also attract someone's attention with **pardon, Monsieur/Madame**.

| | |
|---|---|
| excuse me, please | **excusez-moi, s'il vous plaît** |
| | eks-koo-zay-mwa, seel voo play |
| where is...? | **où est...?** |
| | oo ay...? |
| where is the nearest...? | **où est le/la ... le/la plus proche?** |
| | oo ay luh/la ... luh/la ploo prosh? |
| how do I get to...? | **pour aller à...?** |
| | poor al-ay a...? |
| is this the right way to...? | **c'est la bonne direction pour...?** |
| | say la bon dee-reks-yoñ poor...? |
| the... | **le/la...** |
| | luh/la... |
| is it far? | **c'est loin?** |
| | say lwañ? |
| can I walk there? | **on peut y aller à pied?** |
| | oñ puh ee al-ay a pyay? |
| is there a bus that goes there? | **il y a un bus pour y aller?** |
| | eel ee a uñ boos poor ee al-lay? |
| is there a bus that goes to...? | **il y a un bus pour aller à/au...?** |
| | eel ee a uñ boos poor al-ay a/oh...? |
| we're looking for... | **nous cherchons...** |
| | noo shehr-shoñ... |
| we're lost | **nous sommes perdus** |
| | noo som pehr-doo |
| can you show me on the map? | **pouvez-vous me montrer sur la carte?** |
| | poo-vay-voo muh moñ-tray soor la kart? |

# Asking the way – answers

• Key words are 'right' **droite** (drwat), 'left' **gauche** (gohsh), and 'straight on' **tout droit** (too drwa).
• Learn 'roundabout' **rond-point** (roñ-pwañ), 'crossroads' **carrefour** (kar-foor), 'square' **place** (plass), 'centre of town' **centre ville** (soñ-truh veel), 'exit' **sortie** (sor-tee) and 'follow' **suivre** (sweev-ruh).

| | |
|---|---|
| keep going straight ahead | **continuez tout droit** koñ-tee-n<u>oo</u>-ay too drwa |
| you have to turn round | **vous devez faire demi-tour** voo duh-vay fehr duh-mee-toor |
| turn... | **tournez...** toor-nay... |
| right | **à droite** a drwat |
| left | **à gauche** a gohsh |
| keep going... | **continuez...** koñ-tee-n<u>oo</u>-ay... |
| as far as... | **jusqu'à...** zh<u>oo</u>s-ka... |
| as far as the church | **jusqu'à l'église** zh<u>oo</u>s-ka lay-gleez |
| cross... | **traversez...** tra-ver-say... |
| the street | **la rue** la r<u>oo</u> |
| the square | **la place** la plass |
| take... | **prenez...** pruh-nay... |
| the first/second (road) on the right | **la première/deuxième à droite** la pruhm-yehr/duhz-yem a drwat |

| it's... | c'est... |
| | say... |
| after the traffic lights | après les feux |
| | a-pray lay fuh |
| the road to... | la direction de... |
| | la dee-rek-syon duh... |
| follow the signs for... | suivez les panneaux indicateurs en direction de... |
| | swee-vay lay pan-oh añ-dee-ka-tuhr oñ dee-rek-syoñ duh... |

# Bus

........................................................

• France has a national rail network so coach travel isn't as common as you might expect.
• Don't rely on a bus service in a small airport, the one bus scheduled may have left if there's a delay to your arrival.
• In cities, after the underground has stopped, you find night buses. In Paris the **Noctambus** runs from 1-5.30am at a flat rate.

| where is the bus station? | où est la gare routière? |
| | oo ay la gar root-yehr? |
| I want to go... | je voudrais aller... |
| | zhuh voo-dray al-ay... |
| to the station | à la gare |
| | a la gar |
| to the museum | au musée |
| | oh moo-zay |
| to the city centre | au centre-ville |
| | oh soñ-truh-veel |
| to Paris | à Paris |
| | a pa-ree |
| is there a bus that goes there? | est-ce qu'il y a un bus pour y aller? |
| | ess keel ee a uñ boos poor ee al-ay? |
| which bus do I take for...? | quel bus dois-je prendre pour aller à...? |
| | kel boos dwa-zhuh proñdr poor al-ay a...? |

| where do I get the bus to...? | **où est-ce qu'on prend le bus pour...?** |
| | oo ess koñ proñ luh b<u>oo</u>s poor...? |
| how often are the buses? | **les bus passent tous les combien?** |
| | lay b<u>oo</u>s pass too lay koñ-byañ? |
| can you tell me when to get off? | **pourriez-vous me dire quand descendre?** |
| | poo-ree-ay voo muh deer koñ day-soñdr? |

# Metro

• • • • • • • • • • • • • • • • • • • • • • • • • • • • • • • • • • • • • • • • • • • • • • • • • • • • • •

• A book of 10 tickets (**carnet** kar-nay) is cheaper than buying single tickets. They can be used by a group of people.
• The **Carte Paris Visite** (for 1, 2, 3, or 5 days) is great value.
• Children between 4 and 11 get a reduced rate. Under 4s are free.
• The Paris metro runs until 12.30 at night.

| where is the nearest metro station? | **où est la station de métro la plus proche?** |
| | oo ay la stass-yoñ duh may-troh la pl<u>oo</u> prosh? |
| ten tickets, please | **un carnet, s'il vous plaît** |
| | uñ kar-nay, seel voo play |
| do you have a metro map? | **est-ce que vous avez un plan du métro?** |
| | ess kuh vooz av-ay uñ ploñ d<u>oo</u> may-troh? |
| I want to go to... | **je voudrais aller à...** |
| | zhuh voo-dray al-ay a... |
| can I go by metro? | **est-ce que je peux y aller en métro?** |
| | ess kuh zhuh puh ee al-ay oñ may-troh? |
| do I have to change? | **est-ce qu'il y a un changement?** |
| | ess keel ee a añ shoñ-zuh-moñ? |
| where? | **où?** |
| | oo? |
| which line is it for...? | **c'est quelle ligne pour...?** |
| | say kel leen-yuh poor...? |
| which station is it for the Louvre? | **c'est quelle station pour le Louvre?** |
| | say kel stass-yoñ poor luh loovr? |
| what is the next stop? | **quel est le prochain arrêt?** |
| | kel ay luh pro-shañ ar-reh? |

# Train

................................................................

• France has a highly efficient national rail network. Check offers and info on **www.sncf.com**.
• The highspeed TGV train must be booked in advance.
• Get reductions for 2 (or more) travelling on return trips.
• Tickets must be validated before boarding the train. Machines are orange and at the beginning of the platform.

| | |
|---|---|
| where is the station? | **où est la gare?** |
| | oo ay la gar? |
| to the station, please | **à la gare, s'il vous plaît** |
| | a la gar, seel voo play |
| a single to... | **un aller simple pour...** |
| | uñ al-ay sañ-pluh poor... |
| 2 singles to... | **deux allers simples pour...** |
| | duh-zal-ay sañ-pluh poor... |
| a return to... | **un aller retour pour...** |
| | uñ al-ay ruh-toor poor... |
| 2 returns to... | **deux allers retours pour...** |
| | duh-zal-ay ruh-toor poor... |
| a child's return to... | **un aller retour enfant pour...** |
| | uñ al-ay ruh-toor oñ-foñ poor... |
| 1st class/2nd class | **première classe/seconde classe** |
| | pruhm-yehr klass/suh-goñd klass |
| do I have to pay a supplement? | **je dois payer un supplément?** |
| | zhuh dwa pay-ay uñ soop-lay-moñ? |
| is my pass valid on this train? | **est-ce que ma carte est valable dans ce train?** |
| | ess kuh ma kart ay va-labl doñ suh trañ? |
| I want to book... | **je voudrais réserver...** |
| | zhuh voo-dray ray-zehr-vay... |
| a seat | **une place** |
| | oon plass |
| a couchette | **une couchette** |
| | oon koo-shet |

- Children under 4 travel free.
- A Swiss Pass (for cheap travel on Swiss trains) must be bought before arriving in Switzerland.
- Check **www.raileurope.com** before your trip for different options (including the Swiss Pass).
- Remember to validate tickets for both outward and return trips.

| | |
|---|---|
| do you have a train timetable? | **est-ce que vous avez un horaire des trains?** |
| | ess kuh vooz av-ay un o-rehr day trañ? |
| do I need to change? | **est-ce qu'il y a un changement?** |
| | ess keel ee a añ shoñ-zuh-moñ? |
| where? | **où?** |
| | oo? |
| which platform does it leave from? | **il part de quel quai?** |
| | eel par duh kel kay? |
| does the train to ... leave from this platform? | **le train pour ... part de ce quai?** |
| | luh trañ poor ... par duh suh kay? |
| is this the train for...? | **c'est le train pour...?** |
| | say luh trañ poor...? |
| is this seat free? | **cette place est libre?** |
| | set plass ay leeb-ruh? |
| I think this is my seat | **je crois que c'est ma place** |
| | zhuh krwa kuh say ma plass |
| where is the left-luggage? | **où est la consigne?** |
| | oo ay la koñ-seen-yuh? |

# Taxi

....................................................

- Get a taxi from a taxi stand – generally located at stations. In smaller towns you may have to phone for one.
- The taxi is available if the roof sign is lit.
- In Paris there are 3 fare rates: A, B, and C. These correspond to inner and outer zones. Taxi zone maps can be found near to stands.

| | |
|---|---|
| to the airport, please | **à l'aéroport, s'il vous plaît** <br> a la-ehr-o-por, seel voo play |
| to the station, please | **à la gare, s'il vous plaît** <br> a la gar, seel voo play |
| to this address, please | **à cette adresse, s'il vous plaît** <br> a set a-dress, seel voo play |
| how much will it cost? | **combien ça coûtera?** <br> koñ-byañ sa koo-tra? |
| it's too much | **c'est trop** <br> say troh |
| how much is it to the town centre? | **combien ça coûte pour aller jusqu'au centre-ville?** <br> koñ-byañ sa koot poor al-ay zhoo-skoh soñ-truh-veel? |
| where can I get a taxi? | **où est-ce que je peux prendre un taxi?** <br> oo ess kuh zhuh puh proñdr uñ tak-see? |
| please order me a taxi | **pouvez-vous m'appeler un taxi** <br> poo-vay voo map-lay uñ tak-see |
| can I have a receipt? | **est-ce que je peux avoir un reçu?** <br> ess kuh zhuh puh av-war uñ ruh-soo? |
| I've nothing smaller | **je n'ai pas de monnaie** <br> zhuh nay pa duh mon-ay |
| keep the change | **gardez la monnaie** <br> gar-day la mon-ay |

# Boat

• • • • • • • • • • • • • • • • • • • • • • • • • • • • • • • • • • • • • • • • •

• In Paris take a **batobus** trip along the Seine with 8 sight-seeing stops. Visit their website **www.batobus.com**.
• Other French cities with rivers have adopted **bateaux-mouches**. Ask at the tourist offices about trips.
• In Switzerland the Swiss Pass includes travel on some lake steamers.

| | |
|---|---|
| 1 ticket/2 tickets | **un billet/deux billets**<br>uñ bee-yay/duh bee-yay |
| single | **un aller simple**<br>uñ al-ay sañpl |
| round trip | **un aller retour**<br>uñ al-ay ruh-toor |
| is there a tourist ticket? | **est-ce qu'il y a un billet touristique?**<br>ess keel ee a uñ bee-yay too-rees-teek? |
| are there any boat trips? | **est-ce qu'il y a des excursions en bateau?**<br>ess keel ee a dayz ek-skoors-yoñ oñ ba-toh? |
| how long is the trip? | **le voyage dure combien de temps?**<br>luh vwa-yazh door koñ-byañ duh toñ? |
| when is the next boat? | **à quelle heure part le prochain bateau?**<br>a kel uhr par luh pro-shañ ba-toh? |
| when does the boat leave? | **à quelle heure part le bateau?**<br>a kel uhr par luh ba-toh? |
| have you a timetable? | **vous avez un horaire?**<br>vooz av-ay un o-rehr? |
| can we eat on board? | **on peut manger sur le bateau?**<br>oñ puh moñ-zhay soor luh ba-toh? |
| can we hire a boat? | **on peut louer un bateau?**<br>oñ puh loo-ay uñ ba-toh? |

# Car

## Driving

• In wet weather the French motorway speed limit is reduced from 130 to 110kph and by 10kph on all other roads.
• Don't overtake or cross a solid white line. Speeding and other traffic offences are subject to on-the-spot fines.
• Flashing headlights don't mean 'you go', rather 'I'm coming through'. Take special care at pedestrian crossings.
• Flashing amber lights mean proceed with caution.

can I park here? **on peut se garer ici?**
oñ puh suh gar-ay ee-see?

where can I park? **où est-ce que je peux me garer?**
oo ess kuh zhuh puh muh ga-ray?

will there be a lot of traffic? **Est-ce qu'il y aura beaucoup de circulation?**
ess keel ee oh-ra boh-koo duh seer-ku-la-syoñ?

is there a car park? **est-ce qu'il y a un parking?**
ess keel ee a uñ par-keeng?

we're going to... **nous allons à...**
nooz a-loñ a...

what's the best route? **quelle est le meilleur itinéraire?**
kel ay luh me-yuhr ee-tee-nay-rehr?

how do I get onto the motorway? **pour rejoindre l'autoroute, s'il vous plaît?**
poor ruh-zhwañ-druh loh-toh-root, seel voo play?

which exit is it for...? **c'est quelle sortie pour...?**
say kel sor-tee poor...?

is the pass open? **est-ce que le col est ouvert?**
ess kuh luh kol ayt oo-vehr?

do I need snow chains? **est-ce qu'il faut des chaînes?**
ess keel foh day shen?

# Petrol

- Petrol is more expensive at motorway service stations.
- Big supermarkets sell petrol (24/7).

| | |
|---|---|
| is there a petrol station near here? | est-ce qu'il y a une station-service près d'ici? |
| | ess keel ee a oon stass-yoñ sehr-veess pray dee-see? |
| fill it up, please | le plein, s'il vous plaît |
| | luh plañ, seel voo play |
| ...euros of unleaded/ of diesel | ...euros de sans plomb/de gasoil |
| | ...uh-roh duh soñ ploñ/duh gaz-wal |
| pump number... | pompe numéro... |
| | poñp noo-may-roh... |
| that's my car | voilà ma voiture |
| | wwa-la ma vwa-toor |
| where is the air line/the water? | où se trouve le compresseur/l'eau? |
| | oo suh troov luh koñ-pre-suhr/loh? |
| please check... | s'il vous plaît, vérifiez... |
| | seel voo play vay-reef-yay... |
| the tyre pressure | la pression des pneus |
| | la press-yoñ day pnuh |
| the oil/the water | l'huile/l'eau |
| | lweel/loh |
| do you take credit cards? | vous acceptez les cartes de crédit? |
| | vooz ak-sep-tay lay kart duh kray-dee? |

# Problems/breakdown

- Motorways have emergency phones every 2km. The police will automatically know your location if you use them.
- You must carry a warning triangle, spare light bulbs, flash light and a first aid box. Fluorescent vests are compulsory in most of Europe.
- If you break down, put on hazard lights and place a warning triangle 30m behind the car.
- Dial 112 from mobiles for emergency services.

| my car has broken down | ma voiture est en panne |
| --- | --- |
| | ma vwa-toor ayt oñ pan |
| what do I do? | qu'est-ce que je dois faire? |
| | kes kuh zhuh dwa fehr? |
| I'm on my own (female) | je suis seule |
| | zhuh swee suhl |
| I have children in the car | j'ai des enfants dans la voiture |
| | zhay dayz oñ-foñ doñ la vwa-toor |
| where is the nearest garage? | où est le garage le plus proche? |
| | oo ay luh ga-razh luh ploo prosh? |
| is it serious? | c'est grave? |
| | say grav? |
| can you repair it? | est-ce que vous pouvez le réparer? |
| | ess kuh voo poo-vay luh re-pa-ray? |
| when will it be ready? | ça sera prêt quand? |
| | sa suh-ra pray koñ? |
| how much will it cost? | combien ça va coûter? |
| | koñ-byañ sa va koo-tay? |
| the car won't start | la voiture ne démarre pas |
| | la vwa-toor nuh day-mar pa |
| I have a flat tyre | j'ai un pneu crevé |
| | zhay uñ pnuh kruh-vay |
| the engine is overheating | le moteur surchauffe |
| | luh mo-tuhr soor-shohf |
| the battery is flat | la batterie est à plat |
| | la ba-tree ay ta pla |
| can you replace the windscreen? | pouvez-vous changer le pare-brise? |
| | poo-vay voo shoñzhay luh par-breez? |

# Car hire

. . . . . . . . . . . . . . . . . . . . . . . . . . . . . . . . . . . . . . . . . .

• To avoid problems, book a car in advance. If you buy your air ticket on the internet, many airlines offer car hire.
• Drivers under 25 may have to pay a young driver's supplement.
• Take care driving: in some French towns cars coming from the right have right of way. It usually isn't indicated.

| I would like to hire a car | je voudrais louer une voiture |
| for one day | zhuh voo-dray loo-ay oon vwa-toor |
| | pour un jour |
| for ... days | poor uñ zhoor |
| | pour ... jours |
| I would like... | poor ... zhoor |
| | je voudrais... |
| a large car | zhuh voo-dray... |
| | une grosse voiture |
| a small car | oon grohss vwa-toor |
| | une petite voiture |
| a cheaper car | oon puh-teet vwa-toor |
| | une voiture moins chère |
| an automatic | oon vwa-toor mwañ shehr |
| | une automatique |
| | oon oh-toh-ma-teek |
| is fully comprehensive insurance included? | est-ce que l'assurance tous-risques est comprise? |
| | ess kuh lass-oo-roñss too reesk ay koñ-preez? |
| what do we do if we break down? | qu'est-ce qu'il faut faire si la voiture tombe en panne? |
| | kess keel foh fehr see la vwa-toor toñb oñ pan? |
| when must I return the car by? | quand dois-je rapporter la voiture? |
| | koñ dwazh ra-por-tay la vwa-toor? |
| where do we leave the keys? | où est-ce qu'on laisse les clés? |
| | oo ess kon layss lay klay? |
| can you show me the controls? | pouvez-vous me montrer les commandes? |
| | poo-vay voo muh moñ-tray lay ko-moñd? |
| where are the documents? | où sont les papiers? |
| | oo soñ lay pap-yay? |
| do you have a baby seat? | vous avez un siège-auto? |
| | vooz av-ay uñ syezh oh-toh? |
| where is the nearest petrol station? | où est la station-service la plus proche? |
| | oo ay la stass-yoñ sehr-veess la ploo prosh? |

# Shopping

## Shopping – holiday

● The **tabac** sells a wide range of useful things: stamps, phonecards, transport and lottery tickets.
● Smaller shops close on Mondays.
● When buying presents, most shops will offer to giftwrap free of charge. There is also a gift-wrapping area in many supermarkets. Ask for **un paquet-cadeau** (uñ pa-kay ka-doh)

| | |
|---|---|
| do you sell...? | **est-ce que vous vendez...?** |
| | ess kuh voo voñ-day...? |
| stamps | **des timbres** |
| | day tañb-ruh |
| batteries for this camera | **des piles pour cet appareil** |
| | day peel poor set a-pa-ray |
| where can you buy...? | **où est-ce qu'on peut acheter...?** |
| | oo ess koñ puh ash-tay...? |
| stamps | **des timbres** |
| | day tañb-ruh |
| films | **des pellicules** |
| | day pe-lee-kool |
| 10 stamps | **dix timbres** |
| | dee tañbr |
| for postcards | **pour cartes postales** |
| | poor kart pos-tal |
| to US/Australia | **pour les Etats-Unis/l'Australie** |
| | poor layz eta-zoo-nee/lohss-tra-lee |
| to Britain | **pour la Grande-Bretagne** |
| | poor la groñd bruh-tan-yuh |

43

| a memory card | **une carte mémoire** |
| | <u>oo</u>n kart me-mwar |
| a colour film | **une pellicule couleur** |
| | <u>oo</u>n pe-lee-<u>kool</u> koo-luhr |
| a mini DVD for this video camera | **une cassette mini-DV pour ce caméscope** |
| | <u>oo</u>n ka-set mee-nee-day-vay poor suh ka-may-skop |
| I'm looking for a present | **je cherche un cadeau** |
| | zhuh shehrsh uñ ka-doh |
| have you anything cheaper? | **vous avez quelque chose de moins cher?** |
| | vooz av-ay kel-kuh shohz duh mwañ shehr? |
| it's a gift | **c'est un cadeau** |
| | sayt uñ ka-doh |
| could you wrap it up? | **vous pouvez me l'envelopper?** |
| | voo poo-vay muh loñv-lop-ay? |

# Shopping – clothes

• • • • • • • • • • • • • • • • • • • • • • • • • • • • • • • • • • •

- There are a number of good French department stores. Look out for **Printemps**, **Monoprix** and **Galeries Lafayette**.
- Taking things back to a shop after you've bought them is not as accepted as in the UK. You'll need a good reason for asking for a refund.
- Sunday is not a shopping day in France.

| can I try this on? | **est-ce que je peux l'essayer?** |
| | ess kuh zhuh puh lay-say-yay? |
| where are the changing rooms? | **où sont les cabines d'essayage?** |
| | oo soñ lay ka-been day-say-yazh? |
| it's too big | **c'est trop grand** |
| | say troh groñ |
| have you a smaller size? | **vous l'avez en plus petit?** |
| | voo lav-ay oñ <u>ploo</u> puh-tee? |
| it's too small | **c'est trop petit** |
| | say troh puh-tee |
| have you a larger size? | **vous l'avez en plus grand?** |
| | voo lav-ay oñ <u>ploo</u> groñ? |

| it's too expensive | **c'est trop cher** |
| | say troh shehr |
| I'm just looking | **je regarde seulement** |
| | zhuh ruh-gard suhl-moñ |
| I'll take this one | **je prends celui-ci** |
| | zhuh proñ suhl-wee-see |
| I take a size 6 shoe | **je fais du trente-neuf** |
| | zhuh fay <u>doo</u> troñt-nuhf |
| what shoe size are you? | **quelle pointure faites-vous?** |
| | kel pwañ-<u>toor</u> fet-voo? |
| does it fit? | **ça vous va?** |
| | sa voo va? |

# Shopping – food

• Smaller shops generally close between 12 and 2pm. Many shops are closed on Mondays.
• Supermarkets are generally open all day Monday-Saturday. Sunday opening is not as common as in the UK.
• Supermarkets include **Géant**, **Casino**, **Intermarché** and **Carrefour**.
• You will need euro coins to release the shopping trolley.

| where can I buy...? | **où est-ce que je peux acheter...?** |
| | oo ess kuh zhuh puh ash-tay...? |
| fruit | **des fruits** |
| | day frwee |
| bread | **du pain** |
| | <u>doo</u> pañ |
| milk | **du lait** |
| | <u>doo</u> lay |
| where is the supermarket? | **où est le supermarché?** |
| | oo ay luh <u>soo</u>-pehr-mar-shay? |
| where is the baker's? | **où est la boulangerie?** |
| | oo ay la boo-loñzh-ree? |
| where is the market? | **où est le marché?** |
| | oo ay luh mar-shay? |

| | |
|---|---|
| which day is the market? | **c'est quel jour, le marché?**<br>say kel zhoor luh mar-shay? |
| it's me next | **c'est à moi**<br>sayt a mwa |
| that's enough | **ça suffit**<br>sa soo-fee |
| a litre of... | **un litre de...**<br>uñ leetr duh... |
| milk | **lait**<br>lay |
| beer | **bière**<br>byehr |
| water | **eau**<br>oh |
| a bottle of... | **une bouteille de...**<br>oon boo-tay duh... |
| wine | **vin**<br>vañ |
| beer | **bière**<br>byehr |
| water | **eau**<br>oh |
| a can of... | **une canette de...**<br>oon ka-nayt duh... |
| coke | **coca**<br>ko-ka |
| beer | **bière**<br>byehr |
| tonic water | **tonic**<br>to-neek |
| a packet of... | **un paquet de...**<br>uñ pa-kay duh... |
| biscuits | **biscuits**<br>bee-skwee |
| sugar | **sucre**<br>sookr |

- Fruit and veg must usually be weighed and stickered before taking it to the check-out.
- Bread is generally bought daily from the local baker's, **boulangerie** (boo-loñzh-ree) where it is made and baked on the premises.
- Supermarkets don't sell medicine. For paracetamol, cough medicine, etc, you will need to go to a pharmacy.

| | |
|---|---|
| 100 grams of... | **cent grammes de...** |
| | soñ gram duh... |
| cheese | **fromage** |
| | fro-mazh |
| ham | **jambon** |
| | zhoñ-boñ |
| 250 grams of... | **250 grammes de...** |
| | duh soñ sañ-koñt gram duh... |
| butter | **beurre** |
| | buhr |
| mince | **viande hachée** |
| | vyoñd ash-ay |
| a kilo of... | **un kilo de...** |
| | uñ kee-loh duh... |
| potatoes | **pommes de terre** |
| | pom duh ter |
| apples | **pommes** |
| | pom |
| 8 slices of... | **huit tranches de...** |
| | wee troñsh duh... |
| ham | **jambon** |
| | joñ-boñ |
| salami | **saucisson** |
| | soh-see-soñ |
| a loaf of bread | **un pain** |
| | uñ pañ |
| a baguette | **une baguette** |
| | oon ba-get |
| six eggs | **six œufs** |
| | seez uh |

| | |
|---|---|
| a tin of... | **une boîte de...** |
| | <u>oo</u>n bwat duh... |
| tomatoes | **tomates** |
| | to-mat |
| peas | **petits pois** |
| | puh-tee pwa |
| a jar of... | **un pot de...** |
| | uñ poh duh... |
| jam | **confiture** |
| | koñ-fee-t<u>oo</u>r |
| honey | **miel** |
| | myel |
| can I help you? | **vous désirez?** |
| | voo day-zee-ray? |
| is that everything? | **ce sera tout?** |
| | suh suh-ra too? |
| would you like a bag? | **vous voulez un sac?** |
| | voo voo-lay uñ sak? |

# Daylife

## Sightseeing

• The French Tourist Office website is **www.franceguide.com**. Most French national museums close on Tuesday. Local museums generally close Monday.
• In Paris a **carte musées et monuments** (valid for 1, 3 or 5 days) lets you visit over 60 museums and monuments. See **www.intermusees.com**.

| | |
|---|---|
| where is the tourist office? | **où est le syndicat d'initiative?** <br> oo ay luh sañ-dee-ka dee-nees-ya-teev? |
| do you have a town guide? | **vous avez un plan de la ville?** <br> vooz av-ay uñ ploñ duh la veel? |
| we want to visit... | **nous voulons visiter...** <br> noo voo-loñ vee-zee-tay... |
| have you any leaflets? | **vous avez des brochures?** <br> vooz av-ay day bro-shoor? |
| is it open to the public? | **est-ce que c'est ouvert au public?** <br> ess kuh say oo-vehr oh poob-leek? |
| are there any sightseeing tours? | **est-ce qu'il y a des visites guidées?** <br> ess keel ee a day vee-zeet gee-day? |
| when does it leave? | **à quelle heure part-il?** <br> a kel uhr part-eel? |
| where does it leave from? | **il part d'où?** <br> eel par doo? |
| how much is it to get in? | **c'est combien l'entrée?** <br> say koñ-byañ loñ-tray? |
| are there reductions for...? | **est-ce qu'il y a des réductions pour...?** <br> ess keel ee a day ray-dooks-yoñ poor...? |
| students/children/ senior citizens | **les étudiants/les enfants/les seniors** <br> layz ay-tood-yoñ/layz oñ-foñ/lay sayñ-yor |

# Beach

- Many French beaches have lifeguards during the tourist season. These beaches will also generally have showers.
- Most French towns have a municipal pool. Males may be refused entry with swimming trunks that are like long baggy shorts (because they may have been worn as shorts rather than just for swimming).

| | |
|---|---|
| can you recommend a quiet beach? | **est-ce que vous connaissez une plage tranquille?** |
| | ess kuh voo ko-ness-ay <u>oo</u>n plazh troñ-keel? |
| is there a swimming pool? | **est-ce qu'il y a une piscine?** |
| | ess keel ee a <u>oo</u>n pee-seen? |
| can we swim in the river? | **on peut se baigner dans la rivière?** |
| | oñ puh suh be-nyay doñ la reev-yehr? |
| is the water clean? | **est-ce que l'eau est propre?** |
| | ess kuh loh ay propr? |
| is the water deep? | **est-ce que l'eau est profonde?** |
| | ess kuh loh ay pro-foñd? |
| is the water cold? | **est-ce que l'eau est froide?** |
| | ess kuh loh ay frwad? |
| is it dangerous? | **est-ce que c'est dangereux?** |
| | ess kuh say doñ-zhuh-ruh? |
| are there currents? | **est-ce qu'il y a des courants?** |
| | ess keel ee a day koo-roñ? |
| where can we...? | **où est-ce qu'on peut faire...?** |
| | oo ess koñ puh fehr...? |
| surf/scuba dive | **du surf/de la plongée** |
| | d<u>oo</u> suhrf/duh la ploñ-zhay |
| can we hire...? | **est-ce qu'on peut louer...?** |
| | ess koñ puh loo-ay...? |
| a sunshade/ a deck chair | **un parasol/un transat** |
| | uñ pa-ra-sol/uñ troñ-zat |
| a beach hut | **une cabine** |
| | <u>oo</u>n ka-been |

# Sport

................................................................

• Local tourist offices have details of sporting facilities. There is also information in the local regional magazine.
• **Location** (loh-ka-syoñ) means hire.
• **Initiation** (ee-nee-sya-syoñ) means beginners.
• French towns signpost their sporting facilities (**tennis, piscine, complexe sportif**).

| | |
|---|---|
| where can we...? | **où est-ce qu'on peut...?** |
| | oo ess koñ puh...? |
| play tennis/golf | **jouer au tennis/golf** |
| | zhway oh ten-ees/golf |
| go riding | **faire du cheval** |
| | fehr <u>doo</u> shuh-val |
| go fishing | **pêcher** |
| | pesh-ay |
| how much is it...? | **c'est combien...?** |
| | say koñ-byañ...? |
| per hour/per day | **l'heure/la journée** |
| | luhr/la zhoor-nay |
| can I hire...? | **je peux louer...?** |
| | zhuh puh loo-ay...? |
| rackets | **des raquettes** |
| | day ra-ket |
| golf clubs | **des clubs de golf** |
| | day kluhb duh golf |
| how do I book a court? | **comment dois-je faire pour réserver un court?** |
| | ko-moñ dwazh fehr poor ray-zehr-vay uñ koor? |
| do I need a fishing permit? | **est-ce qu'il faut avoir un permis de pêche?** |
| | ess keel foh av-war uñ per-mee duh pesh? |
| is there a football match? | **est-ce qu'il y a un match de football?** |
| | ess keel ee a uñ match duh foot-bol? |
| where is there a sports shop? | **où est-ce qu'il y a un magasin de sports?** |
| | oo ess keel ee a uñ ma-ga-zañ duh spor? |

# Skiing

• • • • • • • • • • • • • • • • • • • • • • • • • • • • • • • • • • • • • • • • •

- Take some passport-sized photos with you. It will save time when getting your ski pass organized.
- For cross-country skiing, visit **www.ski-nordic-france.com**.
- Check **www.snow-forecast.com** or **www.bbc.co.uk/ weather/sports/skiing**.
- A map of the ski runs is **une carte des pistes** (<u>oo</u>n kart day peest).

| | |
|---|---|
| I'd like to hire skis | **je voudrais louer des skis** |
| | zhuh voo-dray loo-ay day skee |
| how much is a pass? | **c'est combien le forfait?** |
| | say koñ-byañ luh for-fay? |
| I'm a beginner | **je suis débutant(e)** |
| | zhuh swee day-boo-toñ(t) |
| is there a map of the ski runs? | **il y a une carte des pistes?** |
| | eel ee a <u>oo</u>n kart day peest? |
| which is an easy run? | **laquelle de ces pistes est facile?** |
| | la-kel duh say peest ay fa-seel? |
| my skis are... | **mes skis sont...** |
| | may skee soñ... |
| too long/too short | **trop longs/trop courts** |
| | troh loñ/trooh koor |
| my bindings... | **mes fixations...** |
| | may feek-sass-yoñ... |
| are too loose | **ne sont pas assez serrées** |
| | nuh soñ pa as-ay ser-ay |
| are too tight | **sont trop serrées** |
| | soñ troh ser-ay |
| can you adjust my bindings? | **pourriez-vous régler mes fixations?** |
| | poo-ree-ay voo ray-glay may feek-sass-yoñ? |
| where can we go cross-country skiing? | **où est-ce qu'on peut faire du ski de fond?** |
| | oo ess koñ puh fehr <u>doo</u> skee duh foñ? |
| what is your shoe size? | **quelle pointure faites-vous?** |
| | kel pwañ-<u>too</u>r fet voo? |

# Nightlife

## Nightlife – popular

- Check what's on from posters, the tourist office or if you are in Paris from **Pariscope** (similar to London's Time Out). Many other towns and cities also have a small paper with lists of events.
- French people don't generally follow a 'round' system. They might just have one or two drinks when out.
- Try night-time rollerblading in Paris. Ask at the tourist office about **randonnée en roller**.

| | |
|---|---|
| what is there to do at night? | **qu'est-ce qu'on peut faire le soir?** <br> kess koñ puh fehr luh swar? |
| which is a good bar? | **vous connaissez un bon bar?** <br> voo ko-ness-ay uñ boñ bar? |
| which is a good night club? | **vous connaissez une bonne boîte?** <br> voo ko-ness-ay <u>oon</u> bon bwat? |
| where do local people go at night? | **où est-ce que les gens du coin vont le soir?** <br> oo ess kuh lay zhoñ <u>doo</u> kwañ voñ luh swar? |
| it isn't a dangerous area? | **ce n'est pas un quartier dangereux?** <br> suh nay paz uñ kart-yay doñ-zhuh-ruh? |
| are there any good concerts? | **est-ce qu'il y a de bons concerts?** <br> ess keel ee a duh boñ koñ-sehr? |
| do you want to dance? | **tu veux danser?** <br> <u>too</u> vuh doñ-say? |
| my name is... | **je m'appelle...** <br> zhuh ma-pel... |
| what's your name? | **comment t'appelles-tu?** <br> ko-moñ ta-pel <u>too</u>? |

# Nightlife – cultural

• Blockbuster films are usually dubbed, arty ones subtitled.
**VO** = original version (subtitled); **VF** = French version (dubbed).
• The first day of summer (21 June) is music night (**fête de la musique**). Anyone can go into the street and play music so you see lots of bands. Some towns organize big concerts. Everything is free.

| | |
|---|---|
| are there any local festivals? | **est-ce qu'il y a des festivals dans la région?** ess keel ee a day fes-tee-val doñ la rezh-yon? |
| we'd like to go... | **nous voudrions aller...** noo voo-dree-oñ al-ay... |
| to the theatre/ to the opera | **au théâtre/à l'opéra** oh tay-atr/a lo-pay-ra |
| to the cinema/ to a concert | **au cinéma/à un concert** oh see-nay-ma/a uñ koñ-sehr |
| what's on? | **quels sont les spectacles à l'affiche?** kel soñ lay spek-takl a la-feesh? |
| do I need to book? | **est-ce qu'il faut réserver?** ess keel foh ray-zehr-vay? |
| how much are tickets? | **c'est combien l'entrée?** say koñ-byañ loñ-tray? |
| when does the performance end? | **quand finit la représentation?** koñ fee-nee la ruh-pray-zoñ-tass-yoñ? |
| is there an interval? | **est-ce qu'il y a un entracte?** ess keel ee a uñ oñ-trakt? |
| 2 tickets... | **deux billets...** duh bee-yay... |
| for tonight | **pour ce soir** poor suh swar |
| for tomorrow night | **pour demain soir** poor duh-mañ swar |
| for 5th August | **pour le cinq août** poor luh sañk oot |

54

# Accommodation

## Hotel

- **Chambres d'hôte** (shoñ-bruh doht) is like bed and breakfast. If they provide evening meals, it is **table d'hôte**.
- Local tourist offices can help with local accommodation.
- Most French towns signpost hotels.
- No frills hotels such as **Formule 1** and **Étap Hôtel** offer good rates.

| | |
|---|---|
| have you a room for tonight? | **vous avez une chambre pour ce soir?** vooz av-ay <u>oo</u>n shoñb-ruh poor suh swar? |
| a single room | **une chambre pour une personne** <u>oo</u>n shoñ-bruh poor <u>oo</u>n pehr-son |
| a double room | **une chambre pour deux personnes** <u>oo</u>n shoñ-bruh poor duh pehr-son |
| a family room | **une famille** <u>oo</u>n fa-mee-yuh |
| with a bath | **avec bain** a-vek bañ |
| with a shower | **avec douche** a-vek doosh |
| how much is it per night? | **c'est combien par nuit?** say koñ-byañ par nwee? |
| is breakfast included? | **le petit déjeuner est compris?** luh puh-tee day-zhuh-nay ay koñ-pree? |
| I booked a room | **j'ai réservé une chambre** zhay ray-zehr-vay <u>oo</u>n shoñb-ruh |
| my name is... | **je m'appelle...** zhuh ma-pel... |
| I'd like to see the room | **je voudrais voir la chambre** zhuh voo-dray vwar la shoñb-ruh |

| | |
|---|---|
| are the rooms air-conditioned? | **les chambres sont climatisées?** |
| | lay shoñb-ruh soñ klee-ma-tee-zay? |
| have you anything less expensive? | **vous avez quelque chose de moins cher?** |
| | vooz av-ay kel-kuh shohz duh mwañ shehr? |
| can I leave this in the safe? | **je peux laisser cela dans le coffre?** |
| | zhuh puh less-ay suh-la doñ luh kof-ruh? |
| can I have my key, please | **ma clé, s'il vous plaît** |
| | ma klay, seel voo play |
| are there any messages for me? | **il y a des messages pour moi?** |
| | eel ee a day mess-azh poor mwa? |
| come in! | **entrez!** |
| | oñ-tray! |
| please come back later | **s'il vous plaît, revenez plus tard** |
| | seel voo play, ruh-vuh-nay ploo tar |
| I'd like breakfast in my room | **je voudrais le petit déjeuner dans ma chambre** |
| | zhuh voo-dray luh puh-tee day-zhuh-nay doñ ma shoñb-ruh |
| please bring... | **pouvez-vous m'apporter...** |
| | poo-vay voo ma-por-tay... |
| toilet paper | **du papier hygiénique** |
| | doo pap-yay ee-zhyen-eek |
| soap | **du savon** |
| | doo sa-voñ |
| clean towels | **des serviettes propres** |
| | day sehr-vyet propr |
| a glass | **un verre** |
| | uñ vehr |
| please clean... | **pouvez-vous nettoyer...** |
| | poo-vay voo ne-twa-yay... |
| my room | **ma chambre** |
| | ma shoñb-ruh |
| the bath | **la baignoire** |
| | la ben-war |
| please call me... | **pouvez-vous m'appeler...** |
| | poo-vay voo map-lay... |

| | |
|---|---|
| at 7 o'clock | **à sept heures** |
| | a set uhr |
| is there a laundry service? | **vous avez un service de blanchisserie?** |
| | vooz av-ay uñ sehr-veess duh bloñ-shees-ree? |
| I'm leaving tomorrow | **je pars demain** |
| | zhuh par duh-mañ |
| could you prepare the bill? | **pouvez-vous préparer la note?** |
| | poo-vay-voo pray-pa-ray la not? |

# Self-catering

......................................................

• Voltage in France and Switzerland is 220 with 2-pronged plugs. Take an adaptor for any electrical appliances you pack.
• Rubbish is collected from collection bins in the street and not from houses. Bins are easy to spot and emptied daily in towns.
• The word for neighbours is **les voisins** (lay vwah-zañ).

| | |
|---|---|
| which is the key for this door? | **quelle est la clé de cette porte?** |
| | kel ay la klay duh set port? |
| please show us how this works | **montrez-nous comment ça marche, s'il vous plaît** |
| | moñ-tray-noo ko-moñ sa marsh, seel voo play |
| how does ... work? | **comment fonctionne...?** |
| | ko-moñ foñks-yon...? |
| the cooker | **la cuisinière** |
| | la kwee-zeen-yehr |
| the heating | **le chauffage** |
| | luh shoh-fazh |
| the washing machine | **la machine à laver** |
| | la ma-sheen a lav-ay |
| the dryer | **le séchoir** |
| | luh saysh-war |
| who do I contact if there are any problems? | **qui faut-il contacter s'il y a un problème?** |
| | kee foht-eel koñ-tak-tay seel ee a uñ prob-lem? |

| we need extra... | **il nous faudrait encore des...** |
| | eel noo foh-dray oñ-kor day... |
| is there always hot water? | **il y a toujours de l'eau chaude?** |
| | eel ee a too-zhoor duh loh shohd? |
| cutlery | **couverts** |
| | koo-vehr |
| sheets | **draps** |
| | dra |
| the gas has run out | **il n'y a plus de gaz** |
| | eel nee a ploo duh gaz |
| what do I do? | **qu'est-ce qu'il faut faire?** |
| | kes keel foh fehr? |
| where are the fuses? | **où sont les fusibles?** |
| | oo soñ lay foo-zee-bluh? |
| where do I put the rubbish? | **où est-ce que je dois mettre la poubelle?** |
| | oo ess kuh zhuh dwa metr la poo-bel? |

# Camping and caravanning

. . . . . . . . . . . . . . . . . . . . . . . . . . . . . . . . . . . . . . . . . . . . . . . . . . .

- There is an additional charge for caravans on French motorways.
- Speed limits for cars towing caravans are lower than normal speed limits.
- In Switzerland it is 50kph in built-up areas and 80kph on other roads.

| we're looking for a campsite | **nous cherchons un camping** |
| | noo shehr-shoñ uñ koñ-peeng |
| have you a list of campsites? | **avez-vous un guide des campings?** |
| | av-ay-voo uñ geed day koñ-peeng? |
| where is the campsite? | **où est le camping?** |
| | oo ay luh koñ-peeng? |
| have you any vacancies? | **il vous reste des places?** |
| | eel voo rest day plass? |
| how much is it per night? | **c'est combien la nuit?** |
| | say koñ-byañ la nwee? |

| | |
|---|---|
| we'd like to stay for ... nights | **nous voudrions rester ... nuits**<br>noo voo-dree-oñ res-tay ... nwee |
| is the campsite near the beach? | **est-ce que le camping est près de la plage?**<br>ess kuh luh koñ-peeng ay pray duh la plazh? |
| can we have a more sheltered site? | **est-ce que nous pouvons avoir un emplacement plus abrité?**<br>ess kuh noo poo-voñ av-war un oñ-plass-moñ pl<u>oo</u>z ab-ree-tay? |
| this site is very muddy | **ce terrain est très boueux**<br>suh tay-rañ ay tray boo-uh |
| is there another site? | **il y a un autre emplacement?**<br>eel ee a un ohtr oñ-plass-moñ? |
| can we camp here? | **est-ce qu'on peut camper ici?**<br>ess koñ puh koñ-pay ee-see? |
| can we park our caravan here? | **est-ce que nous pouvons mettre notre caravane ici?**<br>ess kuh noo poo-voñ metr notr ka-ra-van ee-see? |

# Different travellers

## Children

- The word for child is **enfant** (oñ-foñ).
- Generally children under 4 travel free on public transport. Between 4 and 12, they pay half price.
- In France children under 10 must travel in the back of the car and be strapped in using an appropriate restraint or child seat.

| | |
|---|---|
| a child's ticket | **un billet tarif enfant**<br>uñ bee-yay ta-reef oñ-foñ |
| he/she is ...<br>years old | **il/elle a ... ans**<br>eel/el a ... oñ |
| is there a reduction<br>for children? | **est-ce qu'il y a une réduction pour les<br>enfants?**<br>ess keel ee a <u>oo</u>n ray-d<u>oo</u>ks-yoñ poor layz oñ-foñ? |
| do you have a<br>children's menu? | **est-ce que vous avez un menu enfant?**<br>ess kuh vooz av-ay uñ muh-n<u>oo</u> oñ-foñ? |
| do you have...? | **est-ce que vous avez...?**<br>ess kuh vooz av-ay...? |
| a high chair/a cot | **une chaise de bébé/un lit d'enfant**<br><u>oo</u>n shehz duh bay-bay/uñ lee doñ-foñ |
| what is there for<br>children to do? | **quelles sont les activités prévues pour<br>les enfants?**<br>kel soñ layz ak-tee-vee-tay pray-v<u>oo</u> poor layz oñ-foñ? |
| is there a playpark<br>near here? | **il y a une aire de jeux près d'ici?**<br>eel ee a <u>oo</u>n ehr duh zhuh pray dee-see? |
| is it safe for<br>children? | **c'est sans danger pour les enfants?**<br>say soñ doñ-zhay poor layz oñ-foñ? |
| he/she is 10 years<br>old | **il/elle a dix ans**<br>eel/el a deez oñ |

| do you have children? | **est-ce que vous avez des enfants?** |
| | ess kuh vooz av-ay dayz oñ-foñ? |
| I have two children | **j'ai deux enfants** |
| | zhay duhz oñ-foñ |

# Special needs

• • • • • • • • • • • • • • • • • • • • • • • • • • • • • • • • • • • • •

• Visit **www.handicap.gouv.fr** (French only) to check facilities for the disabled.
• The word for disabled is **handicapé** (oñ-dee-ka-pay). There are often discounts for entrance fees, etc.
• The French Tourist Office has a list of hotels which offer facilities.

| is it possible to visit ... with a wheelchair? | **est-ce qu'on peut visiter ... en fauteuil roulant?** |
| | ess koñ puh vee-zee-tay ... oñ foh-tuhy roo-loñ? |
| do you have toilets for the disabled? | **est-ce que vous avez des toilettes pour handicapés?** |
| | ess kuh vooz av-ay day twa-let poor oñ-dee-ka-pay? |
| I need a bedroom on the ground floor | **j'ai besoin d'une chambre au rez-de-chaussée** |
| | zhay buhz-wañ doon shoñbr oh ray duh shoh-say |
| is there a lift? | **est-ce qu'il y a un ascenseur?** |
| | ess keel ee a uñ ass-oñ-suhr? |
| where is the lift? | **où est l'ascenseur?** |
| | oo ay lass-oñ-suhr? |
| I can't walk far | **je ne peux pas aller très loin à pied** |
| | zhuh nuh puh paz al-ay tray lwañ a pyay |
| are there many steps? | **il y a beaucoup de marches?** |
| | eel ee a boh-koo duh marsh? |
| is there an entrance for wheelchairs? | **est-ce qu'il y a une entrée pour les fauteuils roulants?** |
| | ess keel ee a oon oñ-tray poor lay foh-tuhy roo-loñ? |
| can I travel on this train with a wheelchair? | **est-ce que je peux prendre ce train avec un fauteuil roulant?** |
| | ess kuh zhuh puh proñdr suh trañ a-vek uñ foh-tuhy roo-loñ? |

| is there a reduction for the disabled? | **est-ce qu'il y a une réduction pour les handicapés?** |
| | ess keel ee a <u>oon</u> ray-d<u>oo</u>ks-yoñ poor lay oñ-dee-kap-ay? |

# Exchange visitors

• • • • • • • • • • • • • • • • • • • • • • • • • • • • • • • • • • • • • • • • • •

• These phrases are intended for families hosting French-speaking visitors. We've used the familiar **tu** (rather than the formal **vous**) form.
• French people generally eat dinner about 7.30-8pm so visitors might not be used to eating early. Eating in front of the TV is almost unheard of in France!

| what would you like for breakfast? | **qu'est-ce que tu veux manger pour le petit déjeuner?** |
| | kess kuh <u>too</u> vuh moñ-zhay poor luh puh-tee day-zhuh-nay? |
| what would you like to eat/drink? | **qu'est-ce que tu veux manger/boire?** |
| | kess kuh <u>too</u> vuh moñ-zhay/bwar? |
| did you sleep well? | **tu as bien dormi?** |
| | <u>too</u> a byañ dor-mee? |
| would you like to take a shower? | **tu veux prendre une douche?** |
| | <u>too</u> vuh proñdr <u>oon</u> doosh? |
| what would you like to do today? | **qu'est-ce que tu veux faire aujourd'hui?** |
| | kess kuh <u>too</u> vuh fehr oh-zhoor-dwee? |
| do you want to go shopping? | **tu veux aller faire du shopping?** |
| | <u>too</u> vuh al-ay fehr d<u>oo</u> shop-eeng? |
| I will pick you up at... | **je passerai te prendre à...** |
| | zhuh pass-ray tuh proñd-ruh a... |
| did you enjoy yourself? | **est-ce que tu t'es bien amusé?** |
| | ess kuh <u>too</u> tay byan a-m<u>oo</u>-zay? |
| take care | **fais attention à toi** |
| | fay a-toñs-yon a twa |
| please be back by... | **tâche de rentrer avant...** |
| | tash duh roñ-tray a-voñ... |
| we'll be in bed when you get back | **nous serons au lit lorsque tu rentreras** |
| | noo suh-roñ oh lee lors-kuh <u>too</u> roñ-truh-ra |

- If invited to a French family for a meal, take chocolates or flowers, rather than wine. They will probably have chosen the wine to go with the food. You can also offer to bring one course of the meal: the dessert for example.
- Take care to use the more formal **vous** form until you are invited to **tutoyer** (use the informal **tu**), especially with older people.
- You can call someone by their first name even if you use '**vous**' with them; this will sound friendlier.

| | |
|---|---|
| I like... | **j'aime bien...** |
| | zhem byañ... |
| I don't like... | **je n'aime pas...** |
| | zhuh nem pa... |
| that was delicious | **c'était délicieux** |
| | say-tay day-lee-syuh |
| thank you very much | **merci beaucoup** |
| | mehr-see boh-koo |
| may I phone home? | **est-ce que je peux téléphoner chez moi?** |
| | ess kuh zhuh puh tay-lay-foh-nay shay mwa? |
| can you take me by car? | **est-ce que vous pouvez m'emmener en voiture?** |
| | ess kuh voo poo-vay monm-nay oñ vwa-<u>toor</u>? |
| can I borrow...? | **je peux emprunter...?** |
| | zhuh puh oñ-pruñ-tay...? |
| an iron/a hairdryer | **un fer à repasser/un sèche-cheveux** |
| | uñ fehr a ruh-pass-ay/uñ sesh-shuh-vuh |
| what time do I have to get up? | **à quelle heure faut-il que je me lève?** |
| | a kel uhr foht-eel kuh zhuh muh lev? |
| could you call me at...? | **pouvez-vous m'appeler à...?** |
| | poo-vay voo map-lay at...? |
| I'm leaving in a week | **je m'en vais dans une semaine** |
| | zhuh moñ vay doñz <u>oon</u> suh-men |
| thanks for everything | **merci pour tout** |
| | mehr-see poor too |
| I've had a great time | **j'ai passé des moments formidables** |
| | zhay pass-ay day mo-moñ for-mee-dabl |

# Difficulties

## Problems

• Always try to speak in French – however bad! And then ask if there is someone who does speak some English.
• Try to stay calm. Not understanding each other can often aggravate the situation.
• Try to be as polite as possible, using **monsieur** or **madame** and the polite **vous** form.

| | |
|---|---|
| can you help me? | **pouvez-vous m'aider?** |
| | poo-vay voo may-day? |
| I don't speak French | **je ne parle pas français** |
| | zhuh nuh parl pa froñ-say |
| do you speak English? | **parlez-vous anglais?** |
| | par-lay voo oñ-glay? |
| does anyone speak English? | **il y a quelqu'un qui parle anglais?** |
| | eel ee a kel-kuñ kee parl oñ-glay? |
| I'm lost | **je me suis perdu** |
| | zhuh muh swee pehr-doo |
| how do I get to...? | **pour aller à...?** |
| | poor al-ay a...? |
| I'm late | **je suis en retard** |
| | zhuh swee oñ ruh-tar |
| I need to get to... | **je dois aller à...** |
| | zhuh dwa al-ay a... |
| I've missed... | **j'ai manqué...** |
| | zhay moñ-kay... |
| my plane | **mon avion** |
| | mon av-yoñ |

| my connection | **ma correspondance** |
| | ma ko-res-poñ-doñs |
| I've lost... | **j'ai perdu...** |
| | zhay pehr-doo... |
| my money | **mon argent** |
| | mon ar-zhoñ |
| my passport | **mon passeport** |
| | moñ pass-por |
| my luggage has not arrived | **mes bagages ne sont pas arrivés** |
| | may ba-gazh nuh soñ paz a-ree-vay |
| I've left my bag in... | **j'ai laissé mon sac dans...** |
| | zhay less-ay moñ sak doñ... |
| I have no money | **je n'ai pas d'argent** |
| | zhuh nay pa dar-zhoñ |
| leave me alone! | **laissez-moi tranquille!** |
| | less-ay-mwa troñ-keel! |
| go away! | **allez-vous-en!** |
| | al-ay voo-zoñ! |

# Complaints

• You can try complaining, but you may find that French shop-keepers and waiters aren't as worried about customers' opinions as they are in the UK.
• You'll need a good reason for getting a refund from a shop. You might be surprised at the way people queue in France – it's usually every man (or woman) for himself!

| the light | **la lumière** |
| | la loom-yehr |
| the air conditioning | **la climatisation** |
| | la klee-ma-tee-zas-yoñ |
| ...doesn't work | **...ne marche pas** |
| | ...nuh marsh pa |
| the room is dirty | **la chambre est sale** |
| | la shoñb-ruh ay sal |

| | | |
|---|---|---|
| the bath is dirty | **la baignoire est sale** | |
| | la ben-war ay sal | |
| there is no... | **il n'y a pas...** | |
| | eel nee a pa... | |
| hot water | **d'eau chaude** | |
| | doh shohd | |
| toilet paper | **de papier hygiénique** | |
| | duh pap-yay ee-zhyen-eek | |
| it is too noisy | **il y a trop de bruit** | |
| | eel ee a troh duh brwee | |
| the room is too small | **la chambre est trop petite** | |
| | la shoñb-ruh ay troh puh-teet | |
| this isn't what I ordered | **ce n'est pas ce que j'ai commandé** | |
| | suh nay pa suh kuh zhay ko-moñ-day | |
| there is a mistake | **il y a une erreur** | |
| | eel ee a <u>oo</u>n e-ruhr | |
| I want to complain | **je veux faire une réclamation** | |
| | zhuh vuh fehr <u>oo</u>n ray-kla-mass-yoñ | |
| I want a refund | **je veux être remboursé** | |
| | zhuh vuh etr roñ-boor-say | |
| we've been waiting for a very long time | **nous attendons depuis très longtemps** | |
| | nooz a-toñ-doñ duh-pwee tray loñ-toñ | |
| this is broken | **c'est cassé** | |
| | say kass-ay | |
| can you repair it? | **pouvez-vous le réparer?** | |
| | poo-vay-voo luh ray-pa-ray? | |

# Emergencies

- Emergency numbers in France: Police – 17, Ambulance – 15, Fire brigade – 18.
- Dial 112 from a mobile for all emergency numbers. This is the EU emergency number.
- You find **Gendarmerie** in villages, **Police** in towns.
- If you've been robbed or attacked, go to the police station to report it and fill in a form. A copy is needed for insurance.

| | |
|---|---|
| help! | **au secours!** |
| | oh suh-koor! |
| can you help me? | **pouvez-vous m'aider?** |
| | poo-vay-voo may-day? |
| there's been an accident | **il y a eu un accident** |
| | eel ee a oo un ak-see-doñ |
| someone is injured | **il y a un blessé** |
| | eel ee a uñ bless-ay |
| call... | **appelez...** |
| | ap-lay... |
| the police | **la police** |
| | la po-leess |
| an ambulance | **une ambulance** |
| | oon oñ-boo-loñs |
| the fire brigade | **les pompiers** |
| | lay poñ-pyay |
| he was driving too fast | **il allait trop vite** |
| | eel al-ay troh veet |
| I need a report for my insurance | **il me faut un constat pour mon assurance** |
| | eel muh foh uñ koñ-sta poor mon ass-oo-roñss |
| I've been robbed | **on m'a volé** |
| | oñ ma vol-ay |
| I have no money | **je n'ai pas d'argent** |
| | zhuh nay pa dar-zhoñ |
| my car has been broken into | **ma voiture a été forcée** |
| | ma vwa-toor a ay-tay for-say |

| | |
|---|---|
| my car has been stolen | **on m'a volé ma voiture** |
| | oñ ma vol-ay ma vwa-t<u>oo</u>r |
| I've been attacked | **J'ai été agressé(e)** |
| | zhay ay-tay ag-ress-ay |
| I've been raped | **on m'a violée** |
| | oñ ma vyol-ay |
| that man keeps following me | **cet homme me suit** |
| | set om muh swee |
| how much is the fine? | **c'est combien l'amende?** |
| | say koñ-byañ lam-oñd? |
| can I pay at the police station? | **est-ce que je peux payer au commissariat de police?** |
| | ess kuh zhuh puh pay-ay oh ko-mee-sar-ya duh po-leess? |
| I would like to phone my embassy | **je voudrais appeler mon ambassade** |
| | zhuh voo-dray ap-lay mon oñ-ba-sad |
| where is the British/ Australian/ American/ Canadian consulate? | **où est le consulat britannique/ d'Australie/des Etats-Unis/du Canada?** |
| | oo ay luh koñ-<u>soo</u>-la bree-ta-neek/ doh-stra-lee/dayz-ay-ta-z<u>oo</u>-nee/ d<u>oo</u> ka-na-da? |
| I'm very sorry, officer | **je suis vraiment désolé(e), monsieur l'agent** |
| | zhuh swee vray-moñ day-zoh-lay, muh-syuh la-zhoñ |
| we're on our way | **nous arrivons** |
| | nooz a-ree-voñ |

# Health

## Health

....................................................

• EU citizens are entitled to free emergency care. You need a European Health Insurance Card. (available from **www.dh.gov.uk/travellers**).
• If you need a doctor, look for one who is **conventionné** (working within French national health). Get a signed statement of treatment to reclaim any expenses. This only applies for emergency treatment.

| | |
|---|---|
| have you something for...? | **avez-vous quelque chose contre...?** |
| | av-ay-voo kel-kuh shohz koñtr...? |
| flu | **la grippe** |
| | la greep |
| diarrhoea | **la diarrhée** |
| | la dee-ar-ay |
| is it safe to give to children? | **c'est sans danger pour les enfants?** |
| | say soñ doñ-zhay poor layz oñ-foñ? |
| I don't feel well | **je me sens mal** |
| | zhuh muh soñ mal |
| I need a doctor | **j'ai besoin d'un médecin** |
| | zhay buhz-wañ duñ mayd-sañ |
| my son/daughter is ill | **mon fils/ma fille est malade** |
| | moñ feess/ma fee ay ma-lad |
| he/she has a temperature | **il/elle a de la fièvre** |
| | eel/el a duh la fyehv-ruh |
| I'm taking these drugs | **je prends ces médicaments** |
| | zhuh proñ say may-dee-ka-moñ |
| I have high blood pressure | **j'ai de la tension** |
| | zhay duh la toñss-yoñ |
| I'm pregnant | **je suis enceinte** |
| | zhuh sweez oñ-sañt |

| | |
|---|---|
| I'm on the pill | **je prends la pilule** |
| | zhuh proñ la pee-<u>lool</u> |
| I'm allergic to penicillin | **je suis allergique à la pénicilline** |
| | zhuh sweez a-lehr-zheek a la pe-nee-see-leen |
| my blood group is... | **mon groupe sanguin est...** |
| | moñ groop soñ-gañ ay... |
| I'm breastfeeding | **j'allaite mon enfant** |
| | zha-let mon oñ-foñ |
| can I take this medicine? | **est-ce que je peux prendre ce médicament?** |
| | ess kuh zhuh puh proñd-ruh suh may-dee-ka-moñ? |
| will he/she have to go to hospital? | **est-ce qu'il/qu'elle devra aller à l'hôpital?** |
| | ess keel/kel duhv-ra al-ay a lop-ee-tal? |
| I need to go to casualty | **je dois aller aux urgences** |
| | zhuh dwa al-ay ohz <u>oor</u>-zhoñss |
| where is the hospital? | **où est l'hôpital?** |
| | oo ay lop-ee-tal? |
| when are visiting hours? | **quelles sont les heures de visite?** |
| | kel soñ layz uhr duh vee-zeet? |
| which ward? | **quel service?** |
| | kel sehr-veess? |
| I need to see a dentist | **j'ai besoin de voir un dentiste** |
| | zhay buhz-woñ duh vwar uñ doñ-teest |
| I have toothache | **j'ai mal aux dents** |
| | zhay mal oh doñ |
| the filling has come out | **le plombage est parti** |
| | luh ploñ-bazh ay par-tee |
| it hurts | **ça me fait mal** |
| | sa muh fay mal |
| my dentures are broken | **mon dentier est cassé** |
| | moñ doñt-yay ay kass-ay |
| can you repair them? | **vous pouvez le réparer?** |
| | voo poo-vay luh ray-par-ay? |
| I have an abscess | **j'ai un abcès** |
| | zhay un ab-seh |
| can you write me a prescription? | **pouvez-vous me faire une ordonnance?** |
| | poo-vay voo muh fehr <u>oon</u> or-donn-oñs? |

# Business

## Business

• Office hours in France are generally 9am to 12pm and 1.30 to 5pm. Long lunches rather than formal meetings might be the best way of finding out about a French business.
• If a French bank holiday falls on a Thursday, Friday also becomes a holiday, making it into a long weekend.

| | |
|---|---|
| where can I plug in my laptop? | **où est-ce que je peux brancher mon (ordinateur) portable?** |
| | oo ess kuh zhuh puh broñ-shay moñ (ohr-dee-na-tuhr) por-tabl? |
| what is your website address? | **quelle est l'adresse de votre site?** |
| | kel ay la-dress duh votr seet? |
| I'm... | **je suis...** |
| | zhuh swee... |
| here's my card | **voici ma carte de visite** |
| | vwa-see ma kart duh vee-zeet |
| I'm from Jones Ltd | **je suis de la compagnie Jones** |
| | zhuh swee duh la koñ-pan-yee Jones |
| I'd like to arrange a meeting with Mr/Ms... | **j'aimerais arranger une entrevue avec Monsieur/Madame...** |
| | zhay-muh-ray a-roñ-zhay oon oñ-truh-voo a-vek muh-syuh/ma-dam... |
| on 4 May at 11 o'clock | **pour le quatre mai à onze heures** |
| | poor luh kat-ruh may a oñz uhr |
| can we meet at a restaurant? | **est-ce que nous pouvons nous rencontrer dans un restaurant?** |
| | ess kuh noo poo-voñ noo roñ-koñ-tray doñz uñ res-toh-roñ? |

| | |
|---|---|
| I will confirm by e-mail | je confirmerai par e-mail |
| | zhuh koñ-feer-muh-ray par ee-mehl |
| I'm staying at Hotel... | je suis à l'Hôtel... |
| | zhuh swee a loh-tel... |
| how do I get to your office? | comment se rend-on à votre bureau? |
| | ko-moñ suh roñ-toñ a votr boo-roh? |
| here is some information about my company | voici de la documentation concernant ma compagnie |
| | vwa-see duh la do-koo-moñ-tass-yoñ koñ-sehr-noñ ma koñ-pan-yee |
| I have an appointment with... | j'ai rendez-vous avec... |
| | zhay roñ-day-voo a-vek... |
| at ... o'clock | à ... heures |
| | a ... uhr |
| I'm delighted to meet you | je suis enchanté de faire votre connaissance |
| | zhuh sweez oñ-shoñ-tay duh fehr votr ko-nay-soñs |
| my French isn't very good | mon français n'est pas très bon |
| | moñ froñ-say nay pa tray boñ |
| I need an interpreter | j'ai besoin d'un interprète |
| | zhay buhz-wañ dun añ-tehr-pret |
| what is the name of the managing director? | comment s'appelle le directeur? |
| | ko-moñ sa-pel luh dee-rek-tuhr? |
| I would like some information about the company | je voudrais des renseignements sur l'entreprise |
| | zhuh voo-dray day roñ-sen-yuh-moñ soor loñ-truh-preez |
| do you have a press office? | est-ce que vous avez un service de presse? |
| | ess kuh vooz av-ay uñ sehr-veess duh press? |
| can you photocopy this for me? | pouvez-vous me photocopier ça? |
| | poo-vay voo muh fo-to-kop-yay sa? |
| is there a business centre? | est-ce qu'il y a un service de secrétariat? |
| | ess keel ee a uñ sehr-veess duh suh-kray-ta-ree-a? |
| do you have an appointment? | est-ce que vous avez rendez-vous? |
| | ess kuh vooz a-vay roñ-day-voo? |

# Phoning

• International dialling codes: UK 0044; USA/Canada 001; Australia 0061.
• Cheap rates are from 7pm to 8am Monday-Friday, all day Saturday/Sunday and hols.
• Most phone boxes don't take coins, just cards.
• You can buy phonecards at 50 or 120 units.
• All French phone numbers include the area code. Leave out the first zero if you are phoning to France from abroad.

| | |
|---|---|
| a phonecard | **une télécarte** |
| | <u>oo</u>n tay-lay-kart |
| I want to make a phone call | **je voudrais téléphoner** |
| | zhuh voo-dray tay-lay-foh-nay |
| I wish to make a reverse charge call | **je voudrais téléphoner en PCV** |
| | zhuh voo-dray tay-lay-foh-nay oñ pay-say-vay |
| can I speak to...? | **je peux parler à...?** |
| | zhuh puh par-lay a...? |
| this is... | **c'est...** |
| | say... |
| Monsieur Citron please | **Monsieur Citron s'il vous plaît** |
| | muh-syuh see-troñ seel voo play |
| I'll call back later | **je vais rappeler plus tard** |
| | zhuh vay rap-lay pl<u>oo</u> tar |
| can you give me and outside line, please? | **est-ce que vous pouvez me passer une ligne extérieure s'il vous plaît?** |
| | ess kuh voo poo-vay muh pas-say <u>oo</u>n lee-nyuh eks-tayr-yuhr seel-voo-play? |
| hello? | **allô?** |
| | a-loh? |
| who is calling? | **c'est de la part de qui?** |
| | say duh la par duh kee? |
| it's engaged | **c'est occupé** |
| | say o-k<u>oo</u>-pay |

| | |
|---|---|
| do you have a mobile? | **vous avez un portable?** |
| | vooz a-vay uñ por-tab-luh? |
| my mobile number is... | **mon numéro de mon portable est le...** |
| | moñ noo-may-ro duh por-tab-luh ay luh... |
| I'll text you | **je t'enverrai un SMS** |
| | zuh toñ-vay-ray uñ ess-em-ess |
| can you text me? | **tu peux m'envoyer un SMS?** |
| | too puh moñ-vwa-je uñ ess-em-ess? |

# E-mail/fax

---

- Internet cafés are on the increase. Visit **www.cybercafes.com**. www. is **trois w point** (trwa doob-luh vay pwañ).
- The French for @ is **arrobase** (a-roh-baz).
- The ending for French e-addresses is **.fr**
- **Mél** on a form is for e-mail address (like **Tél** for phone number).

| | |
|---|---|
| I want to send an e-mail | **je voudrais envoyer un e-mail** |
| | zhuh voo-dray oñ-vwa-yay uñ ee-mehl |
| what's your e-mail address? | **quelle est votre addresse e-mail?** |
| | kel ay votr a-dress ee-mehl? |
| my e-mail address is... | **mon adresse e-mail est...** |
| | moñ a-dress ee-mehl ay... |
| caz.smith@ anycompany.co.uk | **caz point smith arrobase anycompany point co point uk** |
| | caz pwañ smith a-roh-baz anycompany pwañ say oh pwañ oo ka |
| did you get my e-mail? | **est-ce que vous avez reçu mon e-mail?** |
| | ess kuh vooz av-ay ruh-soo mon ee-mehl? |
| I want to send a fax | **je voudrais envoyer un fax** |
| | zhuh voo-dray oñ-vwa-yay uñ faks |
| do you have a fax? | **vous avez un fax?** |
| | vooz av-ay uñ faks? |
| what's your fax number? | **quel est votre numéro de fax?** |
| | kel ay votr noo-may-ro duh faks? |

| did you get my fax? | **vous avez reçu mon fax?** |
| | vooz av-ay ruh-<u>soo</u> moñ faks? |
| how do you spell it? | **comment est-ce que ça s'écrit?** |
| | koh-moñ ess kuh sa seh-kree? |
| all one word? | **en un seul mot?** |
| | oñ uñ suhl moh? |
| all lower case | **tout en minuscules** |
| (small letters) | too toñ mee-n<u>oo</u>s-kul |

# Internet/cybercafé

• Broadband is widely available in France. Internet cafés in larger towns and cities often open late (10pm, sometimes 2am) and offer a wide range of services. Prices range between 2 and 4 euros per half hour but there are special deals (**un forfait**) for users who need more time.

• If you take your laptop (**le portable**) with you, remember the mains voltage is 230V so make sure you have the right adaptor. Look for 'hotspots' – places where you can connect to a wireless network. Many hotels, cafés, restaurants and railway stations provide this service (sometimes free of charge).

• Internet access in public libraries and universities is usually restricted to research purposes.

• French website addresses end with **.fr** (pwã ayf-ayr) or **.gouv.fr** (pwã goov pwã ayf-ayr) for governmental websites.

| I'd like to use the internet | **je voudrais utiliser internet** |
| | zuh voo-dray <u>oo</u>-tee-lee-zay ã-tehr-nayt |
| I want to check my email | **je voudrais relever mes e-mails** |
| | zhuh voo-dray ruh-luh-vay may zee-mayl |
| how much is it... for 15 minutes/ for one hour/to print something out? | **c'est combien... pour un quart d'heure/ pour une heure/pour imprimer quelque chose?** |
| | say kon-byañ... poor uñ kar duhr/poor <u>oo</u>n uhr/ poor añ-pree-may kel-kuh shoz? |

| | |
|---|---|
| I'd like to put these photos onto CD | j'aimerais mettre ces photos sur CD |
| | zhem-ray met-ruh say foh-toh soor say-day |
| can you print it out? | est-ce que vous pourriez l'imprimer? |
| | ess kuh voo poo-ree-ay lañ-pree-may? |
| where can I buy a memory stick? | où est-ce que je peux acheter uné carte mémoire? |
| | oo ess kuh zhuh puh ash-tay oon kart may-mwhar? |
| can you help me please? | est-ce que vous pouvez m'aider s'il vous plaît? |
| | ess kuh voo poo-vay may-day seel voo play? |
| it doesn't work | ça ne marche pas |
| | sa nuh marsh pa |
| this computer has crashed | cet ordinateur a planté |
| | set or-dee-na-tuhr a ploñ-tay |

# Practical info

## Numbers

........................................................

| | | |
|---|---|---|
| 0 | zéro | zay-ro |
| 1 | un | uñ |
| 2 | deux | duh |
| 3 | trois | trwa |
| 4 | quatre | kat-ruh |
| 5 | cinq | sañk |
| 6 | six | seess |
| 7 | sept | set |
| 8 | huit | weet |
| 9 | neuf | nuhf |
| 10 | dix | deess |
| 11 | onze | oñz |
| 12 | douze | dooz |
| 13 | treize | trez |
| 14 | quatorze | ka-torz |
| 15 | quinze | kañz |
| 16 | seize | sez |
| 17 | dix-sept | dees-set |
| 18 | dix-huit | deez-weet |
| 19 | dix-neuf | deez-nuhf |
| 20 | vingt | vañ |
| 21 | vingt et un | vañt-ay-uñ |
| 22 | vingt-deux | vañ-duh |
| 30 | trente | troñt |
| 40 | quarante | ka-roñt |
| 50 | cinquante | sañ-koñt |
| 60 | soixante | swa-soñt |
| 70 | soixante-dix | swa-soñt-deess |

| 80 | quatre-vingts | kat-ruh-vañ |
| 90 | quatre-vingt-dix | kat-ruh-vañ-deess |
| 100 | cent | soñ |
| 110 | cent dix | soñ deess |
| 200 | deux cents | duh soñ |
| 250 | deux cents cinquante | duh soñ sañ-koñt |
| 500 | cinq cents | sañ soñ |
| 1,000 | mille | meel |
| 1,000,000 | un million | uñ meel-yoñ |

| 1st | premier | pruhm-yay |
| 2nd | deuxième | duhz-yem |
| 3rd | troisième | trwaz-yem |
| 4th | quatrième | katree-yem |
| 5th | cinquième | sañk-yem |
| 6th | sixième | seez-yem |
| 7th | septième | set-yem |
| 8th | huitième | weet-yem |
| 9th | neuvième | nuhv-yem |
| 10th | dixième | deez-yem |

# Days and months

| Monday | lundi | luñ-dee |
| Tuesday | mardi | mar-dee |
| Wednesday | mercredi | mer-kruh-dee |
| Thursday | jeudi | zhuh-dee |
| Friday | vendredi | voñ-druh-dee |
| Saturday | samedi | sam-dee |
| Sunday | dimanche | dee-moñsh |

| January | janvier | zhoñv-yay |
| February | février | fayv-ree-ay |
| March | mars | mars |
| April | avril | av-reel |
| May | mai | may |

| June | juin | zhwañ |
| July | juillet | zhwee-yay |
| August | août | oot |
| September | septembre | sep-toñ-bruh |
| October | octobre | ok-toh-bruh |
| November | novembre | noh-voñ-bruh |
| December | décembre | day-soñ-bruh |

| what's the date? | quelle est la date d'aujourd'hui? |
| | kel ay la dat doh-zhoor-dwee? |
| which day? | quel jour? |
| | kel zhoor? |
| which month? | quel mois? |
| | kel mwa? |
| day | jour |
| | zhoor |
| week | semaine |
| | suh-mayn |
| month | mois |
| | mwa |
| year | année |
| | a-nay |
| March 5th | le cinq mars |
| | luh sañk marss |
| July 6th | le six juillet |
| | luh see jwee-yay |
| 2008 | deux mille huit |
| | duh meel weet |
| on Saturday | samedi |
| | sam-dee |
| on Saturdays | le samedi |
| | luh sam-dee |
| every Saturday | tous les samedis |
| | too lay sam-dee |
| this Saturday | samedi qui vient |
| | sam-dee kee vyañ |

| | |
|---|---|
| next Saturday | **samedi prochain**<br>sam-dee pro-shañ |
| last Saturday | **samedi dernier**<br>sam-dee dern-yay |
| please can you confirm the date? | **vous pouvez me confirmer la date, s'il vous plaît?**<br>voo poo-vay muh koñ-feer-may la dat, seel voo play? |

## Time

- am = **du matin** (<u>doo</u> ma-tañ)
- pm = **de l'après-midi** (duh lap-ray-mee-dee)
- The 24-hour clock is used a lot more in Europe than in Britain.
- With the 24-hour clock the words **quart** (quarter) and **demie** (half) aren't used. 15 (**quinze**) and 30 (**trente**) are used.

| | |
|---|---|
| what time is it, please? | **quelle heure est-il, s'il vous plaît?**<br>kel uhr ayt-eel, seel voo play? |
| it's 1 o'clock | **il est une heure**<br>eel ay <u>oo</u>n uhr |
| it's 3 o'clock | **il est trois heures**<br>eel ay trwaz uhr |
| it's half past 8 | **il est huit heures et demie**<br>eel ay weet uhr ay duh-mee |
| in an hour | **dans une heure**<br>doñz <u>oo</u>n uhr |
| half an hour | **une demi-heure**<br><u>oo</u>n duh-mee uhr |
| until 8 o'clock | **jusqu'à huit heures**<br><u>joo</u>s-ka weet uhr |
| it is half past 10 | **il est dix heures et demie**<br>eel ay deez uhr ay duh-mee |
| at 10 am | **à dix heures**<br>a deez uhr |

| at 2200 | à vingt-deux heures |
| | a vañ-duhz uhr |
| at midday | à midi |
| | a mee-dee |
| at midnight | à minuit |
| | a meen-wee |
| soon | bientôt |
| | byañ-toh |
| later | plus tard |
| | ploo tar |
| am | du matin |
| | doo ma-tañ |
| pm | du soir |
| | doo swar |

# Eating out

## Eating out

French cuisine is among the best in the world. The French take their food very seriously and what they eat largely depends on what is available locally and in season.

In Brittany with its craggy coastline, you find fish and superb seafood, along with sweet and savoury pancakes. Normandy boasts apples and rich dairy produce which you can sample in **tarte normande** (apple tart), cider and **calvados** (apple brandy).

Southern France enjoys the flavours of the sun and Mediterranean – tomatoes, olives, basil, garlic, anchovies and saffron. Try **pissaladière** (similar to pizza) and **tapenade** (rich anchovy and olive paste). Corsica mingles the flavours of France and Italy and makes use of wild boar.

Eastern France shares border and tastes with its German neighbours. You find sauerkraut and pork as well as **quiche lorraine**.

Western France boasts Bordeaux wine, truffles and goose liver. Stews are cooked in red wine with wild mushrooms.

Central France, a largely rural area, specialises in heavy, hearty dishes to see through the long winter months. Taste the earthy flavours in the Puy lentils, potatoes, cheese and pork.

The Pyrenees separate France and Spain but not influences. You find them in the bean and vegetable stews with spicy pork sausage similar to **chorizo**.

Paris, naturally, takes a pinch from here, a **soupçon** from there, and serves them up elegantly in rich smooth sauces.

Breakfast (**le petit déjeuner**) is a light meal, usually fresh bread or croissants with butter and jam and strong black coffee, with or without hot milk. The main meal of the day in France used to be lunch (**le déjeuner**), served between 12.30 and 2pm. Nowadays lunch may be lighter with the evening meal (**le dîner**) being the main meal, usually served between 7.30 and 8.30pm.

# Ordering drinks

• You don't need to order at the bar. Take a seat and a waiter will take your order.
• Try a shandy, **un panaché** (uñ pan-a-shay), or cordial and lemonade, **un diabolo** (uñ dee-a-bo-lo): either mint, **menthe** (moñt) or strawberry, **fraise** (frehz).
• 'Cheers!' in French is **santé** (soñ-tay).

| | |
|---|---|
| a black coffee | **un café noir**<br>uñ ka-fay nwar |
| a white coffee | **un café crème/un café au lait**<br>uñ ka-fay krem/uñ ka-fay oh lay |
| a tea | **un thé**<br>uñ tay |
| with milk | **au lait**<br>oh lay |
| with lemon | **au citron**<br>oh see-troñ |
| a bottle of mineral water | **une bouteille d'eau minérale**<br><u>oo</u>n boo-tay doh mee-nay-ral |
| sparkling | **gazeuse**<br>gaz-uhz |
| still | **plate**<br>plat |

| a beer | **une bière** |
| | oon byehr |
| a shandy | **un panaché** |
| | uñ pa-na-shay |
| a half pint | **un demi** |
| | uñ duh-mee |
| what beers do you have? | **qu'est-ce que vous avez comme bières?** |
| | kess kuh vooz a-vay kom byehr? |
| the wine list, please | **la carte des vins, s'il vous plaît** |
| | la kart day vañ, seel voo play |
| a bottle of house wine | **un pichet de vin** |
| | uñ pee-shay duh vañ |
| a glass of wine ... white/red | **un verre de vin ... blanc/rouge** |
| | uñ vehr duh vañ ... bloñ/roozh |
| a bottle of red wine | **une bouteille de vin rouge** |
| | oon boo-tay duh vañ roozh |
| a bottle of white wine | **une bouteille de vin blanc** |
| | oon boo-tay duh vañ bloñ |
| would you like a drink? | **voulez-vous boire quelque chose?** |
| | voo-lay voo bwar kel-kuh shoz? |
| what will you have? | **qu'est-ce que vous prenez?** |
| | kess kuh voo pruh-nay? |

# Ordering food

- By law, French restaurants must offer one set-price menu, many offer 2 or 3.
- **Au choix** (oh shwah) means 'choice of'.
- A children's menu is **un menu enfant** (uñ muh-noo oñ-foñ).
- It is polite to wish **bon appétit** (boñ a-pay-tee). The reply is 'you, too', either **vous** or **toi aussi** (vooz/twah oh-see).

| can you recommend a good restaurant? | **pouvez-vous nous recommander un bon restaurant?** |
| | poo-vay voo noo ruh-ko-moñ-day uñ boñ res-toh-roñ? |

| I'd like to book a table | **je voudrais réserver une table** |
| | zhuh voo-dray ray-zehr-vay oon tabl |
| for ... people | **pour ... personnes** |
| | poor ... pehr-son |
| for tonight | **pour ce soir** |
| | poor suh swar |
| at 8pm | **à huit heures** |
| | a weet uhr |
| the menu, please | **le menu, s'il vous plaît** |
| | luh muh-noo, seel voo play |
| is there a dish of the day? | **est-ce qu'il y a un plat du jour?** |
| | ess keel ee a uñ pla doo zhoor? |
| have you a set-price menu? | **avez-vous un menu à prix fixe?** |
| | av-ay voo uñ muh-noo a pree feeks? |
| the 26-euro menu | **le menu à vingt-six euros** |
| | luh muh-noo a vañ-seess uh-roh |
| I'll have this | **je vais prendre ça** |
| | zhuh vay proñdr sa |
| what do you recommend? | **qu'est-ce que vous me conseillez?** |
| | kess kuh voo muh koñ-say-ay? |
| I don't eat meat | **je ne mange pas de viande** |
| | zhuh nuh moñ-zh pa duh vyoñd |
| do you have any vegetarian dishes? | **avez-vous des plats végétariens?** |
| | av-ay voo day pla vay-zhay-tar-yañ? |
| excuse me! | **excusez-moi!** |
| | eks-koo-zay mwa! |
| some bread please | **du pain s'il vous plaît** |
| | doo pañ seel voo play |
| some water please | **de l'eau s'il vous plaît** |
| | duh loh seel voo play |
| the bill, please | **l'addition, s'il vous plaît** |
| | la-dees-yoñ, seel voo play |

# Special requirements

- The words for gluten free are **sans gluten** (soñ gloo-ten).
- **Fait avec du lait cru** means made with unpasteurised milk.
- **Biologique** (bee-o-loh-zheek) or **bio** means organic.
- On labels, **glucides** (gloo-seed) are carbohydrates. **Lipides** (lee-peed) are fats.
- Decaffeinated is **décaféiné** (day-ka-fay-ee-nay).

| | |
|---|---|
| what's in this? | **quels sont les ingrédients?** |
| | kel soñ lay añ-gray-dyoñ? |
| I'm vegetarian | **je suis végétarien(ne)** |
| | zhuh swee vay-zhay-tar-yañ(-yeñ) |
| I don't eat fish | **je ne mange pas de poisson** |
| | zhuh nuh moñzh pa duh pwa-soñ |
| I don't eat pork | **je ne mange pas de porc** |
| | zhuh nuh moñzh pa duh por |
| I can't eat liver | **je ne peux pas manger de foie** |
| | zhuh nuh puh pa moñ-zhay duh fwah |
| I'm allergic to shellfish | **je suis allergique aux crustacés** |
| | zhuh swee a-lehr-zheek oh kroos-ta-say |
| I am allergic to peanuts | **je suis allergique aux cacahuètes** |
| | zhuh swee a-lehr-zheek oh ka-ka-wet |
| I can't eat raw eggs | **je ne peux pas manger d'œufs crus** |
| | zhuh nuh puh pa moñ-zhay duh kroo |
| is it raw? | **c'est cru?** |
| | say kroo? |
| I am on a diet | **je suis au régime** |
| | zhuh swee oh ray-zheem |
| I don't drink alcohol | **je ne bois pas d'alcool** |
| | zhuh nuh bwa pa dal-kol |

# Eating photoguide

## Eating places

**Baker's Boulangeries** open very early and sell sandwiches and snacks.

**Cake Shops** Often have a tearoom (**Salon de thé**), serving mouth-watering cakes and generally weak tea with lemon. Try **chocolat chaud** (hot chocolate).

**Market** There are daily and weekly markets, selling fruit, vegetables, cheese and local specialities.

**Grocer and Cheesemonger** There are over 350 varieties of French cheese. Ask for **un morceau** uñ mor-soh, a bit.

**Butcher, Pork and Poultry Traiteur** means that they are also a deli and have dishes to take away.

**Brasseries** and **Bistros** serve a **plat du jour** (dish of the day) at any time of the day. Restaurants generally open at meal times.

Ice-cream Parlour

**Plats du Jour** A café serving food will have one or more daily dishes. If they are in popular areas, it is worth going early before they run out.

**Menu du Jour**
A set-price daily menu. This is good value and often includes drink. Bread is always provided.

**Tabacs** often have a bar or restaurant attached. They are usually good value and frequented by locals.

Food is expensive at service stations compared to other eating places. If you can, go to a village bakery, or take food with you.

Supermarket cafés offer standard kids' food – hamburger (**steak haché**) or fish fingers (**bâtonnets de colin pané**), with chips, dessert and toy.

**Frites 500m** **Chips** Signals roadside café 500 metres away. Mediocre food, mostly chips.

**Logis de France** A chain of smallish hotels (around 18 rooms), usually family-run and with restaurants making the most of regional produce and specialities.

## Table d'hôte

B & B (**chambres d'hôtes**) may offer meals – generally home-cooked dishes using local produce.

Eating places

Hotels often have a restaurant open to non-residents. They tend to be shut on Sunday.

A more traditional-style hotel, usually in the country. They often have restaurants open to the public which tend to be more expensive than the norm.

**Take-away**
**pain** = bread
**viennoiserie** = Danish pastries
**tartes** = tarts, pies
**sucrées** = sweet
**salées** = savoury
**poulets rôtis** = spit-roasted chickens
**à emporter** = take-away

Pizzas and Take-Away Dishes

**In a Hurry?** Meals don't always have to be slow affairs. Here you can have a salad (made up of your own choice) and drink. A drink (**boisson**) is included in the price.

**Sandwiches** are widely available. Half or whole baguettes. Vegetarians may have little choice and should ask for a '**sandwich emmental**'.

**Pancakes** Make a delicious meal of 2 or 3 crêpes as different courses with either savoury (**galette**) or sweet fillings.

# Reading the menu

**Restaurant** By law French restaurants must display their menus outside. You will be able to judge the type of food and cost before you go in. As well as displaying the menu, restaurants and hotels display awards. They are usually open 12-2pm and 7-9.30pm.

### La Carte Menu

POTAGES *soups*

ENTRÉES *starter*

POISSONS *fish*

FRUITS DE MER *seafood*

VIANDES *meat*

GIBIER et VOLAILLE *game and poultry*

LÉGUMES *vegetables*

FROMAGES *cheeses*

DESSERTS *sweet*

BOISSONS *drinks*

---

**Du lundi au vendredi**
**Menu du midi**
**7.5⁰**
**ENTREE + PLAT + CAFE**

Restaurants usually have different menus, varying in price. Some are only available at lunchtime (**du midi**). The menu above is lunchtimes only Mon–Fri. **Entrée** = starter, **plat** = main dish, **café** = coffee (usually of the strong dark, variety).

---

Salade compo...
Boisson *
* ¹/4 de Vin
ou. Bière Pression
ou. Eau Minérale
ou. Soda

Many set-price menus include drink (**boisson**). Here the choice is between ¹/4 litre of wine (**vin**), draught lager (**bière pression**), mineral water (**eau minérale**) or a soft fizzy drink (**soda**).

Choosing dishes from the à la carte menu tends to be more expensive than opting for a set price menu. Restaurants generally offer several set price menus. There may be two menus of differing prices, a regional (**du terroir**) menu which lets you sample local dishes, and for the foodies, a **menu gourmand**.

**MENUS à 26 € ET 28,50 €**

26,00 € avec fromage ou dessert
28,50 € avec fromage et dessert

Amuse-bouche

Foie gras de canard maison     ou     Fricassée d'escargots en cocotte
aux épices douces                              et champignons au beurre d'herbe
                                                                Croûtons dorés

ou

Terrine de rouget et Saint Jacques
en gelée parfumée aux algues

Saumon cuit à l'huile d'olive     ou     Baron de lapin rôti à la moutarde,
morilles au jus,                                      jeunes carottes, pommes nouvelles
pommes écrasées                                   et oignons grelots

ou

Pièce de bœuf épaisse
servie saignante,
réduction de Mâcon rouge aux échalotes

Assortiment de nos fromages     ou     Fromage frais de vache
sur le plateau                                        en faisselle à la crème
                                                               ou au coulis de fruits rouges

Un dessert au choix sur la carte

Prix nets

Watch out for the little words –
**ou** = or, **et** = and.

**amuse-bouche** = appetisers

**maison** = home-made

**au choix** = choice of, there may be a couple of options to choose from.

**prix** = price

**MENU ENFANT (- 10 ANS)**

9,00 € (prix net)

Salade verte et tomates     ou     rosette beurre

Steak haché avec sa garniture     ou     blanc de volaille avec sa garniture

Yaourth nature     ou     Glaces

**Menu Enfant**
Children's menu – this menu is for children under 10. There is a choice between two set meals.

**avec sa garniture** usually means with chips or rice and veg.
**Garnis** means the same thing.

*Menu du Terroir*     Regional Dishes

Reading the menu

91

# Drinks and bill

**Coffee** If you ask for **un café** you'll get it small, strong and black. For a white coffee, ask for **un café au lait** uñ ka-fay oh lay or **un cappuccino**.

Eau Fraîche et Boissons Chaudes

**Cold Water and Hot Drinks** Mineral water will be either sparkling or still.

You don't have to go to the bar to order your drinks in a café. Sit at a table and the waiter will take your order. In small towns and villages you won't be asked to pay straight-away, but when you've finished. It's usual to leave any loose change on the table.

It is cheaper to drink inside. If you are looking for a toilet and can only see a café or bar, you should buy a cheap drink at the bar, like a coffee, or a small glass of wine.

To ask for the bill, attract the waiter's attention with **pardon** and ask for **l'addition**, **s'il vous plaît** lad-ees-yoñ seel voo play.

**service non compris** = service not included. If you wish to tip, about 10% of the bill is fairly standard.

*Carte des vins*

**Wine List**

**Reading The Wine Label Appellation contrôlee** guarantees that the wine is from a demarcated area (not its quality). In this case, Côtes de Bourg.

Alcohol content. 11.5% is average, 14% would be pretty hefty.

**mis en bouteille au** = bottled at

## Apéritifs et Digestifs

French people love aperitifs. They can be a simple glass of Pernod with water or can involve Champagne, canapés and long chats.

**Vin de pays** simply means the wine has come from one area i.e. not blended. **Vin de table**, or **vin ordinaire** indicates that the wine has been blended and is usually sold in plastic bottles.

You can buy a wide selection of French champagne at most supermarkets. It makes a good gift to take to French friends when invited for a meal. **Brut** = very dry, **sec** = dry, **demi-sec** = sweet, **doux** = very sweet.

Beer in France is generally lager. Draught beer is **bière pression** byehr pray-syoñ. Half a pint is **un demi** uñ duh-mee.

# Menu reader

...à la/à l'/au/aux... 'in the style of...', or 'with...'

**au feu de bois** cooked over a wood fire

**au four** baked

**au porto** in port

**abats** offal, giblets

**abricot** apricot

**Abricotine** liqueur brandy with apricot flavouring

**agneau** lamb

**agrumes** citrus fruit

**aïado** roast shoulder of lamb stuffed with garlic and other ingredients

**aïgo boulido** garlic soup

**ail** garlic

**aile** wing

**aïoli** rich garlic mayonnaise originated in the south and gives its name to the dish it is served with: cold steamed fish and vegetables. The mayonnaise is served on the side

**airelles** bilberries, cranberries

**aligot** puréed potato with cheese

**allumettes** very thin chips

**amande** almond

**amuse-bouche** nibbles

**arlésienne, à l'** with tomatoes, onions, aubergines, potatoes and rice

**armagnac** fine grape brandy from the Landes area

**armoricaine, ...à l'** cooked with brandy, wine, tomatoes and onions

**ananas** pineapple

**anchoïade** anchovy paste usually served on grilled French bread

**anchois** anchovies

**andouille** (eaten cold), **andouillette** (eaten hot) spicy tripe sausage

**anglaise, ...à l'** poached or boiled

**anguille** eel

**anis** aniseed

**arachide** peanut (uncooked)

**araignée de mer** spider crab

**artichaut** artichoke

**artichauts à la barigoule** artichokes in wine, with carrots, garlic, onions

**asperge** asparagus

**aspic de volaille** chicken in aspic

**assiette** dish, platter

**assiette anglaise** plate of assorted cold meats

**assiette de charcuterie** plate of assorted pâtés and salami

**assiette de crudités** selection of raw vegetables served with a dip

**assiette du pêcheur** assorted fish or seafood

**aubergine** aubergine

**aubergines farcies** stuffed aubergines

**auvergnate, ...à l'** with cabbage, sausage and bacon

**avocat** avocado

**baba au rhum** rum baba

**baccala frittu** dried salt cod fried Corsica style

**Badoit** mineral water, very slightly sparkling

**baekenofe** hotpot of pork, mutton and beef baked in white wine with potato layers from Alsace

**baguette** stick of French bread

**banane** banana

**bananes flambées** bananas flambéed in brandy

**bar** sea-bass

**barbue** brill

**bardatte** cabbage stuffed with rabbit or hare

**barquette** small boat-shaped flan

**basilic** basil

**baudroie** fish soup with vegetables, garlic and herbs

**bavarois** moulded cream and custard pudding, usually served with fruit

**Béarnaise, à la** sauce similar to mayonnaise but flavoured with tarragon and white wine. Traditionally served with steak

**bécasse** woodcock

**béchamel** classic white sauce made with milk, butter and flour

**beignets** fritters, doughnuts

**Bénédictine** herb liqueur on a brandy base

**betterave** beetroot

**beurre** butter

**beurre blanc, ...à la** sauce of white wine and shallots with butter

**bien cuit** well done

**bière** beer

**bière blonde** lager

**bière brune** bitter

**bière pression** draught beer

**bifteck** steak

**bigorneau** periwinkle

**biologique** organic

**bis** wholemeal (of bread or flour)

**biscuit de Savoie** sponge cake

**bisque** smooth rich seafood soup

**bisque de homard** lobster soup

**blanquette** white meat stew served with a creamy white sauce

**blanquette de veau** veal stew in white sauce

**blanquette de volaille** chicken stew in white sauce

**blé** wheat

**blette** Swiss chard

**bleu** very rare

**bœuf** beef

**bœuf bourguignon** beef in burgundy, onions and mushrooms

**bœuf en daube** rich beef stew with wine, olives, tomatoes and herbs

**bombe** moulded ice cream dessert

**bonite** bonito, small tuna fish

**bonne femme, ...à la** cooked in white wine with mushrooms

**bordelaise, ...à la** cooked in a sauce of red wine, shallots and herbs

**bouchée** vol-au-vent

**bouchée à la reine** vol-au-vent filled with chicken or veal and mushrooms in a white sauce

**boudin** pudding

**boudin blanc** white pudding

**boudin noir** black pudding
**bouillabaisse** rich seafood dish flavoured with saffron originally from Marseilles
**bouilleture d'anguilles** eels cooked with prunes and red wine
**bouilli** boiled
**bouillon** stock
**bouillon de légumes** vegetable stock
**bouillon de poule** chicken stock
**boulangère, ...à la** baked with potatoes and onions
**boulettes** meatballs
**bourgeoise, ...à la** with carrots, onions, bacon, celery and braised lettuce
**bourguignonne, ...à la** cooked in red wine, with onions, bacon and mushrooms
**bourride** fish stew traditionally served with garlic mayonnaise (**aïoli**)
**brandade de morue** dried salt cod puréed with potatoes and olive oil
**brème** bream
**brioche** sweet bun
**brioche aux fruits** sweet bun with glacé fruit
**brochet** pike
**brocoli** broccoli
**brugnon** nectarine
**bugne** doughnut from the Lyons area
**bulot** whelk
**cabillaud** fresh cod
**cacahuète** peanut
**café** coffee

**café au lait** coffee with hot milk
**café crème** white coffee
**café décaféiné** decaffeinated coffee
**café glacé** iced coffee
**café irlandais** Irish coffee
**café noir** black coffee
**caille** quail
**caille sur canapé** quail served on toast
**caillettes** rolled liver stuffed with spinach
**cajou, noix de** cashew nut
**calisson** almond sweet
**calmar** (or **calamar**) squid
**calvados** apple brandy made from apples (Normandy)
**canard** duck
**canard à l'orange** roast duck with orange sauce
**canard périgourdin** roast duck with prunes, pâté de **foie gras** and truffles
**canard Rouennais** stuffed roast duck covered in red wine sauce
**caneton** duckling
**cannelle** cinnamon
**câpres** capers
**carbonnade de bœuf** braised beef
**cardon** cardoon
**cari** curry
**carotte** carrot
**carottes Vichy** carrots cooked in butter and sugar
**carpe** carp
**carpe farcie** carp stuffed with mushrooms or **foie gras**

**carré persillé** roast lamb Normandy style (with parsley)

**carrelet** plaice

**carte des vins** wine list

**cassis** blackcurrant, blackcurrant liqueur

**cassoulet** bean stew with pork or mutton, confit and sausages. There are many regional variations

**caviar** caviar

**caviar blanc** mullet roe

**caviar niçois** a paste made with anchovies and olive oil

**cédrat** large citrus fruit, similar to a lemon

**céleri** celery; celeriac

**céleri rémoulade** celeriac in a mustard and herb dressing

**céleri-rave** celeriac

**cèpes** boletus mushrooms, wild mushrooms

**cèpes marinés** wild mushrooms marinated in oil, garlic and herbs

**cerfeuil** chervil

**cerise** cherry

**cervelas** smoked pork sausages, saveloy

**cervelle** brains (usually lamb or calf)

**cervelle de Canut** savoury dish of fromage frais, goat's cheese, herbs and white wine

**champignon** mushroom

**champignons à la grecque** mushrooms cooked in wine, olive oil, herbs and tomato

**champignons de Paris** button mushrooms

**champignons périgourdine** mushrooms with truffles and **foie gras**

**chanterelle** chanterelle (wild golden-coloured mushroom)

**chantilly** sweetened whipped cream

**charlotte** custard and fruit in lining of almond fingers

**Chartreuse** aromatic herb liqueur made by Carthusian monks

**chasseur** literally hunter-style, cooked with white wine, shallots, mushrooms and herbs

**châtaigne** chestnut

**châteaubriand** thick fillet steak

**châtelaine, ...à la** with artichoke hearts

**chaud(e)** hot

**chaudrée rochelaise** a selection of fish stewed in white wine

**chauffé** heated

**chausson** a pasty filled with meat or seafood

**chausson aux pommes** apple turnover

**cheval, à** topped with a fried egg

**chèvre** goat

**chevreuil** venison

**chichi** doughnut shaped in a stick

**chicorée** chicory, endive

**chocolat** chocolate

**chocolat chaud** hot chocolate

**chou** cabbage

**choucroute** sauerkraut

**choucroute garnie** sauerkraut with various types of sausages

**chou-fleur** cauliflower

**choux brocolis** broccoli
**choux de Bruxelles** Brussels sprouts
**ciboule** (or **cive**) spring onions
**ciboulette** chives
**cidre** cider
**cidre brut** dry cider
**cidre doux** sweet cider
**citron** lemon
**citron pressé** freshly squeezed lemon juice with water and sugar
**citron vert** lime
**citrouille** pumpkin
**civet** thick stew
**civet de langouste** crayfish in wine sauce
**civet de lièvre** hare stewed in wine, onions and mushrooms
**clafoutis** cherry pudding
**clou de girofle** clove
**cochon** pig
**coco** coconut
**cocotte, en** cooked in a small earthenware casserole
**cœur** heart
**cœurs d'artichauts** artichoke hearts
**cœurs de palmier** palm hearts
**cognac** high quality white grape brandy
**coing** quince
**Cointreau** orange-flavoured liqueur
**colbert,...à la** fried, with a coating of egg and breadcrumbs
**colin** hake
**compote de fruits** mixed stewed fruit

**concombre** cucumber
**condé** rich rice pudding with fruits
**confit** pieces of meat preserved in fat
**confit d'oie** goose meat preserved in its own fat
**confit de canard** duck meat preserved in its own fat
**confiture** jam
**confiture d'oranges** marmalade
**congre** conger eel
**consommé** clear soup, generally made from meat or fish stock
**contre-filet** sirloin fillet (beef)
**coq au vin** chicken and mushrooms cooked in red wine
**coquelet** cockerel
**coques** cockles
**coquillages** shellfish
**coquilles Saint-Jacques** scallops
**coquilles Saint-Jacques à la Bretonne** scallops cooked in shell with a bread-crumb and white sauce topping
**coquilles Saint-Jacques à la provençale** scallops with garlic sauce
**coquillettes** pasta shells
**cornichon** gherkin
**côtelette** cutlet
**côtelettes d'agneau** lamb cutlets
**côte** rib, chop
**côtes de porc** pork chops
**cotriade** fish stew (Brittany)
**cou** neck
**coulibiac** salmon cooked in puff pastry
**coulis** puréed fruit sauce

**coupe** goblet with ice cream
**courge** marrow
**cousinat** chestnut and cream soup
**crabe** crab
**craquelots** smoked herring
**crémant** sparkling wine
**crème** cream
**crème anglaise** fresh custard
**crème au beurre** butter cream with egg yolks and sugar
**crème brûlée** rich custard with caramelised sugar on top
**crème caramel** baked custard with caramelised sugar sauce
**crème chantilly** sweetened whipped cream
**crème pâtissière** thick fresh custard used in tarts and desserts
**crème renversée** (or **crème caramel**) custard with a caramelised top
**crème de** cream of... (soup)
**crème d'Argenteuil** white asparagus soup
**crème de cresson** watercress soup
**crème de marrons** chestnut purée
**crème de menthe** peppermint-flavoured liqueur
**crêpes** sweet and savoury pancakes
**crêpes fourrées** filled pancakes
**crêpes Suzette** pancakes with a Cointreau or Grand Marnier sauce usually flambéed
**crépinette** type of sausage
**crevette** prawn
**crevette grise** shrimp
**crevette rose** large prawn

**croque-madame** grilled gruyère cheese and ham sandwich with a fried egg on top
**croque-monsieur** grilled gruyère cheese and ham sandwich
**croûte, en** in pastry
**croûtes, croûtons, ...aux** served with cubes of toasted or fried bread
**cru** raw
**crudités** assortment of raw vegetables (grated carrots, sliced tomatoes, etc) served as a starter
**crustacés** shellfish
**cuisses de grenouille** frogs' legs
**cuit** cooked
**culotte** rump steak
**Curaçao** orange-flavoured liqueur
**darne** fish steak
**datte** date
**daube** casserole with wine, herbs, garlic, tomatoes and olives
**dauphinoise, ...à la** baked in milk
**daurade** sea bream
**diable, ...à la** strong mustard seasoning
**diabolo menthe** mint cordial and lemonade
**dinde** turkey
**diots au vin blanc** pork sausages in white wine
**duxelles** fried mushrooms onions and shallots
**eau** water
**eau de Seltz** soda water
**eau-de-vie** brandy (often made from plum, pear, etc)
**eau minérale** mineral water

**eau minérale gazeuse** sparkling mineral water

**eau du robinet** tap water

**échalote** shallot

**échine** loin of pork

**écrevisse** freshwater crayfish

**églefin** haddock

**emballé** wrapped

**en brochette** cooked like a kebab (on a skewer)

**encornet** squid

**endive** chicory

**entrecôte** rib steak

**entrées** starters

**entremets** sweets (desserts)

**épaule** shoulder

**éperlan** whitebait

**épice** spice

**épinards** spinach

**escalope** escalope

**escargots** snails (generally cooked with strong seasonings)

**escargots à la bourguignonne** snails with garlic butter

**espadon** swordfish

**estouffade de boeuf** beef stew cooked in red wine, herbs, onions, mushrooms and diced bacon

**estragon** tarragon

**esturgeon** sturgeon

**faisan** pheasant

**far aux pruneaux** prune cake from Brittany

**farci(e)** stuffed

**farigoule** thyme (in provençal dialect)

**faux-filet** sirloin

**fenouil** fennel

**feuille** leaf

**feuilleté** in puff pastry

**fèves** broad beans

**fiadone** ewe's cheese and lemon dish from Corsica

**figue** fig

**filet** fillet steak

**filet de bœuf** tenderloin

**filet de bœuf en croûte** steak in pastry

**filet mignon** small pork fillet steak

**financière, ...à la** rich sauce made with Madeira wine and truffles

**fine de claire** type of oyster

**fines herbes** mixed, chopped herbs

**flageolet** type of small green haricot bean

**flamande, ...à la** served with potatoes, cabbage, carrots and pork

**flambé(e)** doused with brandy or another spirit and set alight, usually cooked at your table

**flammenküche** onion, bacon and cream tartlet from Alsace

**flétan** halibut

**flocons d'avoine** oat flakes

**florentine** with spinach, usually served with mornay sauce

**foie** liver (usually calf's)

**foie de volailles** chicken livers

**foie gras** goose liver

**fond d'artichaut** artichoke heart

**fondue** a shared dish which is served in the middle of the table. Each person uses a long fork to dip their bread or meat into the pot

**fondue (au fromage)** melted cheeses with white wine into which chunks of bread are dipped

**fondue bourguignonne** small chunks of beef dipped into boiling oil and eaten with different sauces. The meat equivalent to cheese fondue

**forestière, ...à la** with bacon and mushrooms

**fougasse** type of bread with various fillings (olives, anchovies)

**fourré(e)** stuffed

**frais (fraîche)** fresh

**fraise** strawberry

**fraises des bois** wild strawberries

**framboise** raspberry

**frappé** iced

**fricassée** a stew, usually chicken or veal, and vegetables

**frisée** curly endive

**frit(e)** fried

**friture** fried food, usually small fish

**froid(e)** cold

**fromage** cheese

**fromage blanc** soft white cheese

**fromage frais** creamy fresh cheese

**froment** wheat

**fruit** fruit

**fruit de la passion** passion fruit

**fruits de mer** shellfish, seafood

**fumé(e)** smoked

**fumet** fish stock

**galantine** meat in aspic

**galette** savoury buckwheat pancake

**gambas** large prawns

**ganache** chocolate cream filling

**garbure** thick vegetable and meat soup

**gargouillau** pear tart

**garni(e)** garnished i.e. served with something (vegetables)

**garnitures** side dishes

**gâteau** cake, gateau

**gâteau Saint-Honoré** choux pastry cake filled with custard

**gaufres** waffles (often cream-filled)

**gazeuse** sparkling

**gelée** jelly, aspic

**genièvre** juniper berry

**génoise** sponge cake

**germes de soja** bean sprouts

**gésier** gizzard

**gibier** game

**gigot d'agneau** leg of lamb

**gigot de mer** large fish baked whole

**gingembre** ginger

**glace** ice cream

**gougères** choux pastry with cheese

**goyave** guava

**Grand Marnier** tawny-coloured, orange-flavoured liqueur

**gratin, au** topped with cheese and breadcrumb and grilled

**gratin dauphinois** potatoes cooked in cream, garlic and Swiss cheese

**gratinée Lyonnaise** clear soup with eggs flavoured with Port wine and served with toasted french bread and grated cheese

**grenade** pomegranate

**grecque, ...à la** cooked in olive oil, garlic, tomatoes and herbs, can be served hot or cold

grenouille frog usually frogs' legs

grenouilles à la mode de Boulay frogs' legs cooked with butter, shallots and parsley

grillade grilled meat

grillé(e) grilled

groseille redcurrant

groseille à maquereau gooseberry

hachis mince

hareng herring

haricots beans

haricots beurre butter beans

haricots blancs haricot beans

haricots rouges red kidney beans

haricots verts green beans, French beans

herbes (fines herbes) herbs

hollandaise, sauce sauce made of butter, egg yolks and lemon juice, served warm

homard lobster

homard à l'armoricaine lobster cooked with onions, tomatoes and wine

homard thermidor lobster served in cream sauce, topped with parmesan

hors d'œuvre variés selection of appetizers

huile oil

huile d'arachide groundnut oil

huile de tournesol sunflower oil

huître oyster

îles flottantes soft meringues floating on fresh custard

Izarra vert green-coloured herb liqueur

jambon ham

jambon de Bayonne cured raw ham from the Basque country

jambon de Paris boiled ham

jardinière, ...à la with peas and carrots, or other fresh vegetables

julienne vegetables cut into fine strips

jus juice, meat-based glaze or sauce

jus de pomme apple juice

jus d'orange orange juice

kig-ha farz meat stew from Brittany

kir white wine and cassis aperitif

kirsch a kind of eau-de-vie made from cherries (Alsace)

kouglof hat-shaped sugar-covered cake from Alsace

kouign-amann cake from Brittany

lait milk

lait demi-écrémé semi-skimmed milk

lait écrémé skimmed milk

lait entier full-cream milk

laitue lettuce

lamproie à la bordelaise lamprey in red wine

langouste crayfish (saltwater)

langouste froide crayfish served cold with mayonnaise and salad

langoustines large prawn

langue tongue (veal, beef)

lapin rabbit

lard fat, streaky bacon

lard fumé smoked bacon

lardon strip of fat, diced bacon

laurier bayleaf

légumes vegetables

**lentilles** lentils
**levure** yeast
**lièvre** hare
**limande** lemon sole
**limousine, ...à la** cooked with chestnuts and red cabbage
**lotte** monkfish
**loup de mer** sea-bass
**Lyonnaise, ...à la** with onions
**macaron** macaroon
**macédoine (de fruits)** fresh fruit salad
**macédoine de légumes** mixed cooked vegetables
**madeleine** small sponge cake
**magret de canard** duck breast
**maïs, maïs doux** maize, sweetcorn
**mange-tout** sugar peas
**mangue** mango
**maquereau** mackerel
**marcassin** young wild boar
**marinière, ...à la** a sauce of white wine, onions and herbs (mussels or clams)
**marmite** casserole
**marjolaine** marjoram
**marron** chestnut
**marrons glacés** candied chestnuts
**marrons Mont Blanc** chestnut purée and cream
**matelote** fresh-fish stew
**matelote à la normande** sea-fish stew with cider, calvados and cream
**médaillon** thick, medal-sized slices of meat
**melon** melon

**menthe** mint, mint tea
**merguez** spicy, red sausage
**meringues à la chantilly** meringues filled with whipped cream
**merlan** whiting
**merluche** hake
**mérou** grouper
**merveilles** fritters flavoured with brandy
**mignonnette** small fillet of lamb
**mijoté** stewed
**millefeuille** thin layers of pastry filled with custard
**mirabelle** small yellow plum, plum brandy from Alsace
**mont-blanc** pudding made with chestnuts and cream
**Mornay, sauce** béchamel and cheese sauce
**morue** dried salt cod
**moules** mussels
**moules marinière** mussels cooked in white wine
**moules poulette** mussels in wine, cream and mushroom sauce
**mourtairol** beef, chicken, ham and vegetable soup
**mousse au chocolat** chocolate mousse
**mousseline** mashed potatoes with cream and eggs
**moutarde** mustard
**mouton** mutton or sheep
**mûre** blackberry
**muscade** nutmeg
**myrtille** bilberry
**navet** turnip

nectarine nectarine

niçoise, ...à la with garlic and tomatoes

noisette hazelnut

noisettes d'agneau small round pieces of lamb

noix walnut, general term for a nut

nouilles noodles

œuf egg

œufs à la coque soft-boiled eggs

œufs au plat fried eggs

œufs Bénédicte poached eggs on toast, with ham and hollandaise sauce

œufs brouillés scrambled eggs

œufs durs hard-boiled eggs

œufs en cocotte eggs baked in individual containers with wine

œufs frits fried eggs and bacon

oie goose

oie farcie aux pruneaux goose stuffed with prunes

oignon onion

olive olive

omelette omelette

omelette brayaude cheese and potato omelette

omelette nature plain omelette

omelette norvégienne baked Alaska

onglet cut of beef (steak)

orange orange

orangeade orangeade

orge barley

os bone

oseille sorrel

oursin sea urchin

pain bread, loaf of bread

pain au chocolat croissant with chocolate filling

pain bagnat bread roll with egg, olives, salad, tuna, anchovies and olive oil

pain bis brown bread

pain complet wholemeal bread

pain d'épices ginger cake

pain de mie white sliced loaf

pain de seigle rye bread

pain grillé toast

palmier caramelized puff pastry

palombe wood pigeon

palourde clam

pamplemousse grapefruit

panais parsnip

pané(e) with breadcrumbs

panini toasted Italian sandwich

panisse thick chickpea flour pancake

pannequets au fromage pancakes filled with white sauce and cheese (Brittany)

papillote, en cooked in a parcel

parfait rich home-made ice cream

Paris Brest ring-shaped cake filled with praline-flavoured cream

parisienne, ...à la sautéed in butter with white wine, sauce and shallots

parmentier with potatoes

pastèque watermelon

pastis aniseed-based aperitif

patate douce sweet potato

pâté pâté

pâté de foie de volailles chicken liver pâté

pâté en croûte pâté in pastry

**pâtes** pasta
**pâtes fraîches** fresh pasta
**patranque** central France dish of bread cubes, garlic and cheese
**paupiettes** meat slices stuffed and rolled
**pavé** thick slice
**pays d'auge, ...à la** in cream and cider or Calvados
**paysanne, ...à la** cooked with diced bacon and vegetables
**pêche** peach
**pêches melba** poached peaches served with a raspberry sauce and vanilla ice cream or whipped cream
**perche** perch (fish)
**perche du Menon** perch cooked in champagne
**perdreau (perdrix)** partridge, grouse
**Périgueux, sauce** with truffles
**Pernod** aperitif with aniseed flavour (**pastis**)
**persil** parsley
**persillé(e)** with parsley
**petit-beurre** butter biscuit
**petits farcis** stuffed tomatoes, aubergines, courgettes and peppers
**petit pain** roll
**petits fours** bite-sized cakes and pastries
**petits pois** garden peas
**petit-suisse** thick fromage frais
**pieds et paquets** mutton or pork tripe and trotters
**pigeon** pigeon
**pignons** pine nuts

**pilon** drumstick (chicken)
**piment** chilli
**piment doux** sweet pepper
**piment fort** chilli
**pimenté** peppery hot
**pintade/pintadeau** guinea fowl
**pipérade** tomato, pepper and onion omelette
**piquant** spicy
**pissaladière** a kind of pizza made mainly in the Nice region, filled with onions, anchovies and black olives
**pistache** pistachio
**pistou** garlic, basil and olive oil sauce from Provence – similar to **pesto**
**plat** dish
**plat principal** main course
**plate** still
**plie** plaice
**poché(e)** poached
**poêlé** pan-fried
**point, ...à** medium rare
**poire** pear
**poires belle Hélène** poached pears with vanilla ice cream and chocolate sauce
**poireau** leek
**pois** peas
**pois cassés** split peas
**pois-chiches** chickpeas
**poisson** fish
**poitrine** breast (lamb or veal)
**poivre** pepper
**poivron** sweet pepper
**poivron rouge** red pepper
**poivron vert** green pepper
**pomme** apple

**pomme (de terre)** potato
**pommes à l'anglaise** boiled potatoes
**pommes à la vapeur** steamed potatoes
**pommes allumettes** very thin chips
**pommes dauphine** potato croquettes
**pommes duchesse** potato mashed then baked in the oven
**pommes frites** french fries, chips
**pommes Lyonnaise** potatoes fried with onions
**pommes mousseline** potatoes mashed with cream
**pommes rissolées** small potatoes deep-fried
**pompe aux grattons** pork flan
**porc** pork
**pot-au-feu** beef and vegetable stew
**potage** soup, generally creamed or thickened
**potée auvergnate** cabbage and meat soup
**potiron** type of pumpkin
**poularde** fattened chicken
**poulet** chicken
**poulet basquaise** chicken stew with tomatoes, mushrooms and peppers
**poulet célestine** chicken cooked in white wine with mushrooms and onion
**poulet Vallée d'Auge** chicken cooked with cider, calvados, apples and cream
**poulpe à la niçoise** octopus in

tomato sauce
**pousses de soja** bean sprouts
**poussin** baby chicken
**poutargue** mullet roe paste
**praire** clam
**praliné** hazelnut flavoured
**primeurs** spring vegetables
**provençale, ...à la** cooked with tomatoes, peppers, garlic and white wine
**prune** plum, plum brandy
**pruneau** prune, damson (Switz.)
**purée** mashed potatoes; purée
**quatre-quarts** cake made with equal parts of butter, flour, sugar and eggs
**quenelles** poached fish or meat mousse balls served in a sauce
**quenelles de brochet** pike mousse in cream sauce
**quetsch** type of plum
**queue de bœuf** oxtail
**quiche Lorraine** flan with egg, fresh cream and diced back bacon
**râble** saddle
**radis** radishes
**ragoût** stew, casserole
**raie** skate
**raifort** horseradish
**raisin** grape
**raisin sec** sultana, raisin
**raïto** red wine, olive, caper, garlic and shallot sauce
**ramier** wood pigeon
**râpé(e)** grated
**rascasse** scorpion fish
**ratatouille** tomatoes, aubergines,

courgettes and garlic cooked in olive oil

**rave** turnip

**raviolis** pasta parcels of meat

**reine-claude** greengage

**rillettes** coarse pork pâté

**rillettes de canard** coarse duck pâté

**ris de veau** calf sweetbread

**riz** rice

**rognon** kidney

**rognons blancs** testicles

**rognons sautés sauce madère** sautéed kidneys served in Madeira sauce

**romaine** cos lettuce

**romarin** rosemary

**rond de gigot** large slice of leg of lamb

**rosbif** roast beef

**rôti** roast

**rouget** red mullet

**rouille** spicy version of garlic mayonnaise (**aïoli**) served with fish stew or soup

**roulade** meat or fish, stuffed and rolled

**roulé** sweet or savoury roll

**rumsteak** rump steak

**rutabaga** swede

**sabayon** dessert made with egg yolks, sugar and Marsala wine

**sablé** shortbread

**safran** saffron

**saignant** rare

**Saint-Hubert** game consommé flavoured with wine

**salade** lettuce, salad

**salade aveyronnaise** cheese salad (made with Roquefort)

**salade de fruits** fruit salad

**salade de saison** mixed salad and/or greens in season

**salade lyonnaise** vegetable salad (cooked), dressed with eggs, bacon and croutons

**salade niçoise** many variations on a famous theme: the basic ingredients are green beans, anchovies, black olives, green peppers

**salade russe** mixed cooked vegetables in mayonnaise

**salade verte** green salad

**salé** salted/spicy

**salsifis** salsify

**sandwich** sandwich

**sanglier** wild boar

**sarrasin** buckwheat

**sarriette** savoury (herb)

**sauce** sauce

**sauce piquante** gherkins, vinegar and shallots

**saucisse/saucisson** sausage

**saumon** salmon

**saumon fumé** smoked salmon

**saumon poché** poached salmon

**sauté(e)** sautéed

**sauté d'agneau** lamb stew

**savarin** a filled ring-shaped cake

**savoyarde, ...à la** with gruyère cheese

**scarole** endive, escarole

**sec** dry or dried

**seiche** cuttlefish

**sel** salt
**selle d'agneau** saddle of lamb
**semoule** semolina
**socca** thin chickpea flour pancake
**sole** sole
**sole Albert** sole in cream sauce with mustard
**sole cardinal** sole cooked in wine, served with lobster sauce
**sole Normande** sole cooked in a cream, cider and shrimp sauce
**sole Saint Germain** grilled sole with butter and tarragon sauce
**sole-limande** lemon sole
**soufflé** light fluffy dish made with egg yolks and stiffly beaten egg whites combined with cheese, ham, fish, etc
**soufflé au Grand Marnier** soufflé flavoured with Grand Marnier liqueur
**soufflé au jambon** ham soufflé
**soupe** hearty and chunky soup
**soupe à l'oignon** onion soup usually served with a crisp chunk of French bread in the dish with grated cheese piled on top
**soupe à la bière** beer soup
**soupe au pistou** vegetable soup with garlic and basil
**soupe aux choux** cabbage soup with pork
**soupe de poisson** fish soup
**steak** steak
**steak au poivre** steak with peppercorns
**steak tartare** minced raw steak mixed with raw egg, chopped

onion, tartare or worcester sauce, parsley and capers
**sucre** sugar
**sucré** sweet
**suprême de volaille** breast of chicken in cream sauce
**tajine** North African casserole
**tapenade** olive paste
**tarte** open tart, generally sweet
**tarte aux fraises** strawberry tart
**tarte aux pommes** apple tart
**tarte flambée** thin pizza-like pastry topped with onion, cream and bacon (Alsace)
**tarte Normande** apple tart
**tarte tatin** upside down tart with caramelized apples or pears
**tarte tropézienne** sponge cake filled with custard cream topped with almonds
**tartiflette** cheese, cured ham and potato dish from the Savoie
**tartine** open sandwich
**terrine** terrine, pâté
**terrine de campagne** pork and liver terrine
**terrine de porc et gibier** pork and game terrine
**tête de veau** calf's head
**thé** tea
**thé au citron** tea with lemon
**thé au lait** tea with milk
**thé sans sucre** tea without sugar
**thermidor** lobster grilled in its shell with cream sauce
**thon** tuna fish
**tian provençal** baked tomatoes

and courgettes with cheese

**tilleul** lime tea

**timbale** round dish in which a mixture of usually meat or fish is cooked. Often lined with pastry and served with a rich sauce

**timbale d'écrevisses** crayfish in a cream, wine and brandy sauce

**timbale de fruits** pastry base covered with fruits

**tiramisu** mascarpone cheese, coffee, chocolate and cream

**tisane** herbal tea

**tomate** tomato

**tomates à la provençale** grilled tomatoes steeped in garlic

**tomates farcies** stuffed tomatoes

**tomme** type of cheese

**tournedos** thick fillet steak

**tournedos Rossini** thick fillet steak on fried bread with goose liver and truffles on top

**tourte à la viande** meat pie usually made with veal and pork

**tripe** tripe

**tripes à la mode de Caen** tripe cooked with vegetables, herbs, cider and calvados

**tripoux** mutton tripe

**truffade** sautéed potatoes with cheese and bacon (central France)

**truffe** truffle

**truffiat** potato cake

**truite** trout

**truite aux amandes** trout covered with almonds

**turbot** turbot

**vacherin** large meringue filled with cream, ice cream and fruit

**vapeur, ...à la** steamed

**veau** calf, veal

**veau sauté Marengo** veal cooked in a casserole with white wine, garlic, tomatoes and mushrooms

**velouté** thick creamy white sauce made with fish, veal or chicken stock. Also used in soups

**venaison** venison

**verdure, en** garnished with green vegetables

**verjus** juice of unripe grapes

**vermicelle** vermicelli

**verveine** herbal tea made with verbena

**viande** meat

**viande séchée** thin slices of cured beef

**vichyssoise** leek and potato soup, served cold

**viennoise** fried in egg and breadcrumbs

**vin** wine

**vin blanc** white wine

**vin de pays** local regional wine

**vin de table** table wine

**vin rosé** rosé wine

**vin rouge** red wine

**vinaigrette** French dressing of oil and vinegar

**vinaigre** vinegar

**violet** sea squirt

**volaille** poultry

**yaourt** yoghurt

**zewelwai** onion flan

# Grammar

## Nouns

A noun is a word such as 'car', 'horse' or 'Mary' which is used to refer to a person or thing.

Unlike English, French nouns have a gender: they are either masculine (le) or feminine (la). Therefore words for 'the' and 'a(n)' must agree with the noun they accompany – whether masculine, feminine or plural.

|        | masculine | feminine | plural |
|--------|-----------|----------|--------|
| the    | le chat   | la rue   | les chats, les rues |
| a, an  | un chat   | une rue  | des chats, des rues |

If the noun begins with a vowel (a, e, i, o or u) or a silent h, le and la shorten to l', i.e. l'avion *(m)*, l'école *(f)*, l'hôtel *(m)*.

**Note**: when le and les are used after the prepositions à (to, at) and de (any, some, of) they contract as follows:

à + le = au (au cinéma but à la gare)
à + les = aux (aux magasins – applies to both *(m)* and *(f)*)
de + le = du (du pain but de la confiture)
de + les = des (des pommes – applies to both *(m)* and *(f)*)

There are some broad rules with noun endings which indicate whether they are masculine or feminine.

Generally masculine endings:
-er, -ier, -eau, -t, -c, -age, -ail, -oir, -é, -on, -acle, -ège, -ème, -o, -ou

Generally feminine endings:
**-euse**, **-trice**, **-ère**, **-ière**, **-elle**, **-te**, **-tte**, **-de**, **-che**, **-age**, **-aille**, **-oire**, **-ée**, **-té**, **-tié**, **-onne**, **-aison**, **-ion**, **-esse**, **-ie**, **-ine**, **-une**, **-ure**, **-ance**, **-anse**, **-ence**, **-ense**

# Plurals

The general rule is to add an **s** to the singular.

> **le chat** = **les chats**

Exceptions occur with the following noun endings: **-eau**, **-eu**, **-al**.

> **le bateau** = **les bateaux**
> **le neveu** = **les neveux**
> **le cheval** = **les chevaux**

Nouns ending in **-s**, **-x**, or **-z** do not change in the plural.

> **le dos** = **les dos**
> **le prix** = **les prix**
> **le nez** = **les nez**

# Adjectives

An adjective is a word such as 'small', 'pretty' or 'practical' that describes a person or thing, or gives extra information about them.

Adjectives normally follow the noun they describe in French.

> **la pomme verte** the green apple

Some common exceptions which go before the noun are:
**beau** beautiful, **bon** good, **grand** big, **haut** high, **jeune** young, **long** long, **joli** pretty, **mauvais** bad, **nouveau** new, **petit** small, **vieux** old.

> **un bon livre** a good book

French adjectives have to reflect the gender of the noun they describe. To make an adjective feminine, an e is added to the masculine form unless this already ends in an e, i.e. jeune.

**Note**: The addition of an e to the final consonant (which is usually silent in the masculine) means that you should pronounce the ending in the feminine.

| masculine | le livre vert | feminine | la pomme verte |
|---|---|---|---|
| | luh leevr vehr | | la pom vehrt |
| | the green book | | the green apple |

To make an adjective plural, an s is added to the singular form: masculine plural – verts (the ending is still silent: vehr) or feminine plural – vertes (because of the e, the t ending is sounded: vehrt).

## My, your, his, her, our, their

These words also reflect the gender and number of the noun they accompany (whether masculine, feminine or plural) and not the sex of the 'owner'.

| | with masc. sing. noun | with fem. sing. noun | with plural nouns |
|---|---|---|---|
| my | mon | ma | mes |
| your (familiar, singular) | ton | ta | tes |
| his/her | son | sa | ses |
| our | notre | notre | nos |
| your (polite and plural) | votre | votre | vos |
| their | leur | leur | leurs |

# Pronouns

. . . . . . . . . . . . . . . . . . . . . . . . . . . . . . . . . . . . . . . .

A pronoun is a word that you use to refer to someone or something when you do not need to use a noun, usually because the person or thing has been mentioned earlier. Examples are 'it', 'she', 'something' and 'myself'.

| subject | | object | |
|---|---|---|---|
| I | je, j' | me | me, m' |
| you (familiar) | tu | you | te, t' |
| you (polite and plural) | vous | you | vous |
| he/it | il | him/it | le, l' |
| she/it | elle | her/it | la, l' |
| we | nous | us | nous |
| they (masculine) | ils | them | les |
| they (feminine) | elles | them | les |

In French there are two forms for 'you' – tu and vous. Tu is the familiar form which is used with children and people you know as friends. Vous, as well as being the plural form for 'you', is also the polite form of addressing someone. You should probably use this form until the other person invites you to use the more familiar tu ('on se dit 'tu'?').

Object pronouns are placed before the verb.

> il vous aime (he loves <u>you</u>)
> nous la connaissons (we know <u>her</u>)

However, in commands or requests object pronouns follow the verb.

> écoutez-le (listen to <u>him</u>)
> aidez-moi (help <u>me</u>)

**Note**: this does not apply to negative commands or requests.

> ne le faites pas (don't do <u>it</u>)

The object pronouns shown above are also used to mean 'to me', 'to us', etc. except, le and la which become lui (to him, to her) and les which becomes leur (to them).

il le lui donne (he gives it <u>to him</u>)

# Verbs

A verb is a word such as 'sing', 'walk' or 'cry' which is used with a subject to say what someone or something does or what happens to them. Regular verbs follow the same pattern of endings. Irregular verbs do not follow a regular pattern so you need to learn the different endings.

There are three main patterns of endings for verbs in French – those ending -er, -ir and -re.

| | |
|---|---|
| donner | **to give** |
| je donne | I give |
| tu donnes | you give |
| il/elle donne | he/she gives |
| nous donnons | we give |
| vous donnez | you give |
| ils/elles donnent | they give |
| past participle: donné (with avoir) | |

| | |
|---|---|
| finir | **to finish** |
| je finis | I finish |
| tu finis | you finish |
| il/elle finit | he/she finishes |
| nous finissons | we finish |
| vous finissez | you finish |
| ils/elles finissent | they finish |
| past participle: fini (with avoir) | |

| répondre | **to reply** |
|---|---|
| je réponds | I reply |
| tu réponds | you reply |
| il/elle répond | he/she replies |
| nous répondons | we reply |
| vous répondez | you reply |
| ils/elles répondent | they reply |

past participle: répondu (with avoir)

## Irregular verbs

Among the most important irregular verbs are the following:

| être | **to be** |
|---|---|
| je suis | I am |
| tu es | you are |
| il/elle est | he/she is |
| nous sommes | we are |
| vous êtes | you are |
| ils/elles sont | they are |

past participle: été (with avoir)

| avoir | **to have** |
|---|---|
| j'ai | I have |
| tu as | you have |
| il/elle a | he/she has |
| nous avons | we have |
| vous avez | you have |
| ils/elles ont | they have |

past participle: eu (with avoir)

| aller | **to go** |
|---|---|
| je vais | I go |
| tu vas | you go |
| il/elle va | he/she goes |
| nous allons | we go |
| vous allez | you go |
| ils/elles vont | they go |

past participle: allé (with être)

| venir | **to come** |
|---|---|
| je viens | I come |
| tu viens | you come |
| il/elle vient | he/she comes |
| nous venons | we come |
| vous venez | you come |
| ils/elles viennent | they come |

past participle: venu (with être)

| faire | **to do** |
|---|---|
| je fais | I do |
| tu fais | you do |
| il/elle fait | he/she does |
| nous faisons | we do |
| vous faites | you do |
| ils/elles font | they do |

past participle: fait (with avoir)

| vouloir | **to want** |
|---|---|
| je veux | I want |
| tu veux | you want |
| il/elle veut | he/she wants |
| nous voulons | we want |
| vous voulez | you want |
| ils/elles veulent | they want |

past participle: voulu (with avoir)

| pouvoir | **to be able to** |
|---|---|
| je peux | I can |
| tu peux | you can |
| il/elle peut | he/she can |
| nous pouvons | we can |
| vous pouvez | you can |
| ils/elles peuvent | they can |

past participle: pu (with avoir)

| devoir | **to have to** |
|---|---|
| je dois | I have to |
| tu dois | you have to |
| il/elle doit | he/she has to |
| nous devons | we have to |
| vous devez | you have to |
| ils/elles doivent | they have to |

past participle: dû (with avoir)

# Past tense

To make a simple past tense, you need an auxiliary verb with the past participle of the main verb, e.g. 'I have' (auxiliary) 'been' (past participle), 'I have' (auxiliary) 'eaten' (past participle). In French the basic auxiliary verbs are avoir (to have) and être (to be). A reflexive verb is one where the subject and object are the same e.g. 'to enjoy yourself', 'to dress yourself'. These verbs take être as their auxiliary verb.

To form the simple past tense, 'I gave/I have given', 'I finished/ I have finished', combine the present tense of the verb avoir – 'to have' with the past participle of the verb (donné, fini, répondu).

| j'ai donné | I gave/I have given |
|---|---|
| j'ai fini | I finished/I have finished |
| j'ai répondu | I replied/I have replied |

Grammar

Not all verbs take avoir (j'ai..., il a...) as their auxiliary verb. The reflexive verbs (s'amuser, se promener, etc) take être (je me suis..., il s'est...), and so do a dozen or so other verbs which generally express the idea of motion or staying such as aller 'to go' and rester 'to stay'.

| | |
|---|---|
| je me suis amusé | I had fun |
| je suis allé | I went |
| je suis resté | I stayed |

When the auxiliary verb être is used, the past participle (amusé, allé, resté, etc) becomes like an adjective and agrees with the subject of the verb in number and gender.

| | |
|---|---|
| je me suis amusée | I had fun (female) |
| nous nous sommes amusés | we had fun (plural) |
| je suis allée | I went (female) |
| nous sommes allés | we went (plural) |
| je suis restée | I stayed (female) |
| nous sommes restés | we stayed (plural) |

To make a sentence negative e.g. 'I am not eating', you use ne ... pas around the verb or auxilliary verb.

| | |
|---|---|
| je ne mange pas | I am not eating |
| je ne me suis pas amusé | I did not have fun |

# Dictionary

## A

**a(n)** un/une *m/f*
**abbey** l'abbaye *f*
**able:** *to be able to* pouvoir
**abortion** l'avortement *m*
**about** (approximately) vers; environ
(concerning) au sujet de
*about 100 euros* environ cent euros
*about 10 o'clock* vers dix heures
**above** au-dessus *(de)*
*above the bed* au-dessus du lit
*above the farm* au-dessus de la ferme
**abroad** à l'étranger
**abscess** l'abcès *m*
**accelerator** l'accélérateur *m*
**accent** l'accent *m*
**to accept** accepter
*do you accept this card?* vous acceptez
cette carte?
**access** l'accès *m*
**accident** l'accident *m*
**accident & emergency
department (A&E)** les urgences
**accommodation** le logement
**to accompany** accompagner
**account** le compte
**account number** le numéro de compte
**to ache** faire mal
*it aches* ça fait mal
**acid** l'acide *m*
**actor** l'acteur *m*, l'actrice *f*
**adaptor** (electrical) l'adaptateur *m*
**address** l'adresse *f*
*here's my address* voici mon adresse
*what is the address?* quelle est l'adresse?
**address book** le carnet d'adresse
**admission charge** l'entrée *f*
**to admit** (to hospital) hospitaliser
**adult** *m/f* l'adulte
*for adults* pour adultes
**advance:** *in advance* à l'avance
**advertisement** (in paper) l'annonce *f*;
(on TV) la publicité

**to advise** conseiller
**aerial** l'antenne *f*
**aeroplane** l'avion *m*
**aerosol** l'aérosol *m*
**afraid:** *to be afraid of* avoir peur de
**after** après
**afternoon** l'après-midi *m*
*in the afternoon* l'après-midi
*this afternoon* cet après-midi
*tomorrow afternoon* demain après-midi
**aftershave** l'après-rasage *m*
**again** encore
**against** contre
**age** l'âge *m*
**agency** l'agence *f*
**ago:** *a week ago* il y a une semaine
**to agree** être d'accord
**agreement** l'accord *m*
**AIDS** le SIDA
**air ambulance** l'hélicoptère médical *m*
**airbag** (in car) l'airbag *m*
**airbed** le matelas pneumatique
**air-conditioning** la climatisation
**air-conditioning unit** le climatiseur
**air freshener** le désodorisant
**airline** la ligne aérienne
**air mail:** *by airmail* par avion
**airplane** l'avion *m*
**airport** l'aéroport *m*
**airport bus** la navette pour l'aéroport
**air ticket** le billet d'avion
**aisle** le couloir
**alarm** l'alarme *f*
**alarm clock** le réveil
**alcohol** l'alcool *m*
**alcohol-free** sans alcool
**alcoholic drink** la boisson alcoolisée
**all** tout(e)/tous/toutes
**allergic** allergique
*I'm allergic to...* je suis allergique à...
**allergy** l'allergie *f*
**to allow** permettre
*it's not allowed* c'est interdit

**all right** (agreed) d'accord
*are you all right?* ça va?
**almost** presque
**alone** tout(e) seul(e)
**Alps** les Alpes
**already** déjà
**also** aussi
**altar** l'autel *m*
**always** toujours
**a.m.** du matin
**am:** *I am* je suis
**amber** (traffic light) orange
**ambulance** l'ambulance *f*
**America** l'Amérique *f*
**American** américain(e)
**amount** (total) le montant
**anaesthetic** l'anesthésique *m*
*a general anaesthetic* une anesthésie
  générale
*a local anaesthetic* une anesthésie
  locale
**anchor** l'ancre *f*
**and** et
**angina** l'angine de poitrine *f*
**angry** fâché(e)
**animal** l'animal *m*
**aniseed** l'anis *m*
**ankle** la cheville
**anniversary** l'anniversaire *m*
**to announce** annoncer
**announcement** l'annonce *f*
**annual** annuel(-elle)
**another** un(e) autre
*another beer* une autre bière
**answer** la réponse
**to answer** répondre à
**answerphone** le répondeur
**antacid** le comprimé contre les
  brûlures d'estomac
**antenna** l'antenne *f*
**antibiotic** l'antibiotique *m*
**antifreeze** l'antigel *m*
**antihistamine** l'antihistaminique *m*
**antiques** les antiquités
**antique shop** le magasin d'antiquités
**antiseptic** l'antiseptique *m*
**any** de (du/de la/des)

*have you any apples?* vous avez
  des pommes?
**anyone** quelqu'un/personne
**anything** quelque chose/rien
**anywhere** quelque part
**apartment** l'appartement *m*
**appendicitis** l'appendicite *f*
**apple** la pomme
**application form** le formulaire
**appointment** le rendez-vous
*I have an appointment* j'ai rendez-vous
**approximately** environ
**April** avril
**architect** *m/f* l'architecte
**architecture** l'architecture *f*
**are:** *you are* vous êtes
*we are* nous sommes
*they are* ils/elles sont
**arm** le bras
**armbands** (for swimming) les bracelets
  gonflables
**armchair** le fauteuil
**to arrange** arranger
**to arrest** arrêter
**arrival** l'arrivée *f*
**to arrive** arriver
**art** l'art *m*
**art gallery** le musée
**arthritis** l'arthrite *f*
**artificial** artificiel
**artist** l'artiste *m/f*
**ashtray** le cendrier
**to ask** demander
*to ask a question* poser une question
**aspirin** l'aspirine *f*
**asthma** l'asthme *m*
*I have asthma* je suis asthmatique
**at** à
*at 8 o'clock* à huit heures
*at my/your home* chez moi/vous
*at night* la nuit
*at once* tout de suite
**Atlantic Ocean** l'Océan atlantique *m*
**attachment** (e-mail) la pièce jointe *f*
**attack** (mugging) l'agression *f*
(medical) la crise
**to attack** agresser

attic le grenier
attractive séduisant(e)
auction la vente aux enchères
audience le public
August août
aunt la tante
au pair la jeune fille au pair
Australia l'Australie f
Australian australien(ne)
author l'écrivain; l'auteur m
automatic automatique
automatic car la voiture à boîte automatique
auto-teller le distributeur automatique (de billets)
autumn l'automne m
available disponible
avalanche l'avalanche f
avenue l'avenue f
average moyen(ne)
to avoid éviter
awake: I was awake all night je n'ai pas dormi de toute la nuit
awful affreux(-euse)
awning (for caravan etc) l'auvent m
axle (car) l'essieu m

# B

baby le bébé
baby food les petits pots
baby milk (formula) le lait maternisé
baby's bottle le biberon
baby seat (car) le siège pour bébés
babysitter le/la babysitter
baby wipes les lingettes
back (of body) le dos
backpack le sac à dos
bacon le bacon; le lard
bad (food, weather) mauvais(e)
badminton le badminton
bag le sac; (suitcase) la valise
baggage les bagages
baggage allowance le poids (de bagages) autorisé
baggage reclaim la livraison des bagages
bait (for fishing) l'appât m
baked au four

baker's la boulangerie
balcony le balcon
bald (person) chauve; (tyre) lisse
ball (large: football, etc) le ballon
(small: golf, tennis, etc) la balle
ballet le ballet
balloon le ballon
banana la banane
band (music) le groupe
bandage le pansement
bank (money) la banque
(river) la rive; le bord
bank account le compte en banque
banknote le billet de banque
bar le bar
bar of chocolate la tablette de chocolat
barbecue le barbecue
to have a barbecue faire un barbecue
barber's le coiffeur
to bark aboyer
barn la grange
barrel (wine, beer) le tonneau
basement le sous-sol
basil le basilic
basket le panier
basketball le basket-ball
bat (baseball, cricket) la batte
(animal) la chauve-souris
bath le bain
to have a bath prendre un bain
bathing cap le bonnet de bain
bathroom la salle de bains
with bathroom avec salle de bains
battery (for car) la batterie
(for radio, camera, etc) la pile
bay (along coast) la baie
B&B la chambre d'hôte
to be être
beach la plage
private beach la plage privée
sandy beach la plage de sable
nudist beach la plage de nudistes
beach hut la cabine
bean le haricot
beard la barbe
beautiful beau (belle)
beauty salon le salon de beauté

**because** parce que
**to become** devenir
**bed** le lit
*double bed* le grand lit; le lit deux places
*single bed* le lit une place
*sofa bed* le canapé-lit
*twin beds* les lits jumeaux
**bed clothes** les draps et couvertures
**bedroom** la chambre à coucher
**bee** l'abeille *f*
**beef** le bœuf
**beer** la bière
**before** avant
**to begin** commencer
**behind** derrière
**beige** beige
**Belgian** belge
**Belgium** la Belgique
**to believe** croire
**bell** (church, school) la cloche
(doorbell) la sonnette
**to belong to** appartenir à
**below** sous
**belt** la ceinture
**bend** (in road) le virage
**berth** (train, ship, etc) la couchette
**beside** (next to) à côté de
*beside the bank* à côté de la banque
**best** le/la meilleur(e)
**bet** le pari
**to bet on** faire un pari sur
**better** meilleur(e)
*better than* meilleur que
**between** entre
**bib** (baby's) le bavoir
**bicycle** la bicyclette; le vélo
**bicycle pump** la pompe à vélo
**bicycle repair kit** la trousse de
  réparation (pour vélo)
**bidet** le bidet
**big** grand(e), gros(se)
**bike** (pushbike) le vélo
(motorbike) la moto
**bike lock** l'antivol *m*
**bikini** le bikini
**bill** (restaurant) l'addition *f*
(hotel) la note

(for work done) la facture
**bin** (dustbin) la poubelle
**bin liner** le sac poubelle
**binoculars** les jumelles
**bird** l'oiseau *m*
**biro** le stylo
**birth** la naissance
**birth certificate** l'acte de naissance *m*
**birthday** l'anniversaire *m*
*happy birthday!* bon anniversaire!
*my birthday is on...* mon anniversaire
  c'est le...
**birthday card** la carte d'anniversaire
**birthday present** le cadeau d'anniversaire
**biscuits** les biscuits
**bit:** *a bit (of)* un peu *(de)*
**bite** (animal) la morsure
(insect) la piqûre
**to bite** (animal) mordre
(insect) piquer
**bitten** (by animal) mordu(e)
(by insect) piqué(e)
**bitter** amer(-ère)
**black** noir(e)
**black ice** le verglas
**blank** (disk, tape) vierge
**blanket** la couverture
**bleach** l'eau de Javel *f*
**to bleed** saigner
**blender** (for food) le mixeur
**blind** (person) aveugle
(for window) le store
**blister** l'ampoule *f*
**block of flats** l'immeuble *m*
**blocked** bouché(e)
*the sink is blocked* l'évier est bouché
**blond** (person) blond(e)
**blood** le sang
**blood group** le groupe sanguin
**blood pressure** la tension (artérielle)
**blood test** l'analyse de sang *f*
**blouse** le chemisier
**blow-dry** le brushing
**blowout** (of tyre) l'éclatement *m*
**blue** bleu(e)
*dark blue* bleu foncé
*light blue* bleu clair

**BMX** le bicross
**boar** (wild) le sanglier
**to board** (plane, train, etc) embarquer
**boarding card** la carte
 d'embarquement
**boarding house** la pension (de famille)
**boat** le bateau; (rowing) la barque
**boat trip** l'excursion en bateau *f*
**body** le corps
**to boil** faire bouillir
**boiled** bouilli(e)
**boiler** la chaudière
**bomb** la bombe
**bone** l'os *m*; (fish) l'arête *f*
**bonfire** le feu
**book** le livre
**to book** (reserve) réserver
**booking** la réservation
**booking office** le bureau de location
**bookshop** la librairie
**booster: booster seat** le réhausseur
**boots** les bottes
(short) les bottillons
**border** (of country) la frontière
**boring** ennuyeux(-euse)
**born: to be born** naître
**to borrow** emprunter
**boss** le chef
**both** les deux
**bottle** la bouteille
*a bottle of water* une bouteille d'eau
*a bottle of wine* une bouteille de vin
*a half-bottle* une demi-bouteille
**bottle opener** l'ouvre-bouteilles *m*
**bottom** (of pool, etc) le fond
**bowl** (for soup, etc) le bol
**bow tie** le nœud papillon
**box** la boîte
**box office** le bureau de location
**boxer shorts** le caleçon
**boy** le garçon
**boyfriend** le copain
**bra** le soutien-gorge
**bracelet** le bracelet
**brain** le cerveau
**brake(s)** le(s) frein(s)
**to brake** freiner

**brake cable** le câble de frein
**brake fluid** le liquide de freins
**brake lights** les feux de stop
**brake pads** les plaquettes de frein
**branch** (of tree) la branche
(of company, etc) la succursale
**brand** (make) la marque
**brass** le cuivre
**brave** courageux(-euse)
**bread** le pain
(French stick) la baguette
(thin French stick) la ficelle
*sliced bread* le pain de mie en tranches
**bread roll** le petit pain
**to break** casser
**breakable** fragile
**breakdown** (car) la panne
(nervous) la dépression
**breakdown van** la dépanneuse
**breakfast** le petit déjeuner
**breast** le sein
**to breast-feed** allaiter
**to breathe** respirer
**brick** la brique
**bride** la mariée
**bridegroom** le marié
**bridge** le pont
**briefcase** la serviette
**Brillo® pad** le tampon Jex®
**to bring** apporter
**Britain** la Grande-Bretagne
**British** britannique
**broadband** le haut débit
**brochure** la brochure; le dépliant
**broken** cassé(e)
*my leg is broken* je me suis cassé
 la jambe
**broken down** (car, etc) en panne
**bronchitis** la bronchite
**bronze** le bronze
**brooch** la broche
**broom** (brush) le balai
**brother** le frère
**brother-in-law** le beau-frère
**brown** marron
**bruise** le bleu
**brush** la brosse

bubble bath le bain moussant
bucket le seau
buffet car (train) la voiture-buffet
to build construire
building l'immeuble *m*
bulb (light) l'ampoule *f*
bumbag la banane
bumper (on car) le pare-chocs
bunch (of flowers) le bouquet
(of grapes) la grappe
bungee jumping le saut à l'élastique
bureau de change le bureau de change
burger le hamburger
burglar le/la cambrioleur(-euse)
burglar alarm le système d'alarme
to burn brûler
bus le bus; (coach) le car
bus pass la carte de bus
bus station la gare routière
bus stop l'arrêt de bus *m*
bus ticket le ticket de bus
business les affaires
*on business* pour affaires

business card la carte de visite
business centre le centre d'affaires
business class la classe affaires
businessman/woman l'homme/
   la femme d'affaires
business trip le voyage d'affaires
busy occupé(e)
but mais
butcher's la boucherie
butter le beurre
button le bouton
to buy acheter
by (via) par
(beside) à côté de
*by bus* en bus
*by car* en voiture
*by ship* en bateau
*by train* en train
bypass (road) la rocade

## C

cab (taxi) le taxi
cabaret le cabaret
cabin (on boat) la cabine

cabin crew l'équipage *m*
cablecar le téléphérique; la benne
café le café
*internet café* le cybercafé
cafetière la cafetière
cake (large) le gâteau
(small) la pâtisserie; le petit gâteau
cake shop la pâtisserie
calculator la calculatrice
calendar le calendrier
call (telephone) l'appel *m*
to call (speak, phone) appeler
calm calme
camcorder le caméscope
camera l'appareil photo *m*
camera case l'étui *m*
camera phone le téléphone portable-
   appareil photo
camera shop le magasin de photo
to camp camper
camping gas le butane
camping stove le camping-gaz®
campsite le camping
can (to be able to) pouvoir
(to know how to) savoir
*I can* je peux/sais
*we can* nous pouvons/savons
can la boîte
can opener l'ouvre-boîtes *m*
Canada le Canada
Canadian canadien(ne)
canal le canal
to cancel annuler
cancellation l'annulation *f*
cancer le cancer
candle la bougie
canoe le kayak
canoeing: *to go canoeing* faire
   du canoë-kayak
cap (hat) la casquette
(contraceptive) le diaphragme
capital (city) la capitale
cappuccino le cappuccino
car la voiture
car alarm l'alarme de voiture *f*
car ferry le ferry
car hire la location de voitures

**car insurance** l'assurance automobile f
**car keys** les clés de voiture
**car park** le parking
**car parts** les pièces pour voiture
**car phone** le téléphone de voiture
**car port** l'auvent m
**car radio** l'autoradio m
**car seat** (for child) le siège pour enfant
**carwash** le lavage automatique
**carafe** le pichet
**caravan** la caravane
**carburettor** le carburateur
**card** la carte
*birthday card* la carte d'anniversaire
*business card* la carte de visite
*playing cards* les cartes à jouer
**cardboard** le carton
**cardigan** le gilet
**careful: to be careful** faire attention
*careful!* attention!
**carpet** (rug) le tapis
(fitted) la moquette
**carriage** (railway) la voiture
**carrot** la carotte
**to carry** porter
**carton** (cigarettes) la cartouche
(milk, juice) le brick
**case** (suitcase) la valise
**cash** l'argent liquide m
**to cash** (cheque) encaisser
**cash desk** la caisse
**cash dispenser** (ATM) le distributeur
automatique (de billets)
**cashier** le/la caissier(-ière)
**cashpoint** le distributeur automatique
(de billets)
**casino** le casino
**casserole dish** la cocotte
**cassette** la cassette
**castle** le château
**casualty department** les urgences
**cat** le chat
**catalytic converter** le pot catalytique
**cat food** la nourriture pour chats
**catalogue** le catalogue
**catch** (bus, train) prendre
**cathedral** la cathédrale

**Catholic** catholique
**cave** la grotte
**cavity** (in tooth) la carie
**CD** le CD
**CD player** le lecteur de CD
**CD ROM** le CD-Rom
**ceiling** le plafond
**cellar** la cave
**cellphone** le téléphone cellulaire
**cemetery** le cimetière
**centimetre** le centimètre
**central** central(e)
**central heating** le chauffage central
**central locking** le verrouillage central
**centre** le centre
**century** le siècle
**ceramic** la céramique
**cereal** la céréale
**certain** (sure) certain(e)
**certificate** le certificat
**chain** la chaîne
**chair** la chaise
**chairlift** le télésiège
**chalet** le chalet
**chambermaid** la femme de chambre
**champagne** le champagne
**change** (small coins) la monnaie
**to change** changer
*to change bus* changer d'autobus
*to change clothes* se changer
*to change money* changer de l'argent
*to change train* changer de train
**changing room** la cabine d'essayage
**Channel** (English) la Manche
**chapel** la chapelle
**charcoal** le charbon de bois
**charge** (fee) le prix
**charge: I've run out of charge** je n'ai
plus de batterie
**to charge** prendre
**to charge** recharger: *I need to
charge my phone* j'ai besoin de
recharger mon téléphone
**charge card** la carte de paiement
**charger** (battery) le chargeur
**charter flight** le vol charter
**cheap** bon marché

cheaper moins cher
cheap rate (phone) le tarif réduit
to check vérifier
to check in enregistrer
check-in (desk) l'enregistrement des bagages m
(at hotel) la réception
cheek la joue
cheers! santé!
cheese le fromage
chef le chef de cuisine
chemist's la pharmacie
cheque le chèque
cheque book le carnet de chèques
cheque card la carte d'identité bancaire
chest (body) la poitrine
chewing gum le chewing-gum
chicken le poulet
chickenpox la varicelle
child l'enfant m
child safety seat (car) le siège pour enfant
children les enfants
for children pour enfants
chilli (fruit) le piment
(dish) le chili con carne
chimney la cheminée
chin le menton
china la porcelaine
chips les frites
chiropodist le/la pédicure
chocolate le chocolat
drinking-chocolate le chocolat en poudre
hot chocolate le chocolat chaud
chocolates les chocolats
choir la chorale
to choose choisir
chop (meat) la côtelette
chopping board la planche à découper
christening le baptême
Christian name le prénom
Christmas Noël m
merry Christmas! joyeux Noël!
Christmas card la carte de Noël
Christmas Eve la veille de Noël
church l'église f
cigar le cigare
cigarette la cigarette

cigarette lighter le briquet
cigarette paper le papier à cigarette
cinema le cinéma
circle (theatre) le balcon
circuit breaker le disjoncteur
circus le cirque
cistern (toilet) le réservoir de chasse d'eau
city la ville
city centre le centre-ville
class la classe
first-class de première classe
second-class de seconde classe
clean propre
to clean nettoyer
cleaner (person) la femme de ménage
cleanser (for face) le démaquillant
clear clair(e)
client le client/la cliente
cliff (along coast) la falaise
(in mountains) l'escarpement m
to climb (mountain) faire de la montagne
climbing boots les chaussures de montagne
Clingfilm® le film étirable
clinic la clinique
cloakroom le vestiaire
clock l'horloge f
close by proche
to close fermer
closed (shop, etc) fermé(e)
cloth (rag) le chiffon
(fabric) le tissu
clothes les vêtements
clothes line la corde à linge
clothes pegs les pinces à linge
clothes shop le magasin de vêtements
cloudy nuageux(-euse)
club le club
clutch (in car) l'embrayage m
clutch fluid le liquide d'embrayage
coach (bus) le car; l'autocar m
coach station la gare routière
coach trip l'excursion en car f
coal le charbon
coast la côte
coastguard le garde-côte
coat le manteau

126

coat hanger le cintre
cockroach le cafard
cocktail le cocktail
cocktail bar le cocktail-bar
cocoa le cacao
code le code
coffee le café
*coffee-shop* (shop) la brûlerie
*black coffee* le café noir
*decaffeinated coffee* le café décaféiné
*white coffee* le café au lait
digital numérique
*digital camera* l'appareil-photo numérique
(films) le caméscope numérique
coil (IUD) le stérilet
coin la pièce de monnaie
Coke® le Coca®
colander la passoire
cold froid
*I'm cold* j'ai froid
*it's cold* il fait froid
*cold water* l'eau froide *f*
cold (illness) le rhume
*I have a cold* j'ai un rhume
cold sore le bouton de fièvre
collar le col
collar bone la clavicule
colleague le/la collègue
to collect (someone) aller chercher
collection la collection
colour la couleur
colour-blind daltonien(ne)
colour film (for camera) la pellicule couleur
comb le peigne
to come venir
(to arrive) arriver
*to come back* revenir
*to come in* entrer
*come in!* entrez!
comedy la comédie
comfortable confortable
company (firm) la compagnie; la société
compartment le compartiment
compass la boussole
to complain faire une réclamation
complaint la plainte
to complete remplir

compulsory obligatoire
computer l'ordinateur *m*
computer disk (floppy) la disquette
computer game le jeu en réseau
computer program le programme
 informatique
concert le concert
concert hall la salle de concert
concession la réduction
concussion la commotion (cérébrale)
conditioner l'après-shampooing *m*
condom le préservatif
conductor (in orchestra) le chef d'orchestre
conference la conférence
to confirm confirmer
confirmation la confirmation
confused: *I am confused* je m'y perds
congratulations félicitations!
connection (train, bus, etc)
 la correspondance
constipated constipé(e)
consulate le consulat
to consult consulter
to contact contacter
contact details les coordonnées *f*
contact lenses les verres de contact
contact lens cleaner le produit pour
 nettoyer les verres de contact
to continue continuer
contraceptive le contraceptif
contract le contrat
convenient: *it's not convenient*
 ça ne m'arrange pas
convulsions les convulsions
to cook (be cooking) cuisiner
*to cook a meal* préparer un repas
cooked cuisiné
cooker la cuisinière
cool frais (fraîche)
cool-bag (for picnic) le sac isotherme
cool-box (for picnic) la glacière
copper le cuivre
copy (duplicate) la copie
to copy copier
cordless phone le téléphone sans fil
cork le bouchon
corkscrew le tire-bouchon

corner le coin
cornflakes les corn-flakes
corridor le couloir
cortisone la cortisone
cosmetics les produits de beauté
cost le coût
to cost coûter
*how much does it cost?* ça coûte combien?
costume (swimming) le maillot (de bain)
cot le lit d'enfant
cottage la maison de campagne
cotton le coton
cotton bud le coton-tige®
cotton wool le coton hydrophile
couchette la couchette
cough la toux
to cough tousser
cough mixture le sirop pour la toux
cough sweets les pastilles pour la gorge
counter (shop, bar, etc) le comptoir
country (not town) la campagne
(nation) le pays

countryside le paysage
couple (two people) le couple
*a couple of...* deux...
courgette la courgette
courier service le service de messageries
course (syllabus) le cours
(of meal) le plat
cousin le/la cousin(e)
cover charge (restaurant) le couvert
cow la vache
craft fair le marché d'artisanat
crafts les objets artisanaux
craftsperson l'artisan(e)
cramps (period pain) les règles douloureuses
cranberry juice le jus de cranberry
crash (car) l'accident m; la collision
crash helmet le casque
cream (food, lotion) la crème
*soured cream* la crème fermentée
*whipped cream* la crème fouettée
creche (toddlers) la crèche
(older) la garderie
credit (on mobile phone) les unités fpl
credit card la carte de crédit

crime le crime
crisps les chips
croissant le croissant
cross la croix
to cross (road, sea, etc) traverser
cross-country skiing le ski de fond
cross-channel ferry le ferry qui traverse la Manche
crossing (by sea) la traversée
crossroads le carrefour; le croisement
crossword puzzle les mots croisés
crowd la foule
crowded bondé(e)
crown la couronne
cruise la croisière
crutches les béquilles
to cry (weep) pleurer
crystal le cristal
cucumber le concombre
cufflinks les boutons de manchette
cul-de-sac le cul-de-sac
cup la tasse
cupboard le placard
currant le raisin sec
currency (tradition) la devise; la monnaie
current (air, water, etc) le courant
curtain le rideau
cushion le coussin
custom (tradition) la tradition
customer le/la client(e)
customs la douane
(duty) les droits de douane
customs declaration la déclaration de douane
to cut couper
cut la coupure
cutlery les couverts
to cycle faire du vélo
cycle track la piste cyclable
cycling le cyclisme
cyst le kyste
cystitis la cystite

## D

daily (each day) tous les jours
dairy produce les produits laitiers
dam le barrage

damage les dégâts
damp humide
dance le bal
to dance danser
danger le danger
dangerous dangereux(-euse)
dark l'obscurité f
*after dark* la nuit tombée
date la date
date of birth la date de naissance
daughter la fille
daughter-in-law la belle-fille
dawn l'aube f
day le jour
*every day* tous les jours
*per day* par jour
dead mort(e)
deaf sourd(e)
dear (expensive, in letter) cher (chère)
debit card la carte de paiement
debts les créances
decaffeinated décaféiné(e)
*decaffeinated coffee* le café décaféiné
December décembre
deckchair la chaise longue
to declare déclarer
*nothing to declare* rien à déclarer
deep profond(e)
deep freeze le congélateur
deer le cerf
to defrost décongeler
to de-ice (windscreen) dégivrer
delay le retard
*how long is the delay?* il y a combien de retard?
delayed retardé(e)
delicatessen l'épicerie fine f
delicious délicieux(-euse)
demonstration la manifestation
dental floss le fil dentaire
dentist le/la dentiste
dentures le dentier
deodorant le déodorant
to depart partir
department le rayon
department store le grand magasin
departure le départ

departure lounge la salle d'embarquement
deposit les arrhes
to describe décrire
description la description
desk (furniture) le bureau
(information) l'accueil m
dessert le dessert
details les détails
detergent le détergent
detour la déviation
to develop (photos) faire développer
diabetes le diabète
diabetic diabétique
*I'm diabetic* je suis diabétique
to dial (a number) composer
dialling code l'indicatif m
dialling tone la tonalité
diamond le diamant
diapers les couches (pour bébé)
diaphragm le diaphragme
diarrhoea la diarrhée
diary l'agenda m
dice le dé
dictionary le dictionnaire
to die mourir
diesel le gas-oil
diet le régime
*I'm on a diet* je suis au régime
*special diet* le régime spécial
different différent(e)
difficult difficile
to dilute diluer; ajouter de l'eau à
dinghy le canot
dining room la salle à manger
dinner (evening meal) le dîner
*to have dinner* dîner
diplomat le diplomate
direct (train, etc) direct(e)
directions les indications
*to ask for directions* demander le chemin
directory (telephone) l'annuaire m
directory enquiries (le service des) renseignements
dirty sale
disability: *to have a disability* être handicapé(e)

**disabled** (person) handicapé(e)
**to disagree** ne pas être d'accord
**to disappear** disparaître
**disaster** la catastrophe
**disco** la discothèque
**discount** le rabais
**to discover** découvrir
**disease** la maladie
**dish** le plat
**dishtowel** le torchon à vaisselle
**dishwasher** le lave-vaisselle
**disinfectant** le désinfectant
**disk** (floppy) la disquette
**to dislocate** (joint) disloquer
**disposable** jetable
**distant** lointain(e)
**distilled water** l'eau distillée *f*
**district** (of town) le quartier
**to disturb** déranger
**to dive** plonger
**diversion** la déviation
**divorced** divorcé(e)
**DIY shop** le magasin de bricolage
130 **dizzy** pris(e) de vertige
**to do** faire
**doctor** le médecin
**documents** les papiers
**dog** le chien
**dog food** la nourriture pour chiens
**dog lead** la laisse
**doll** la poupée
**dollar** le dollar
**domestic flight** le vol intérieur
**donor card** la carte de donneur d'organes
**door** la porte
**doorbell** la sonnette
**double** double
**double room** la chambre pour deux personnes
**double bed** le grand lit
**doughnut** le beignet
**down: to go down** descendre
**downstairs** en bas
**Down's syndrome** la trisomie
*he/she has Down's syndrome* il/elle est trisomique
**drain** (house) le tuyau d'écoulement

**draught** (of air) le courant d'air
*there's a draught* il y a un courant d'air
**draught lager** la bière pression
**drawer** le tiroir
**drawing** le dessin
**dress** la robe
**to dress** s'habiller
**dressing** (for food) la vinaigrette
(for wound) le pansement
**dressing gown** le peignoir
**drill** (tool) la perceuse électrique
**drink** la boisson
**to drink** boire
**drinking water** l'eau potable *f*
**to drive** conduire
**driver** (of car) le conducteur/ la conductrice
**driving licence** le permis de conduire
**drought** la sécheresse
**to drown** se noyer
**drug** (medicine) le médicament
(narcotics) la drogue
**drunk** ivre; soûl(e)
**dry** sec (sèche)
**to dry** sécher
**dry-cleaner's** le pressing
**dummy** (for baby) la tétine
**during** pendant
**dust** la poussière
**duster** le chiffon
**dustpan and brush** la pelle et la balayette
**duty-free** hors taxe
**duvet** la couette
**duvet cover** la housse de couette
**DVD** le DVD
**DVD player** le lecteur de DVD
**dye** la teinture
**dynamo** la dynamo

# E

**each** chacun/chacune
**ear** l'oreille *f*
**earlier** plus tôt
**early** tôt
**to earn** gagner
**earphones** le casque
**earplugs** les boules Quiès®

**earrings** les boucles d'oreille
**earth** la terre
**earthquake** le tremblement de terre
**east** l'est m
**Easter** Pâques
*happy Easter!* joyeuses Pâques!
**easy** facile
**to eat** manger
**ecological** écologique
**economy** (class) économique
**eco-tourism** l'écotourisme m
**egg** l'œuf m
*fried eggs* les œufs sur le plat
*hard-boiled egg* l'œuf dur
*scrambled eggs* les œufs brouillés
*soft-boiled egg* l'œuf à la coque
**either ... or** soit ... soit
**elastic band** l'élastique m
**elastoplast®** le sparadrap
**elbow** le coude
**electric** électrique
**electric blanket** la couverture chauffante
**electric razor** le rasoir électrique
**electric toothbrush** la brosse à dents électrique
**electrician** l'électricien m
**electricity** l'électricité f
**electricity meter** le compteur électrique
**electronic** électronique
**electronic organizer** l'agenda électronique m
**elevator** l'ascenseur m
**e-mail** l'e-mail m
*to e-mail sb* envoyer un e-mail à qn
**e-mail address** l'adresse électronique (on forms) le mél
**embassy** l'ambassade f
**emergency** l'urgence f
**emergency exit** la sortie de secours
**empty** vide
**end** la fin
**engaged** (to be married) fiancé(e)
(phone, toilet, etc) occupé(e)
**engine** le moteur
**England** l'Angleterre f
**English** anglais(e)
(language) l'anglais m

**Englishman/-woman** l'Anglais(e) m/f
**to enjoy** aimer
*enjoy your meal!* bon appétit!
*I enjoy dancing* j'aime danser
*I enjoy swimming* j'aime nager
**enough** assez
*that's enough* ça suffit
**enquiry desk** les renseignements
**to enter** entrer
**entertainment** les divertissements
**entrance** l'entrée f
**entrance fee** le prix d'entrée
**envelope** l'enveloppe f
**epileptic** épileptique
**epileptic fit** la crise d'épilepsie
**equipment** l'équipement m
**equal** égal
**eraser** la gomme
**error** l'erreur f
**escalator** l'escalator m
**to escape** s'échapper
**essential** indispensable
**estate agency** l'agence immobilière f
**estate car** le break
**Euro** (unit of currency) l'euro m
**eurocheque** l'eurochèque m
**Europe** l'Europe f
**European** européen(ne)
**European Union** l'Union européenne f
**evening** le soir
*7 o'clock in the evening* sept heures du soir
*in the evening* le soir
*this evening* ce soir
*tomorrow evening* demain soir
**evening dress** (man) la tenue de soirée (woman) la robe du soir
**evening meal** le dîner
**every** chaque
**everyone** tout le monde
**everything** tout
**everywhere** partout
**examination** l'examen m
**example:** *for example* par exemple
**excellent** excellent(e)
**except** sauf
**excess baggage** l'excédent de bagages m

exchange l'échange m
to exchange échanger
exchange rate le taux de change
exciting passionnant(e)
excursion l'excursion f
excuse: *excuse me!* excusez-moi!
(to get by) pardon!
exercise l'exercice m
exhaust pipe le pot d'échappement
exhibition l'exposition f
exit la sortie
expenses les frais
expensive cher (chère)
expert l'expert(e) m/f
to expire (ticket, passport) expirer
to explain expliquer
explosion l'explosion f
to export exporter
express (train) le rapide
(parcel, etc) en exprès
extension (electrical) la rallonge
extra (additional) supplémentaire
(more) de plus
eye l'œil m; les yeux pl
eyebrows les sourcils
eye drops les gouttes pour les yeux
eyelashes les cils
eyeliner l'eye-liner m
eye shadow le fard à paupières

## F

fabric le tissu
face le visage
face cloth/glove le gant de toilette
facial les soins du visage
facilities les installations
factor (sunblock) l'indice m
*factor 25* indice 25
factory l'usine f
to faint s'évanouir
fainted évanoui(e)
fair (hair) blond(e)
(just) juste
(funfair) la fête foraine
fake faux (fausse)
fall (autumn) l'automne m
to fall tomber

*he has fallen* il est tombé
false teeth le dentier
family la famille
famous célèbre
fan (handheld) l'éventail m
(electric) le ventilateur
(sports) le supporter
fan belt la courroie de ventilateur
fancy dress le déguisement
far loin
*is it far?* c'est loin?
fare (bus, metro, etc) le prix du billet
farm la ferme
farmer le fermier
farmhouse la ferme
farmers' market le marché fermier
fashionable à la mode
fast rapide
*too fast* trop vite
to fasten (seatbelt) attacher
fat gros (grosse)
(noun) la graisse
father le père
father-in-law le beau-père
fault (defect) un défaut
*it's not my fault* ce n'est pas de ma faute
favour le service
favourite préféré(e)
fax le fax
*by fax* par fax
fax number le numéro de fax
to fax (document) faxer
(person) envoyer un fax à
February février
to feed nourrir
to feel sentir
*I don't feel well* je ne me sens pas bien
*I feel sick* j'ai la nausée
feet les pieds
felt-tip pen le feutre
female (animal) la femelle
ferry le ferry
festival le festival
to fetch aller chercher
fever la fièvre
few peu
*a few* quelques-un(e)s

fiancé(e) le fiancé/la fiancée
field le champ
to fight se battre
file (computer) le fichier
(for papers) le dossier
to fill remplir
to fill in (form) remplir
to fill up (with petrol) faire le plein
*fill it up!* (car) le plein!
fillet le filet
filling (in tooth) le plombage
film le film
(for camera) la pellicule
filter le filtre
to find trouver
fine (penalty) la contravention
finger le doigt
to finish finir
finished fini(e)
fire le feu; l'incendie *m*
fire alarm l'alarme à incendie *f*
fire brigade les pompiers
fire engine la voiture de pompiers
fire escape (staircase) l'échelle de secours *f*
fire exit la sortie de secours
fire extinguisher l'extincteur *m*
fireplace la cheminée
fireworks les feux d'artifice
firm la compagnie
first premier(-ière)
first aid les premiers secours
first aid kit la trousse de secours
first-class de première classe
first name le prénom
fish le poisson
to fish pêcher
fisherman le pêcheur
fishing la pêche
*to go fishing* aller à la pêche
fishing permit le permis de pêche
fishing rod la canne à pêche
fishmonger's le/la marchand(e) de poisson
fit (medical) l'attaque *f*
to fit: *it doesn't fit me* ça ne me va pas
to fix (repair) réparer
*can you fix it?* vous pouvez le réparer?
fizzy gazeux(-euse)

flag le drapeau
flames les flammes
flash (for camera) le flash
flashlight la lampe de poche
flask (vacuum flask) le Thermos®
flat (appartment) l'appartement *m*
(level) plat
(beer) éventé
flat tyre le pneu dégonflé
flavour le goût
(of ice cream) le parfum
flaw le défaut
fleas les puces
fleece la polaire
flesh la chair
flex (electrical) le fil
flight le vol
flip flops les tongs
flippers les palmes
flood l'inondation *f*
flash flood la crue subite
floor (of room) le sol
(storey) l'étage
*(on the) ground floor* (au) rez-de-chaussée
*(on the) first floor* (au) premier étage
*(on the) second floor* (au) deuxième étage
*which floor?* quel étage?
floorcloth la serpillère
florist's shop le magasin de fleurs
flour la farine
flower la fleur
flu la grippe
fly la mouche
to fly (person) aller en avion
(bird) voler
fly sheet le double toit
fog le brouillard
foggy: *it was foggy* il y avait du brouillard
foil le papier alu(minium)
to fold plier
to follow suivre
food la nourriture
food poisoning l'intoxication alimentaire *f*
foot le pied

**to go on foot** aller à pied
**football** le football
**football match** le match de football
**football pitch** le terrain de football
**football player** le/la joueur(-euse)
 de football
**footpath** le sentier
**for** pour
*for him/her* pour lui/elle
*for me/you/us* pour moi/vous/nous
**forbidden** interdit(e)
**forehead** le front
**foreign** étranger(-ère)
**foreign currency** les devises étrangères
**foreigner** l'étranger(ère) *m(f)*
**forest** la forêt
**forever** toujours
**to forget** oublier
**fork** (for eating) la fourchette
(in road) l'embranchement *m*
**form** (document) le formulaire
(shape, style) la forme
**fortnight** la quinzaine
**forward** en avant
**foul** (football) la faute
**four** le quatre
**fountain** la fontaine
**four-wheel drive vehicle** le quatre-
 quatre; le 4x4
**fox** le renard
**fracture** la fracture
**fragile** fragile
**fragrance** le parfum
**frame** (picture) le cadre
**France** la France
*in/to France* en France
**free** (not occupied) libre
(costing nothing) gratuit(e)
**free-range** élevé(e) en plein air
**freezer** le congélateur
**French** français(e)
(language) le français
**French fries** les frites
**French people** les Français
**frequent** fréquent(e)
**fresh** frais (fraîche)
**fresh water** (not salt) l'eau douce *f*

**Friday** vendredi
**fridge** le frigo
**fried** frit(e)
**friend** *m/f* l'ami(e)
**frog** la grenouille
**frogs' legs** les cuisses de grenouille
**from** de
*I'm from England* je suis anglais(e)
*I'm from Scotland* je suis écossais(e)
**front** le devant
*in front of...* devant...
**front door** la porte d'entrée
**frost** le gel
**frozen** gelé(e)
(food) surgelé(e)
**fruit** le fruit
*dried fruit* les fruits secs
**fruit juice** le jus de fruit
**fruit salad** la salade de fruits
**to fry** frire
**frying-pan** la poêle
**fuel** le combustible
**fuel gauge** la jauge de carburant
**fuel pump** la pompe d'alimentation
**fuel tank** le réservoir de carburant
**full** plein(e)
(occupied) complet(-ète)
**full board** la pension complète
**fumes** (exhaust) les gaz d'échappement
**fun:** *to have fun* s'amuser
**funeral** les obsèques
**funfair** la fête foraine
**funny** (amusing) amusant(e)
**fur** la fourrure
**furnished** meublé(e)
**furniture** les meubles
**fuse** le fusible
**fuse box** la boîte à fusibles
**future** l'avenir *m*

## G

**gallery** la galerie
**game** le jeu
(meat) le gibier
**garage** (for petrol) la station-service
(for parking, repair) le garage
**garden** le jardin

**garlic** l'ail *m*
**gas** le gaz
**gas cooker** la gazinière
**gas cylinder** la bouteille de gaz
**gastritis** la gastrite
**gate** la porte
**gay** (person) homo
**gear** la vitesse
*in first gear* en première
*in second gear* en seconde
**gearbox** la boîte de vitesses
**gear cable** le câble d'embrayage
**gear lever** le levier de vitesse
**generous** généreux(-euse)
**gents** (toilet) les toilettes pour hommes
**genuine** authentique
**German** allemand(e)
(language) l'allemand *m*
**German measles** la rubéole
**Germany** l'Allemagne *f*
**to get** (obtain) obtenir
(to fetch) aller chercher
**to get in** (vehicle) monter
**to get off** (bus, etc) descendre
**gift** le cadeau
**gift shop** la boutique de souvenirs
**gigabyte** gigaoctet
**gigahertz** gigahertz
**girl** la fille
**girlfriend** la copine
**to give** donner
**to give back** rendre
**glacier** le glacier
**glass** le verre
*a glass of water* un verre d'eau
**glasses** (spectacles) les lunettes
**glasses case** l'étui à lunettes *m*
**gloves** les gants
**glue** la colle
**gluten** le gluten
**GM-free** sans OGM
**to go** aller
*I'm going to...* je vais...
*we're going to hire a car* nous allons
  louer une voiture
**to go back** retourner
**to go in** entrer

**to go out** (leave) sortir
**goat** la chèvre
**God** Dieu *m*
**goggles** (for swimming) les lunettes
  de natation
**gold** l'or
*is it gold?* c'est en or?
**golf** le golf
**golf ball** la balle de golf
**golf clubs** les clubs de golf
**golf course** le terrain de golf
**good** bon (bonne)
*(that's) good!* (c'est) bien!
**good afternoon** bonjour
**goodbye** au revoir
**good day** bonjour
**good evening** bonsoir
**good morning** bonjour
**good night** bonne nuit
**goose** l'oie *f*
**GPS** (global positioning system) le GPS
**gram** le gramme
**grandchildren** les petits-enfants
**granddaughter** la petite-fille
**grandfather** le grand-père
**grandmother** la grand-mère
**grandparents** les grands-parents
**grandson** le petit-fils
**grapes** le raisin
**grass** l'herbe *f*
**grated** (cheese) râpé(e)
**grater** la râpe
**greasy** gras (grasse)
**great** (big) grand(e)
(wonderful) formidable
**Great Britain** la Grande-Bretagne
**green** vert(e)
**green card** (insurance) la carte verte
**greengrocer's** le magasin de fruits
  et légumes
**greetings card** la carte de vœux
**grey** gris(e)
**grill** (part of cooker) le gril
**grilled** grillé(e)
**grocer's** l'épicerie *f*
**ground** la terre; le sol
**ground floor** le rez-de-chaussée

*on the ground floor* au rez-de-chaussée
**groundsheet** le tapis de sol
**group** le groupe
**guarantee** la garantie
**guard** (on train) le chef de train
**guava** la goyave
**guest** *m/f* (house guest) l'invité(e)
(in hotel) le/la client(e)
**guesthouse** la pension
**guide** (tourist guide) le/la guide
**guidebook** le guide
**guided tour** la visite guidée
**guitar** la guitare
**gun** (rifle) le fusil
(pistol) le pistolet
**gym** (gymnasium) le gymnase
**gym shoes** les chaussures de sport
**gynaecologist** le/la gynécologue

## H

**haemorrhoids** les hémorroïdes
**hail** la grêle
**hair** les cheveux

**hairbrush** la brosse à cheveux
**haircut** la coupe (de cheveux)
**hairdresser** le/la coiffeur(-euse)
**hairdryer** le sèche-cheveux
**hair dye** la teinture pour les cheveux
**hair gel** le gel pour cheveux
**hairgrip** la pince à cheveux
**hair mousse** la mousse coiffante
**hair spray** la laque
**half** la moitié
*half an hour* une demi-heure
**half board** la demi-pension
**half fare** le demi-tarif
**half-price** à moitié prix
**ham** (cooked) le jambon
(cured) le jambon cru
**hamburger** le hamburger
**hammer** le marteau
**hand** la main
**handbag** le sac à main
**handbrake** le frein à main
**hand luggage** les bagages à main
**hand-made** fait main
**handicapped** handicapé(e)

**handkerchief** le mouchoir
**handle** la poignée
**handlebars** le guidon
**hands-free kit** (for phone) le kit mains-libres
**handsome** beau (belle)
**hanger** (coathanger) le cintre
**hangover** la gueule de bois
**to hang up** (telephone) raccrocher
**hang-gliding** le deltaplane
*to go hang-gliding* faire du deltaplane
**to happen** arriver; se passer
*what happened?* qu'est-ce qui s'est passé?
**happy** heureux(-euse)
*happy birthday!* bon anniversaire!
**harbour** le port
**hard** (not soft) dur(e)
(not easy) difficile
**hard disk** le disque dur
**hardware shop** la quincaillerie
**to harm someone** faire du mal à quelqu'un
**harvest** (grape) les vendanges
**hat** le chapeau
**to have** avoir
**to have to** devoir
**hay fever** le rhume des foins
**he** il
**head** la tête
**headache** le mal de tête
*I have a headache* j'ai mal à la tête
**headlights** les phares
**headphones** les écouteurs
**head waiter** le maître d'hôtel
**health** la santé
**health food shop** la boutique de produits diététiques
**healthy** sain(e)
**to hear** entendre
**hearing aid** la prothèse auditive
**heart** le cœur
**heart attack** la crise cardiaque
**heartburn** les brûlures d'estomac
**heater** l'appareil de chauffage *m*, le radiateur
**heating** le chauffage

**to heat up** faire chauffer
**heavy** lourd(e)
**heel** le talon
**heel bar** le talon-minute
**height** la hauteur
**helicopter** l'hélicoptère *m*
**hello** bonjour!
(on telephone) allô?
**helmet** le casque
**help!** au secours!
**to help** aider
*can you help me?* vous pouvez m'aider?
**hem** l'ourlet *m*
**hepatitis** l'hépatite *f*
**her** son/sa/ses
*her passport* son passeport
*her room* sa chambre
*her suitcases* ses valises
**herb** l'herbe *f*
**herbal tea** la tisane
**here** ici
*here is...* voici...
**hernia** la hernie
**hi!** salut!
**to hide** (something) cacher
(oneself) se cacher
**high** haut(e)
**high blood pressure** la tension
**high chair** la chaise de bébé
**high tide** la marée haute
**hill** la colline
**hill-walking** la randonnée (de basse montagne)
**him** il; lui
**hip** la hanche
**hip replacement** la pose d'une prothèse de la hanche
**hire** la location
*bike hire* la location de bicyclettes
*boat hire* la location de bateaux
*car hire* la location de voitures
*ski hire* la location de skis
**to hire** louer
**hired car** la voiture de location
**his** son/sa/ses
*his passport* son passeport
*his room* sa chambre

*his suitcases* ses valises
**historic** historique
**history** l'histoire *f*
**to hit** frapper
**to hitchhike** faire du stop
**HIV** le VIH
**hobby** le passe-temps
**to hold** tenir
(contain) contenir
**hold-up** (in traffic) l'embouteillage *m*
**hole** le trou
**holiday** les vacances
*on holiday* en vacances
**home** la maison
*at my/your/our home* chez moi/vous/nous
**homeopathic** (remedy etc) homéopathique
**homeopathy** l'homéopathie *f*
**homesick: to be homesick** avoir le mal du pays
*I'm homesick* j'ai le mal du pays
**homosexual** homosexuel(le)
**honest** honnête
**honey** le miel
**honeymoon** la lune de miel
**hood** (of car) le capot
**hook** (fishing) l'hameçon *m*
**to hope** espérer
*I hope so/not* j'espère que oui/non
**horn** (of car) le klaxon
**hors d'œuvre** le hors-d'œuvre
**horse** le cheval
**horse racing** les courses de chevaux
**horse-riding: to go horse-riding** faire du cheval
**hosepipe** le tuyau d'arrosage
**hospital** l'hôpital *m*
**hostel** (youth hostel) l'auberge de jeunesse *f*
**hot** chaud(e)
*I'm hot* j'ai chaud
*it's hot* (weather) il fait chaud
**hot-water bottle** la bouillotte
**hotel** l'hôtel *m*
**hour** l'heure *f*
*half an hour* une demi-heure
*1 hour* une heure

**2 hours** deux heures
**house** la maison
**househusband** l'homme au foyer *m*
**housewife** la femme au foyer
**house wine** le vin en pichet
**housework**: *to do the housework* faire le ménage
**hovercraft** l'aéroglisseur *m*
**how?** (in what way) comment?
**how much/many?** combien?
**how are you?** comment allez-vous?
**hungry**: *to be hungry* avoir faim
**I'm hungry** j'ai faim
**to hunt** chasser
**hunting permit** le permis de chasse
**hurry**: *I'm in a hurry* je suis pressé
**to hurt**: *to hurt somebody* faire du mal à quelqu'un
**that hurts** ça fait mal
**husband** le mari
**hut** (bathing/beach) la cabine (mountain) le refuge
**hydrofoil** l'hydrofoil *m*
**hypodermic needle** l'aiguille hypodermique *f*

# I

**I** je
**ice** la glace
(cube) le glaçon
**with/without ice** avec/sans glaçons
**ice cream** la glace
**ice lolly** l'esquimau *m*
**ice rink** la patinoire
**to ice skate** faire du patin (à glace)
**ice skates** les patins (à glace)
**idea** l'idée *f*
**identity card** la carte d'identité
**if** si
**ignition** l'allumage *m*
**ignition key** la clé de contact
**ill** malade
**illness** la maladie
**immediately** immédiatement
**immersion heater** le chauffe-eau électrique
**immigration** l'immigration *f*

**immobilizer** (on car) l'antivol *m*
**immunisation** l'immunisation *f*
**to import** importer
**important** important(e)
**impossible** impossible
**to improve** améliorer
**in** dans
**in 2 hours' time** dans deux heures
**in Canada** au Canada
**in France** en France
**in London** à Londres
**in front of** devant
**included** compris(e)
**inconvenient** gênant
**to increase** augmenter
**indicator** (car) le clignotant
**indigestion** l'indigestion *f*
**indigestion tablets** les comprimés pour les troubles digestifs
**indoors** à l'intérieur
**infection** l'infection *f*
**infectious** infectieux(-euse)
**information** les renseignements
**information desk** les renseignements
**information office** le bureau de renseignements
**ingredients** les ingrédients
**inhaler** l'inhalateur *m*
**injection** la piqûre
**to injure** blesser
**injured** blessé(e)
**injury** la blessure
**inn** l'auberge *f*
**inner tube** la chambre à air
**inquiries** les renseignements
**inquiry desk** le bureau de renseignements
**insect** l'insecte *m*
**insect bite** la piqûre (d'insecte)
**insect repellent** le produit antimoustiques
**inside** à l'intérieur
**instant coffee** le café instantané
**instead of** au lieu de
**instructor** le moniteur/la monitrice
**insulin** l'insuline *f*
**insurance** l'assurance *f*

**insurance certificate** l'attestation d'assurance *f*
**to insure** assurer
**insured** assuré(e)
**to intend to** avoir l'intention de
**interesting** intéressant(e)
**international** international(e)
**internet** l'internet *m*
*internet café* le cybercafé
**internet access** l'accès internet *m*
*do you have internet access?* avez-vous un accès internet?
**interpreter** l'interprète *m/f*
**interval** (theatre) l'entracte *m*
**interview** l'entrevue *f* (TV, etc) l'interview *f*
**into** dans; en
*into town* en ville
**to introduce** présenter
**invitation** l'invitation *f*
**to invite** inviter
**invoice** la facture
**iPod®** l'iPod *m*
**Ireland** l'Irlande *f*
**Irish** irlandais(e)
**iron** (for clothes) le fer à repasser (metal) le fer
**to iron** repasser
**ironing board** la planche à repasser
**ironmonger's** la quincaillerie
**is** est
**island** l'île *f*
**it** il; elle
**Italian** italien(ne)
**Italy** l'Italie *f*
**to itch** démanger
*it itches* ça me démange
**item** l'article *m*
**itemized bill** la facture détaillée
**IUD** le stérilet

## J

**jack** (for car) le cric
**jacket** la veste
*waterproof jacket* l'anorak *m*
**jam** (food) la confiture
**jammed** (stuck) coincé(e)

**January** janvier
**jar** (honey, jam, etc) le pot
**jaundice** la jaunisse
**jaw** la mâchoire
**jealous** jaloux(-ouse)
**jeans** le jean
**jellyfish** la méduse
**jet ski** le jet-ski
**jetty** (landing pier) l'embarcadère *m*
**Jew** le Juif/la Juive
**jeweller's** la bijouterie
**jewellery** les bijoux
**Jewish** juif (juive)
**job** le travail; l'emploi
**to jog** faire du jogging
**to join** (become member) s'inscrire
**to join in** participer
**joint** (body) l'articulation *f*
**to joke** plaisanter
**joke** la plaisanterie
**journalist** le/la journaliste
**journey** le voyage
**judge** le juge
**jug** le pichet
**juice** le jus
*a carton of juice* une brique de jus de fruit
*fruit juice* le jus de fruit
*orange juice* le jus d'orange
**July** juillet
**to jump** sauter
**jumper** le pull
**jump leads** les câbles de raccordement pour batterie
**junction** (road) le croisement; le carrefour
**June** juin
**just:** *just two* deux seulement
*I've just arrived* je viens d'arriver

## K

**to keep** (retain) garder
**kennel** la niche
**kettle** la bouilloire
**key** la clé
*the car key* la clé de la voiture
**keyboard** le clavier
**keycard** (electronic key) la carte-clé électronique

**keyring** le porte-clés
**to kick** donner un coup de pied à
**kid** (child) le gosse
**kidneys** (in body) les reins
**kill** tuer
**kilo(gram)** le kilo
**kilometre** le kilomètre
**kind** (person) gentil(-ille)
**kind** (sort) la sorte
**kiosk** (newsstand) le kiosque
(phone box) la cabine
**kiss** le baiser
**to kiss** embrasser
**kitchen** la cuisine
**kitchen paper** l'essuie-tout *m*
**kite** (toy) le cerf-volant
**kiwi fruit** le kiwi
**knee** le genou
**knickers** la culotte
**knife** le couteau
**to knit** tricoter
**to knock** (on door) frapper
**to knock down** (in car) renverser
**to knock over** (vase, glass, etc) faire tomber
**knot** le nœud
**to know** (be aware of) savoir
(person, place) connaître
*I don't know* je ne sais pas
*I don't know Paris* je ne connais pas Paris
**to know how to do sth** savoir faire quelque chose
*to know how to swim* savoir nager
**kosher** casher

## L

**label** l'étiquette *f*
**lace** la dentelle
**laces** (for shoes) les lacets
**ladder** l'échelle *f*
**ladies** (toilet) les toilettes pour dames
**lady** la dame
**lager** la bière
*bottled lager* la bière en bouteille
*draught lager* la bière pression
**lake** le lac
**lamb** l'agneau *m*

**lamp** la lampe
**lamppost** le réverbère
**lampshade** l'abat-jour *m*
**to land** atterrir
**land** la terre
**landlady** la propriétaire
**landline phone** le (téléphone) fixe
**landlord** le propriétaire
**landslide** le glissement de terrain
**lane** la ruelle
(of motorway) la voie
**language** la langue
**language school** l'école de langues *f*
**laptop** le portable
**laptop bag** la sacoche d'ordinateur portable
**large** grand(e)
**last** dernier(-ière)
*last month* le mois dernier
*last night* (evening/night-time) hier soir; la nuit dernière
*last time* la dernière fois
*last week* la semaine dernière
*last year* l'année dernière
*the last bus* le dernier bus
*the last train* le dernier train
**late** tard
*sorry we are late* excusez-nous d'arriver en retard
*the train is late* le train a du retard
**later** plus tard
**to laugh** rire
**launderette** la laverie automatique
**laundry service** le service de blanchisserie
**lavatory** les toilettes
**lavender** la lavande
**law** la loi
**lawn** la pelouse
**lawyer** *m/f* l'avocat(e)
**laxative** le laxatif
**layby** l'aire de stationnement *f*
**lead** (electric) le fil
(metal) le plomb
**lead-free petrol** l'essence sans plomb *f*
**leaf** la feuille
**leak** la fuite
**to leak:** *it's leaking* il y a une fuite

**to learn** apprendre
**learning disability:** *he/she has a learning disability* il a des difficultés d'apprentissage
**lease** (rental) le bail
**leather** le cuir
**to leave** (depart for) partir
(depart from) quitter
(to leave behind) laisser
*to leave for Paris* partir pour Paris
*to leave London* quitter Londres
**left:** *on/to the left* à gauche
**left-handed** (person) gaucher(-ère)
**left-luggage** (office) la consigne
**left-luggage locker** la consigne automatique
**leg** la jambe
**legal** légal(e)
**leisure centre** le centre de loisirs
**lemon** le citron
**lemonade** la limonade
**lemongrass** la citronnelle
**to lend** prêter
**length** la longueur
**lens** (of camera, etc) l'objectif *m*
(contact lens) la lentille
**lesbian** la lesbienne
**less** moins
*less than* moins de
**lesson** la leçon
**to let** (allow) permettre
(to hire out) louer
**letter** la lettre
**letterbox** la boîte aux lettres
**lettuce** la laitue
**level crossing** le passage à niveau
**library** la bibliothèque
**licence** le permis
**lid** le couvercle
**to lie down** s'allonger
**life belt** la bouée de sauvetage
**lifeboat** le canot de sauvetage
**lifeguard** le maître nageur
**life insurance** l'assurance-vie *f*
**life jacket** le gilet de sauvetage
**life raft** le radeau de sauvetage
**lift** (elevator) l'ascenseur *m*

**lift pass** (on ski slopes) le forfait
**light** (not heavy) léger(-ère)
**light** la lumière
*have you got a light?* avez-vous du feu?
**light bulb** l'ampoule *f*
**lighter** le briquet
**lighthouse** le phare
**lightning** les éclairs
**like** (preposition) comme
*like this* comme ça
**to like** aimer
*I like coffee* j'aime le café
*I don't like coffee* je n'aime pas le café
*I'd like...* je voudrais...
*we'd like...* nous voudrions...
**lilo®** le matelas pneumatique
**lime** (fruit) le citron vert
**line** (mark) la ligne
(row) la file
(telephone) la ligne
**linen** le lin
(sheets, tablecloth) le linge
**lingerie** la lingerie
**lip** la lèvre
**lip-reading** lire sur les lèvres
**lip salve** le baume pour les lèvres
**lipstick** le rouge à lèvres
**liqueur** la liqueur
**list** la liste
**to listen to** écouter
**litre** le litre
**litter** (rubbish) les ordures
**little** petit(e)
*a little...* un peu de...
**to live** (in a place) vivre; habiter
*he lives in a flat* il habite dans un appartement
*I live in London* j'habite à Londres
**liver** le foie
**living room** le salon
**loaf** le pain
**local** local(e)
**lock** la serrure
*the lock is broken* la serrure est cassée
**to lock** fermer à clé
**locker** (for luggage) le casier
**locksmith** le serrurier

**log** (for fire) la bûche
*Yule log* la bûche de Noël
**logbook** (of car) la carte grise
**lollipop** la sucette
**London** Londres
*to/in London* à Londres
**long** long(ue)
*for a long time* longtemps
**long-sighted** hypermétrope
**to look after** garder
**to look at** regarder
**to look for** chercher
**loose** (not fastened) desserré(e)
*it's come loose* (unscrewed) ça s'est desserré
(detached) ça s'est détaché
**lorry** le camion
**to lose** perdre
**lost** (object) perdu(e)
*I've lost...* j'ai perdu...
*I'm lost* je suis perdu(e)
**lost property office** le bureau des objets trouvés
**lot:** *a lot of* beaucoup de
**lotion** la lotion
**lottery** le loto
**loud** fort(e)
**loudspeaker** le haut-parleur
**lounge** (in hotel, airport) le salon
**love** l'amour
**to love** (person) aimer
*I love you* je t'aime
(food, activity, etc) adorer
*I love swimming* j'adore nager
**lovely** beau (belle)
**low** bas (basse)
**low-alcohol** peu alcoolisé(e)
**to lower** baisser
**low-fat** allégé(e)
**low tide** la marée basse
**luck** la chance
**lucky** chanceux(-euse)
**luggage** les bagages
**luggage allowance** le poids maximum autorisé
**luggage rack** le porte-bagages
**luggage tag** l'étiquette à bagages *f*

**luggage trolley** le chariot (à bagages)
**lump** (swelling) la bosse
**lunch** le déjeuner
**lunchbreak** la pause de midi
**lung** le poumon
**luxury** le luxe

## M
**machine** la machine
**mad** fou (folle)
**magazine** la revue
**maggot** l'asticot *m*
**magnet** l'aimant *m*
**magnifying glass** la loupe
**maid** la domestique
**maiden name** le nom de jeune fille
**mail** le courrier
*by mail* par la poste
**mains** (electricity) le secteur
(water) la conduite
**main course** (of meal) le plat principal
**main road** la route principale
**to make** faire
**make-up** le maquillage
**male** (person) masculin
**mallet** le maillet
**man** l'homme *m*
**to manage** (to be in charge of) gérer
**manager** le/la directeur(-trice)
**mango** la mangue
**manicure** la manicure
**manual** (car) manuel(le)
**many** beaucoup de
**map** la carte
*road map* la carte routière
*street map* le plan de la ville
**March** mars
**margarine** la margarine
**marina** la marina
**mark** (stain) la tache
**market** le marché
*when is the market?* le marché, c'est quel jour?
*where is the market?* où est le marché?
**market place** le marché
**marmalade** la marmelade d'oranges

**married** marié(e)
*are you married?* vous êtes marié(e)?
*I'm married* je suis marié(e)
**marsh** le marais
**mascara** le mascara
**mass** (in church) la messe
**massage** le massage
**mast** le mât
**masterpiece** le chef-d'œuvre
**match** (game) la partie
**matches** les allumettes
**material** (cloth) le tissu
**to matter:** *it doesn't matter* ça ne
fait rien
*what's the matter?* qu'est-ce qu'il y a?
**mattress** le matelas
**May** mai
**mayonnaise** la mayonnaise
**mayor** le maire
**maximum** le maximum
**Mb** (megabyte) Mo
**me** moi
**meal** le repas
**to mean** vouloir dire
*what does this mean?* qu'est-ce
que ça veut dire?
**measles** la rougeole
**to measure** mesurer
**meat** la viande
**mechanic** le mécanicien
**medical insurance** l'assurance maladie *f*
**medical treatment** les soins médicaux
**medicine** le médicament
**Mediterranean Sea** la Méditerranée
**medium rare** (meat) à point
**to meet** rencontrer
**meeting** la réunion
**meeting point** le point de rencontre
**megabyte** le mégaoctet
*512 megabytes* 512 mégaoctets
**megahertz** mégahertz
**to melt** fondre
**member** (of club, etc) le membre
**membership card** la carte de membre
**memory** la mémoire
**memory stick** (for camera etc) la carte
mémoire

**men** les hommes
**to mend** réparer
**meningitis** la méningite
**menu** (choices) le menu
(card) la carte
**message** le message
**metal** le métal
**meter** le compteur
**metre** le mètre
**metro** le métro
**metro station** la station de métro
**micro-brewery** la mini-brasserie
**microphone** le micro
**microwave oven** le four à micro-ondes
**midday** midi
*at midday* à midi
**middle** le milieu
**middle-aged** d'un certain âge
**midge** le moucheron
**midnight** minuit
*at midnight* à minuit
**migraine** la migraine
*I have a migraine* j'ai la migraine
**mild** (weather, cheese) doux (douce)
(curry) peu épicé(e)
(tobacco) léger(-ère)
**milk** le lait
*baby milk* (formula) le lait maternisé
*fresh milk* le lait frais
*full cream milk* le lait entier
*hot milk* le lait chaud
*long-life milk* le lait longue conservation
*powdered milk* le lait en poudre
*semi-skimmed milk* le lait demi-écrémé
*skimmed milk* le lait écrémé
*soya milk* le lait de soja
*UHT milk* le lait UHT
*with/without milk* avec/sans lait
**milkshake** le milk-shake
**millimetre** le millimètre
**mince** (meat) la viande hachée
**to mind:** *do you mind if I...?* ça vous
gêne si je...?
*do you mind?* vous permettez?
*I don't mind* ça m'est égal
**mineral water** l'eau minérale *f*
**minibar** le minibar

**minimum** le minimum
**minister** (church) le pasteur
**minor road** la route secondaire
**mint** (herb) la menthe
(sweet) le bonbon à la menthe
**minute** la minute
**mirror** le miroir
(in car) le rétroviseur
**miscarriage** la fausse couche
**to miss** (train, flight, etc) rater
**Miss** Mademoiselle
**missing** (disappeared) disparu(e)
**mistake** l'erreur f
**misty** brumeux(-euse)
**misunderstanding** le malentendu
**to mix** mélanger
**mobile** (phone) le mobile/le portable
**mobile number** le numéro de
mobile/de portable
**mobile phone charger** le chargeur
pour (téléphone) portable
**modem** le modem
**modern** moderne

144

**moisturizer** la crème hydratante
**mole** (on skin) le grain de beauté
**moment: at the moment** en ce moment
**monastery** le monastère
**Monday** lundi
**money** l'argent m
*I have no money* je n'ai pas d'argent
**moneybelt** la ceinture porte-monnaie
**money order** le mandat
**month** le mois
*last month* le mois dernier
*next month* le mois prochain
*this month* ce mois-ci
**monthly** mensuel(-elle)
**monument** le monument
**moon** la lune
**mooring** (place) le mouillage
**mop** (for floor) le balai à franges
**moped** le vélomoteur
**more** encore
*more wine* plus de vin
*more than* plus de
*more than 3* plus de trois
**morning** le matin

*in the morning* le matin
*this morning* ce matin
*tomorrow morning* demain matin
**morning-after pill** la pilule du lendemain
**mosque** la mosquée
**mosquito** le moustique
**mosquito bite** la piqûre de moustique
**mosquito coil** la spirale anti-moustiques
**mosquito net** la moustiquaire
**mosquito repellent** le produit
antimoustiques
**most (of the)** la plupart (de)
**moth** (clothes) la mite
**mother** la mère
**mother-in-law** la belle-mère
**motor** le moteur
**motorbike** la moto
**motorboat** le bateau à moteur
**motorway** l'autoroute f
**mountain** la montagne
**mountain bike** le VTT (vélo tout-terrain)
**mountain biking** le VTT
**mountain rescue** le sauvetage
en montagne
**mountaineering** l'alpinisme m
**mouse** (animal, computer) la souris
**moustache** la moustache
**mouth** la bouche
**mouthwash** le bain de bouche
**to move** bouger
*it's moving* ça bouge
**movie** le film
**MP3 player** le lecteur de MP3
**Mr** Monsieur
**Mrs** Madame
**Ms** Madame
**much** beaucoup
*too much* trop
**muddy** boueux(-euse)
**mug:** *I've been mugged* je me suis
fait agresser
**mugging** l'agression f
**mumps** les oreillons
**muscle** le muscle
**museum** le musée
**mushrooms** les champignons
**music** la musique

**musical** (show) la comédie musicale
**Muslim** musulman(e)
**mussels** les moules
**must** devoir
*I/we must go* il faut que j'y aille/
  que nous y allions
*you must be there* il faut que vous y soyez
**mustard** la moutarde
**my** mon/ma/mes
*my passport* mon passeport
*my room* ma chambre
*my suitcases* mes valises

## N

**nail** (metal) le clou
(finger) l'ongle *m*
**nailbrush** la brosse à ongles
**nail clippers** le coupe-ongles
**nail file** la lime à ongles
**nail polish** le vernis à ongles
**nail polish remover** le dissolvant
**nail scissors** les ciseaux à ongles
**name** le nom
*my name is...* je m'appelle...
*what is your name?* comment vous
  appelez-vous?
**nanny** le/la baby-sitter
**napkin** la serviette de table
**nappy** la couche
**narrow** étroit(e)
**national** national(e)
**nationality** la nationalité
**national park** le parc national
**natural** naturel(le)
**nature reserve** la réserve naturelle
**nature trail** le sentier de grande
  randonnée
**navy blue** bleu marine
**near** près de
*is it near?* c'est près d'ici?
*near the bank* près de la banque
**necessary** nécessaire
**neck** le cou
**necklace** le collier
**nectarine** le brugnon
**to need (to)** avoir besoin de
*I need...* j'ai besoin de...

*I need to phone* j'ai besoin de téléphoner
*we need...* nous avons besoin de...
**needle** l'aiguille *f*
*a needle and thread* du fil et une aiguille
**negative** (photography) le négatif
**neighbour** le/la voisin(e)
**nephew** le neveu
**net** le filet
*the Net* le net; l'internet *m*
**network** le réseau
**neutral** (car) le point mort
*in neutral* au point mort
**never** jamais
*I never drink wine* je ne bois jamais de vin
**new** nouveau(-elle)
**news** (TV, radio, etc) les informations
**newsagent's** le magasin de journaux
**newspaper** le journal
**news stand** le kiosque
**New Year** le Nouvel An
*happy New Year!* bonne année!
**New Year's Eve** la Saint-Sylvestre
**New Zealand** la Nouvelle-Zélande
**next** prochain(e)
(after) ensuite
*next Monday* lundi prochain
*next month* le mois prochain
*next to* à côté de
*next week* la semaine prochaine
*the next train* le prochain train
*we're going to Paris next* ensuite
  nous allons à Paris
**nice** beau (belle)
(enjoyable) bon (bonne)
(person) sympathique
**niece** la nièce
**night** (night-time) la nuit
(evening) le soir
*at night* la nuit/le soir
*last night* hier soir
*tomorrow night* (evening) demain soir
*tonight* ce soir
**nightclub** la boîte de nuit
**nightdress** la chemise de nuit
**night porter** le gardien de nuit
**no** non
(without) sans

*no ice* sans glaçons
*no problem* pas de problème
*no sugar* sans sucre
*no thanks* non merci
**nobody** personne
**noise** le bruit
*it's very noisy* il y a beaucoup de bruit
**non-alcoholic** sans alcool
**none** aucun(e)
**non-smoker:** *I'm a non-smoker*
je ne fume pas
**non-smoking** (seat, compartment)
non-fumeurs
**north** le nord
**Northern Ireland** l'Irlande du Nord *f*
**North Sea** la mer du Nord
**nose** le nez
**not** ne ... pas
*I am not...* je ne suis pas...
**note** (banknote) le billet
(letter) le mot
**note pad** le bloc-notes
**nothing** rien
*nothing else* rien d'autre
**notice** (warning) l'avis *m*
(sign) le panneau
**notice board** le panneau d'affichage
**novel** le roman
**November** novembre
**now** maintenant
**nowhere** nulle part
**nuclear** nucléaire
**number** (quantity) le nombre
(of room, house) le numéro
*phone number* le numéro de téléphone
**numberplate** (of car) la plaque
d'immatriculation
**nurse** *m/f* l'infirmier/l'infirmière
**nursery** la garderie
**nursery slope** la piste pour débutants
**nut** (to eat) la noix
(for bolt) l'écrou *m*

# O

**oar** l'aviron *m*; la rame
**oats** l'avoine *f*
**to obtain** obtenir

**occupation** (work) l'emploi *m*
**ocean** l'océan *m*
**October** octobre
**odd** (strange) bizarre
**of** de
*a glass of...* un verre de...
*made of...* en...
**off** (light) éteint(e)
(rotten) mauvais(e); pourri(e)
**off-piste skiing** le ski hors-piste
**office** le bureau
**often** souvent
**oil** (for car, food) l'huile *f*
**oil filter** le filtre à huile
**oil gauge** la jauge de niveau d'huile
**ointment** la pommade
**OK!** (agreed) d'accord!
**old** vieux (vieille)
*how old are you?* quel âge avez-vous?
*I'm... years old* j'ai... ans
**old-age pensioner** le/la retraité(e)
**olive** l'olive *f*
**olive oil** l'huile d'olive *f*
**on** (light) allumé(e)
(engine, etc) en marche
*on the table* sur la table
*on time* à l'heure
**once** une fois
*at once* tout de suite
**one-way** (street) à sens unique
**onion** l'oignon *m*
**only** seulement
**open** ouvert(e)
**to open** ouvrir
**opera** l'opéra *m*
**operation** (surgical) l'opération *f*
**operator** (phone) le/la standardiste
**opposite** en face de
*opposite the bank* en face de la banque
*quite the opposite* bien au contraire
**optician** *m/f* l'opticien/l'opticienne
**or** ou
**orange** (fruit) l'orange
(colour) orange
**orange juice** le jus d'orange
**orchestra** l'orchestre *m*
**order** (in restaurant) la commande

*out of order* en panne
**to order** (in restaurant) commander
**organic** biologique
**to organize** organiser
**ornament** le bibelot
**other** autre
*have you any others?* vous en avez d'autres?
**our** (sing) notre
(plural) nos
*our baggage* nos bagages
*our passports* nos passeports
*our room* notre chambre
**out** (light) éteint(e)
*he's/she's out* il/elle est sorti(e)
**outdoor** (pool, etc) en plein air
**outside** dehors
**oven** le four
**ovenproof dish** le plat qui va au four
**over** (on top of) au-dessus de
**to overbook** faire du surbooking
**to overcharge** faire payer trop cher
**overdone** (food) trop cuit(e)
**overdose** la surdose
**to overheat** surchauffer
**to overload** surcharger
**to oversleep** se réveiller en retard
**to overtake** (in car) doubler; dépasser
**to owe** devoir
*you owe me...* vous me devez...
**to own** posséder
**owner** le/la propriétaire
**oyster** l'huître *f*

## P

**pace** le pas
**pacemaker** le stimulateur (cardiaque)
**to pack** (luggage) faire les bagages
**package** le paquet
**package tour** le voyage organisé
**packet** le paquet
**padded envelope** l'enveloppe matelassée
**paddling pool** la pataugeoire
**padlock** le cadenas
**page** la page
**paid** payé(e)

*I've paid* j'ai payé
**pain** la douleur
**painful** douloureux(-euse)
**painkiller** l'analgésique *m*
**to paint** peindre
**painting** (picture) le tableau
**pair** la paire
**palace** le palais
**pale** pâle
**palmtop computer** l'ordinateur de poche *m*
**pan** (saucepan) la casserole
(frying pan) la poêle
**pancake** la crêpe
**panniers** (for bike) les sacoches
**panties** la culotte
**pants** (underwear) le slip
**panty liner** le protège-slip
**paper** le papier
**paper hankies** les mouchoirs en papier
**paper napkins** les serviettes en papier
**paragliding** le parapente
**paralysed** paralysé(e)
**paramedic** l'urgentiste *m/f*
**parcel** le colis
**pardon?** comment?
*I beg your pardon!* pardon!
**parents** les parents
**Paris** Paris
**park** le parc
**to park** garer (la voiture)
**parking disk** le disque de stationnement
**parking meter** le parcmètre
**parking ticket** le p.-v.
**part: spare parts** les pièces de rechange
**partner** (business) *m/f* l'associé(e)
(boy/girlfriend) le compagnon/la compagne
**party** (group) le groupe
(celebration) la fête; la soirée
(political) le parti
**pass** (bus, train) la carte
(mountain) le col
**passenger** le passager/la passagère
**passionfruit** le fruit de la passion
**passport** le passeport
**passport control** le contrôle des passeports

pasta les pâtes
pastry la pâte
(cake) la pâtisserie
path le chemin
patient (in hospital) le/la patient(e)
pavement le trottoir
to pay payer
*I'd like to pay* je voudrais payer
*where do I pay?* où est-ce qu'il faut payer?
payment le paiement
payphone le téléphone public
PDA l'organiseur PDA *m*
peace (after war) la paix
peach la pêche
peak rate le plein tarif
peanut allergy l'allergie aux cacahuètes *f*
pear la poire
peas les petits pois
pedal la pédale
pedalo le pédalo®
pedestrian le/la piéton(ne)
pedestrian crossing le passage clouté
to pee faire pipi

to peel (fruit) peler
peg (for clothes) la pince à linge
(for tent) le piquet
pen le stylo
pencil le crayon
penfriend le/la correspondant(e)
penicillin la pénicilline
penis le pénis
penknife le canif
pensioner le/la retraité(e)
people les gens
people carrier le monospace
pepper (spice) le poivre
(vegetable) le poivron
per par
*per day* par jour
*per hour* à l'heure
*per person* par personne
*per week* par semaine
*100 km per hour* 100 km à l'heure
perfect parfait(e)
performance (show) le spectacle
perfume le parfum
perhaps peut-être

period (menstruation) les règles
perm la permanente
permit le permis
person la personne
personal organizer l'agenda *m*
pet l'animal domestique *m*
pet food les aliments pour animaux
pet shop l'animalerie *f*
petrol l'essence *f*
*unleaded* l'essence sans plomb
petrol cap le bouchon de réservoir
petrol pump la pompe à essence
petrol station la station-service
petrol tank le réservoir
pharmacist le/la pharmacien(ne)
pharmacy la pharmacie
phone le téléphone
*by phone* par téléphone
to phone téléphoner
phonebook l'annuaire *m*
phonebox la cabine (téléphonique)
phone call l'appel *m*
phonecard la télécarte
phone inquiries les renseignements
photocopier la photocopieuse
photocopy la photocopie
to photocopy photocopier
photograph la photo
*to take a photograph* prendre une photo
phrase book le guide de conversation
piano le piano
to pick (choose) choisir
(pluck) cueillir
pickpocket le pickpocket
picnic le pique-nique
*to have a picnic* pique-niquer
picnic hamper le panier à pique-nique
picnic rug la couverture
picture (painting) le tableau
(photo) la photo
pie (savoury) la tourte
piece le morceau
pier la jetée
pig le cochon
pill la pilule
*I'm on the pill* je prends la pilule
pillow l'oreiller *m*

pillowcase la taie d'oreiller
pilot le pilote
pin l'épingle *f*
pink rose
PIN number le code confidentiel
pint: *a pint of...* un demi-litre de...
pipe (for water, gas) le tuyau
(smoking) la pipe
pitch (place for tent/caravan)
l'emplacement *m*
pity: *what a pity* quel dommage
pizza la pizza
place l'endroit *m*
place of birth le lieu de naissance
plain (unflavoured) ordinaire
plait la natte
to plan prévoir
plan (map) le plan
plane (aircraft) l'avion *m*
plant (in garden) la plante
plaster (sticking plaster) le sparadrap
(for broken limb, on wall) le plâtre
plastic (made of) en plastique
plastic bag le sac en plastique
plate l'assiette *f*
platform (railway) le quai
*which platform?* quel quai?
play (at theatre) la pièce
to play (games) jouer
play park l'aire de jeux *f*
playroom la salle de jeux
pleasant agréable
please s'il vous plaît
pleased content(e)
*pleased to meet you!* enchanté(e)!
plenty of beaucoup de
pliers la pince
plug (electrical) la prise
(for sink) la bonde
to plug in brancher
plum la prune
plumber le plombier
plumbing la tuyauterie
plunger (to clear sink) le débouchoir
à ventouse
p.m. de l'après-midi
poached poché(e)

pocket la poche
points (in car) les vis platinées
poison le poison
poisonous vénéneux
police (force) la police
policeman le policier
(police woman) la femme policier
police station le commissariat;
la gendarmerie
polish (for shoes) le cirage
pollen le pollen
polluted pollué(e)
pony le poney
pony-trekking la randonnée à cheval
pool (swimming) la piscine
pool attendant le/la surveillant(e)
de baignade
poor pauvre
popcorn le pop-corn
pop socks les mi-bas
popular populaire
pork le porc
port (seaport) le port
(wine) le porto
porter (for luggage) le porteur
portion la portion
Portugal le Portugal
possible possible
post (letters) le courrier
*by post* par courrier
to post poster
postbox la boîte aux lettres
postcard la carte postale
postcode le code postal
poster l'affiche *f*
postman/woman le facteur/la factrice
post office la poste
to postpone remettre à plus tard
pot (for cooking) la casserole
potato la pomme de terre
*baked potato* la pomme de terre cuite
au four
*boiled potatoes* les pommes vapeur
*fried potatoes* les pommes de terres
sautées
*mashed potatoes* la purée
*roast potatoes* les pommes de terre rôties

**potato salad** la salade de pommes de terre
**pothole** le nid de poule
**pottery** la poterie
**pound** (money) la livre
**to pour** verser
**powder** la poudre
**powdered milk** le lait en poudre
**power** (electricity) le courant
**power cut** la coupure de courant
**pram** le landau
**to pray** prier
**to prefer** préférer
**pregnant** enceinte
*I'm pregnant* je suis enceinte
**to prepare** préparer
**to prescribe** prescrire
**prescription** l'ordonnance *f*
**present** (gift) le cadeau
**preservative** le conservateur
**president** le président
**pressure** la pression
*tyre pressure* la pression des pneus
**pretty** joli(e)
**price** le prix
**price list** le tarif
**priest** le prêtre
**print** (photo) la photo
**printer** l'imprimante *f*
**prison** la prison
**private** privé(e)
**prize** le prix
**probably** probablement
**problem** le problème
**professor** le professeur d'université
**programme** (TV, etc) l'émission *f*
**prohibited** interdit(e)
**promise** la promesse
**to promise** promettre
**to pronounce** prononcer
*how's it pronounced?* comment ça se prononce?
**Protestant** protestant(e)
**to provide** fournir
**public** public(-ique)
**public holiday** le jour férié
**pudding** le dessert
**to pull** tirer

**to pull a muscle** se faire une élongation
**to pull over** (car) s'arrêter
**pullover** le pull
**pump** la pompe
**puncture** la crevaison
**puncture repair kit** la boîte de rustines®
**puppet** la marionnette
**puppet show** le spectacle de marionnettes
**purple** violet(-ette)
**purpose** le but
*on purpose* exprès
**purse** le porte-monnaie
**to push** pousser
**pushchair** la poussette
**to put** (place) mettre
**pyjamas** le pyjama
**Pyrenees** les Pyrénées

# Q

**quality** la qualité
**quantity** la quantité
**quarantine** la quarantaine
**to quarrel** se disputer
**quarter** le quart
**quay** le quai
**queen** la reine
**query** la question
**question** la question
**queue** la queue
**to queue** faire la queue
**quick** rapide
**quickly** vite
**quiet** (place) tranquille
**quilt** la couette
**quite** (rather) assez
(completely) complètement
*it's quite expensive* c'est assez cher
*quite good* pas mal
**quiz** le jeu-concours

# R

**rabbit** le lapin
**rabies** la rage
**race** (people) la race
(sport) la course
**race course** le champ de courses
**racket** la raquette

**radiator** le radiateur
**radio** la radio
**raft** le radeau
(sport) le rafting
**railcard** la carte d'abonnement
(de chemin de fer)
**railway** le chemin de fer
**railway station** la gare
**rain** la pluie
**to rain: it's raining** il pleut
**raincoat** l'imperméable *m*
**rake** le râteau
**rape** le viol
**to rape** violer
**raped: to be raped** être violé(e)
**rare** (uncommon) rare
(steak) saignant(e)
**rash** (skin) la rougeur
**rat** le rat
**rate** (price) le tarif
**rate of exchange** le taux de change
**raw** cru(e)
**razor** le rasoir
**razor blades** les lames de rasoir
**to read** lire
**ready** prêt(e)
**real** vrai(e)
**to realize (that...)** se rendre compte
(que...)
**rearview mirror** le rétroviseur
**receipt** le reçu
**receiver** (of phone) le récepteur
**reception** (desk) la réception
**receptionist** le/la réceptionniste
**to recharge** (battery, etc) recharger
**recipe** la recette
**to recognize** reconnaître
**to recommend** recommander
**to record** enregistrer
**to recover** (from illness) se remettre
**to recycle** recycler
**red** rouge
**to reduce** réduire
**reduction** la réduction
**to refer to** parler de
**refill** la recharge
**to refund** rembourser

**to refuse** refuser
**regarding** concernant
**region** la région
**register** le registre
**to register** (at hotel) se présenter
**registered** (letter) recommandé(e)
**registration form** la fiche
**to reimburse** rembourser
**relation** (family) le/la parent(e)
**relationship** les rapports
**to remain** rester
**remember** se rappeler
*I don't remember* je ne m'en rappelle pas
**remote control** la télécommande
**removal firm** les déménageurs
**to remove** enlever
**rent** le loyer
**to rent** louer
**rental** la location
**repair** la réparation
**to repair** réparer
**to repeat** répéter
**to reply** répondre
**report** (of theft, etc) la déclaration
**to report** (theft, etc) déclarer
**request** la demande
**to request** demander
**to require** avoir besoin de
**to rescue** sauver
**reservation** la réservation
**to reserve** réserver
**reserved** réservé(e)
**resident** *m/f* l'habitant(e)
**resort** (seaside) la station balnéaire
*ski resort* la station de ski
**rest** (relaxation) le repos
(remainder) le reste
**to rest** se reposer
**restaurant** le restaurant
**restaurant car** le wagon-restaurant
**retired** retraité(e)
**to return** (to a place) retourner
(to return something) rendre
**return ticket** le billet aller-retour
**to reverse** faire marche arrière
**to reverse the charges** appeler en PCV
**reverse-charge call** l'appel en PCV *m*

**reverse gear** la marche arrière
**rheumatism** le rhumatisme
**rib** la côte
**ribbon** le ruban
**rice** le riz
**rich** (person, food) riche
**to ride** (horse) faire du cheval
**right** (correct) exact(e)
**right** la droite
*on/to the right* à droite
**right of way** la priorité
**ring** (on finger) la bague
**to ring** (bell) sonner
*it's ringing* (phone) ça sonne
**to ring sb** (phone) téléphoner à quelqu'un
**ring road** le périphérique
**ripe** mûr(e)
**river** la rivière
**Riviera** (French) la Côte d'Azur
**road** la route
**road map** la carte routière
**road sign** le panneau
**roadworks** les travaux

**roast** rôti(e)
**roll** (bread) le petit pain
**roller blades** les rollers
**romantic** romantique
**roof** le toit
**roof-rack** la galerie
**room** (in house) la pièce
(in hotel) la chambre
(space) la place
*double room* la chambre pour deux personnes
*family room* la chambre pour une famille
*single room* la chambre pour une personne
**room number** le numéro de chambre
**room service** le service des chambres
**root** la racine
**rope** la corde
**rose** la rose
**rosé wine** le rosé
**rotten** (fruit, etc) pourri(e)
**rough:** *rough sea* la mer agitée
**round** rond(e)
**roundabout** (traffic) le rond-point
**route** la route; l'itinéraire *m*

**row** (theatre, etc) la rangée
**rowing** (sport) l'aviron *m*
**rowing boat** la barque
**rubber** (material) le caoutchouc
(eraser) la gomme
**rubber band** l'élastique *m*
**rubber gloves** les gants en caoutchouc
**rubbish** les ordures
**rubella** la rubéole
**rucksack** le sac à dos
**rug** (carpet) le tapis
**ruins** les ruines
**ruler** (for measuring) la règle
**to run** courir
**rush hour** l'heure de pointe *f*
**rusty** rouillé(e)

## S

**sad** triste
**saddle** la selle
**safe** (for valuables) le coffre-fort
**safe** sûr; sans danger
*is it safe?* ce n'est pas dangereux?
**safety belt** la ceinture de sécurité
**safety pin** l'épingle à nourrice *f*
**sail** la voile
**sailboard** la planche à voile
**sailing** (sport) la voile
**sailing boat** le voilier
**saint** le/la saint(e)
**salad** la salade
*green salad* la salade verte
*mixed salad* la salade composée
*potato salad* la salade de pommes de terre
*tomato salad* la salade de tomates
**salad dressing** la vinaigrette
**salami** le salami
**salary** le salaire
**sale** la vente
**sales** (reductions) les soldes
**salesman/woman** le vendeur/la vendeuse
**sales rep** le/la représentant(e)
**salt** le sel
**salt water** l'eau salée
**salty** salé(e)
**same** même

**sample** l'échantillon *m*
**sand** le sable
**sandals** les sandales
**sandwich** le sandwich
*toasted sandwich* le croque-monsieur
**sanitary towel** la serviette hygiénique
**satellite dish** l'antenne parabolique *f*
**satellite TV** la télévision par satellite
**satnav** (satellite navigation system, for car) le système de navigation satellite
**Saturday** samedi
**sauce** la sauce
**saucepan** la casserole
**saucer** la soucoupe
**sauna** le sauna
**sausage** la saucisse
**to save** (life) sauver
(money) épargner; économiser
**savoury** salé(e)
**saw** la scie
**to say** dire
**scales** (for weighing) la balance
**scarf** (headscarf) le foulard
(woollen) l'écharpe *f*
**scenery** le paysage
**schedule** le programme
**school** l'école *f*
*primary school* l'école primaire
*secondary school* (11-15) le collège
(15-18) le lycée
**scissors** les ciseaux
**score** (of match) le score
**to score** (goal, point) marquer
**Scot** *m/f* l'Écossais(e)
**Scotland** l'Écosse *f*
**Scottish** écossais(e)
**scouring pad** le tampon à récurer
**screen** (computer, TV) l'écran *m*
**screen wash** le lave-glace
**screw** la vis
**screwdriver** le tournevis
*phillips screwdriver* le tournevis cruciforme
**scuba diving** la plongée sous-marine
**sculpture** la sculpture
**sea** la mer
**seafood** les fruits de mer

**seam** (of dress) la couture
**to search** fouiller
**seasickness** le mal de mer
**seaside** le bord de la mer
*at the seaside* au bord de la mer
**season** (of year, holiday time) la saison
*in season* de saison
**seasonal** saisonnier
**season ticket** la carte d'abonnement
**seat** (chair) le siège
(in train) la place
(cinema, theatre) le fauteuil
**seatbelt** la ceinture de sécurité
**second** second(e)
**second** (time) la seconde
**second class** seconde classe
**second-hand** d'occasion
**secretary** le/la secrétaire
**security** la sécurité
**security check** les contrôles de sécurité *mpl*
**security guard** le/la vigile
**sedative** le calmant
**to see** voir
**to seize** saisir
**self-catering flat** l'appartement indépendant (avec cuisine)
**self-employed:** *to be self employed* travailler à son compte
**self-service** le libre-service
**to sell** vendre
*do you sell...?* vous vendez...?
**sell-by date** la date limite de vente
**Sellotape®** le Scotch®
**to send** envoyer
**senior citizen** la personne du troisième âge
**sensible** raisonnable
**separated** séparé(e)
**separately:** *to pay separately* payer séparément
**September** septembre
**serious** grave
**to serve** servir
**service** (church) l'office *m*
(in restaurant, shop, etc) le service
*is service included?* le service est compris?

service charge le service
service station la station-service
set menu le menu à prix fixe
settee le canapé
several plusieurs
to sew coudre
sex le sexe
shade l'ombre *f*
*in the shade* à l'ombre
to shake (bottle, etc) agiter
shallow peu profond(e)
shampoo le shampooing
shampoo and set le shampooing
 et la mise en plis
to share partager
sharp (razor, knife) tranchant
to shave se raser
shaver le rasoir électrique
shaving cream la crème à raser
shawl le châle
she elle
sheep le mouton
sheet (for bed) le drap
shelf le rayon
shell (seashell) le coquillage
sheltered abrité(e)
to shine briller
shingles (illness) le zona
ship le navire
shirt la chemise
shock le choc
shock absorber l'amortisseur *m*
shoe la chaussure
shoelaces les lacets
shoe polish le cirage
shoeshop le magasin de chaussures
shop le magasin
to shop faire du shopping
shop assistant le vendeur/la vendeuse
shop window la vitrine
shopping centre le centre commercial
shore le rivage
short court(e)
shortage le manque
short circuit le court-circuit
short cut le raccourci
shortly bientôt

shorts le short
short-sighted myope
shoulder l'épaule *f*
to shout crier
show le spectacle
to show montrer
shower (wash) la douche
*to take a shower* prendre une douche
shower cap le bonnet de douche
shower gel le gel douche
to shrink (clothes) rétrécir
shut (closed) fermé(e)
to shut fermer
shutter (on window) le volet
shuttle service la navette
sick (ill) malade
*I feel sick* j'ai envie de vomir
side le côté
side dish la garniture
sidelight le feu de position
sidewalk le trottoir
sieve la passoire
sightseeing le tourisme
*to go sightseeing* faire du tourisme
sightseeing tour l'excursion touristique *f*
sign (notice) le panneau
to sign signer
signal: *there's no signal* il n'y a pas
 de réseau, je ne capte pas
signature la signature
signpost le poteau indicateur
silk la soie
silver l'argent *m*
SIM card la carte SIM
similar (to) semblable (à)
since depuis
to sing chanter
single (unmarried) célibataire
(bed, room) pour une personne
single ticket l'aller simple *m*
sink (washbasin) l'évier *m*
sir Monsieur
sister la sœur
sister-in-law la belle-sœur
to sit s'asseoir
*sit down!* asseyez-vous!
site (website) le site internet

**size** (clothes) la taille
(shoe) la pointure
**skates** (ice) les patins à glace
(roller) les patins à roulettes
**to skate** (on ice) patiner
(roller) faire du patin à roulettes
**skateboard** le skate-board
*to go skateboarding* faire du skate-board
**ski** le ski
**to ski** faire du ski
**ski boots** les chaussures de ski
**skid** le dérapage
**to skid** déraper
**skiing** le ski
**ski instructor** le/la moniteur(-trice) de ski
**ski jump** (place) le tremplin de ski
**ski lift** le remonte-pente
**ski pants** le fuseau
**ski pass** le forfait
**ski pole** le bâton (de ski)
**ski run** la piste
**ski suit** la combinaison de ski
**ski tow** le remonte-pente
**skilled** adroit(e); qualifié(e)
**skin** la peau
**skirt** la jupe
**sky** le ciel
**slate** l'ardoise *f*
**sledge** la luge
**to sleep** dormir
**sleeper** (couchette) la couchette
(carriage) la voiture-lit
(train) le train-couchettes
**to sleep in** faire la grasse matinée
**sleeping bag** le sac de couchage
**sleeping car** la voiture-lit
**sleeping mat** le matelas mousse
**sleeping pill** le somnifère
**slice** (bread, cake, etc) la tranche
**sliced bread** le pain de mie en tranches
**slide** (photograph) la diapositive
**to slip** glisser
**slippers** les pantoufles
**slow** lent(e)
**to slow down** ralentir
**slowly** lentement
**small** petit(e)

*smaller than* plus petit(e) que
**smell** l'odeur *f*
*a bad smell* une mauvaise odeur
**smile** le sourire
**to smile** sourire
**smoke** la fumée
**to smoke** fumer
*can I smoke?* on peut fumer?
*I don't smoke* je ne fume pas
**smoke alarm** le détecteur de fumée
**smoked** fumé(e)
**smokers** (sign) fumeurs
**smooth** lisse
**SMS** le SMS
**snack** le casse-croûte
*to have a snack* casser la croûte
**snack bar** le snack-bar
**snail** l'escargot *m*
**snake** le serpent
**snake bite** la morsure de serpent
**to sneeze** éternuer
**snorkel** le tuba
**snorkelling** la plongée (avec masque et tuba)
**snow** la neige
**to snow:** *it's snowing* il neige
**snowboard** le snowboard
**snowboarding** le snowboard
*to go snowboarding* faire du snowboarding
**snow chains** les chaînes
**snowed up** enneigé(e)
**snow tyres** les pneus cloutés
**soap** le savon
**soap powder** (detergent) la lessive
**sober:** *to be sober* ne pas avoir bu
**socket** (for plug) la prise de courant
**socks** les chaussettes
**soda water** l'eau de Seltz *f*
**sofa** le canapé
**sofa bed** le canapé-lit
**soft** doux (douce)
**soft drink** le soda
**software** le logiciel
**soldier** le soldat
**sole** (shoe) la semelle
**soluble** soluble
**some** de (du/de la/des)

**someone** quelqu'un
**something** quelque chose
**sometimes** quelquefois
**son** le fils
**son-in-law** le gendre
**song** la chanson
**soon** bientôt
*as soon as possible* dès que possible
**sore** douloureux(-euse)
**sore throat:** *to have a sore throat* avoir mal à la gorge
**sorry:** *I'm sorry!* excusez-moi!
**sort** la sorte
*what sort?* de quelle sorte?
**soup** le potage; la soupe
**sour** aigre
**soured cream** la crème fermentée
**south** le sud
**souvenir** le souvenir
**spa** la station thermale
**space** la place
**spade** la pelle
**Spain** l'Espagne f
**spam** (email) le spam
**Spanish** espagnol(e)
**spanner** la clé plate
**spare parts** les pièces de rechange
**spare room** la chambre d'amis
**spare tyre** le pneu de rechange
**spare wheel** la roue de secours
**sparkling** (wine) mousseux(-euse)
(water) gazeux(-euse)
**spark plug** la bougie
**to speak** parler
*do you speak English?* vous parlez anglais?
**speaker** (loudspeaker) le haut-parleur
**special** spécial(e)
**specialist** (medical) le/la spécialiste
**speciality** la spécialité
**speeding** l'excès de vitesse m
*a speeding ticket* un p.-v. pour excès de vitesse
**speed limit** la limitation de vitesse
*to exceed speed limit* dépasser la vitesse permise
**speedboat** le hors-bord
**speedometer** le compteur

**SPF** (sun protection factor) l'indice UVA m
**to spell:** *how is it spelt?* comment ça s'écrit?
**to spend** (money) dépenser
(time) passer
**spice** l'épice f
**spicy** épicé(e)
**spider** l'araignée f
**to spill** renverser
**spine** la colonne vertébrale
**spin dryer** le sèche-linge
**spirits** (alcohol) les spiritueux
**splinter** (in finger) l'écharde f
**spoke** (of wheel) le rayon
**sponge** l'éponge f
**spoon** la cuiller
**sport** le sport
**sports centre** le centre sportif
**sports shop** le magasin de sports
**spot** (pimple) le bouton
**sprain** l'entorse f
**spring** (season) le printemps
(metal) le ressort
**square** (in town) la place
**squash** (lemon) la citronnade, (orange) l'orangeade f
(sport) le squash
**squeeze** presser
**squid** le calmar
**stadium** le stade
**stage** la scène
**staff** le personnel
**stain** la tache
**stained glass window** le vitrail
**stairs** l'escalier m
**stale** (bread) rassis(e)
**stalls** (in theatre) l'orchestre m
**stamp** le timbre
**to stand** (get up) se lever
(be standing) être debout
**star** l'étoile f
(celebrity) la vedette
**to start** commencer
**starter** (in meal) le hors d'œuvre
(in car) le démarreur
**station** la gare
**stationer's** la papeterie

statue la statue
stay le séjour
*enjoy your stay!* bon séjour!
**to stay** (remain) rester
(reside for while) loger
*I'm staying at...* je loge à...
steak le bifteck
**to steal** voler
steam la vapeur
steamed cuit(e) à la vapeur
steel l'acier *m*
steep raide
steeple le clocher
steering wheel le volant
step le pas
stepdaughter la belle-fille
stepfather le beau-père
stepmother la belle-mère
stepson le beau-fils
stereo la chaîne (stéréo)
sterling la livre sterling
steward le steward
stewardess l'hôtesse *f*
sticking-plaster le sparadrap
still: *still water* l'eau plate *f*
still (yet) encore
sting la piqûre
**to sting** piquer
stitches (surgical) les points de suture
stockings les bas
stolen volé(e)
stomach l'estomac *m*
stomachache: *to have a stomachache* avoir mal au ventre
stomach upset l'estomac dérangé
stone la pierre
**to stop** arrêter
store (shop) le magasin
storey l'étage *m*
storm l'orage *m*
story l'histoire *f*
straightaway tout de suite
straight on tout droit
strange bizarre
straw (for drinking) la paille
strawberries les fraises
stream le ruisseau

street la rue
street map le plan des rues
strength la force
stress le stress
strike (of workers) la grève
string la ficelle
striped rayé(e)
stroke (haemorrhage) l'attaque (d'apoplexie)
*to have a stroke* avoir une attaque
strong fort(e)
stuck bloqué(e)
student (male) l'étudiant
(female) l'étudiante
student discount le tarif étudiant
stuffed farci(e)
stung piqué(e)
stupid stupide
subscription l'abonnement *m*
subtitles les sous-titres
subway le passage souterrain
suddenly soudain
suede le daim
sugar le sucre
sugar-free sans sucre
**to suggest** suggérer
suit (man's) le costume
(woman's) le tailleur
suitcase la valise
sum la somme
summer l'été *m*
summer holidays les vacances d'été
summit le sommet
sun le soleil
**to sunbathe** prendre un bain de soleil
sunblock l'écran total *m*
sunburn le coup de soleil
suncream la crème solaire
Sunday le dimanche
sunflower le tournesol
sunglasses les lunettes de soleil
sunny: *it's sunny* il fait beau
sunrise le lever du soleil
sunroof le toit ouvrant
sunscreen (lotion) l'écran solaire *m*
sunset le coucher de soleil
sunshade le parasol
sunstroke l'insolation *f*

**suntan** le bronzage
**suntan lotion** le lait solaire
**supermarket** le supermarché
**supper** (dinner) le souper
**supplement** le supplément
**to supply** fournir
**to surf** faire du surf
*to surf the Net* surfer sur Internet
**surfboard** la planche de surf
**surfing** le surf
**surgery** (operation) l'opération chirurgicale *f*
**surname** le nom de famille
**surprise** la surprise
**to survive** survivre
**suspension** (car) la suspension
**to swallow** avaler
**to sweat** transpirer
**sweater** le pull
**sweatshirt** le sweat-shirt
**sweet** sucré(e)
**sweetener** l'édulcorant *m*
**sweets** les bonbons
**to swell** (bump, eye, etc) enfler
**to swim** nager
**swimming pool** la piscine
**swimsuit** le maillot de bain
**swing** (for children) la balançoire
**swipecard** la carte magnétique
**Swiss** suisse
**switch** le bouton
**to switch off** éteindre
**to switch on** allumer
**Switzerland** la Suisse
**swollen** enflé(e)
**synagogue** la synagogue
**syringe** la seringue

## T

**table** la table
**tablecloth** la nappe
**table tennis** le tennis de table
**table wine** le vin de table
**tablet** le comprimé
**to take** (something) prendre
**to take away** (something) emporter
**to take off** (clothes) enlever

**talc** le talc
**to talk (to)** parler (à)
**tall** grand(e)
**tampons** les tampons hygiéniques
**tangerine** la mandarine
**tank** (petrol) le réservoir
(fish) l'aquarium *m*
**tap** le robinet
**tap water** l'eau du robinet *f*
**tape measure** le mètre à ruban
**tart** la tarte
**taste** le goût
**to taste** goûter
*can I taste some?* je peux goûter?
**tax** l'impôt *m*
**taxi** le taxi
**taxi driver** le chauffeur de taxi
**taxi rank** la station de taxis
**tea** le thé
*herbal tea* la tisane
*lemon tea* le thé au citron
*tea with milk* le thé au lait
**teabag** le sachet de thé
**teapot** la théière
**teaspoon** la cuiller à café
**tea towel** le torchon
**to teach** enseigner
**teacher** le professeur
**team** l'équipe *f*
**tear** (in material) la déchirure
**teat** (on bottle) la tétine
**teenager** l'adolescent(e)
**teeth** les dents
**telegram** le télégramme
**telephone** le téléphone
**to telephone** téléphoner
**telephone box** la cabine téléphonique
**telephone call** le coup de téléphone
**telephone card** la télécarte
**telephone directory** l'annuaire *m*
**telephone number** le numéro de téléphone
**television** la télévision
**to tell** dire
**temperature** la température
*to have a temperature* avoir de la fièvre
**temporary** temporaire

**tenant** le/la locataire
**tendon** le tendon
**tennis** le tennis
**tennis ball** la balle de tennis
**tennis court** le court de tennis
**tennis racket** la raquette de tennis
**tent** la tente
**tent peg** le piquet de tente
**terminal** (airport) l'aérogare *f*
**terrace** la terrasse
**terracotta** la terre cuite
**to test** (try out) tester
**testicles** les testicules
**tetanus injection** la piqûre antitétanique
**text message** le SMS
**to text** envoyer un SMS à
*I'll text you* je t'enverrai un SMS
**than** que
**to thank** remercier
**thank you** merci
*thank you very much* merci beaucoup
**that** cela
*that one* celui-là/celle-là
**the** le/la/l'/les
**theatre** le théâtre
**theft** le vol
**their** (sing) leur
(plural) leurs
**them** eux
**there** là
**there is/are...** il y a...
**thermometer** le thermomètre
**these** ces
*these ones* ceux-ci/celles-ci
**they** ils/elles
**thick** (not thin) épais(se)
**thief** le voleur/la voleuse
**thigh** la cuisse
**thin** (person) mince
**thing** la chose
*my things* mes affaires
**to think** penser
**thirsty:** *I'm thirsty* j'ai soif
**this** ceci
*this one* celui-ci/celle-ci
**thorn** l'épine *f*
**those** ces

*those ones* ceux-là/celles-là
**thread** le fil
**throat** la gorge
**throat lozenges** les pastilles pour la gorge
**through** à travers
**thumb** le pouce
**thunder** le tonnerre
**thunderstorm** l'orage *m*
**Thursday** jeudi
**thyme** le thym
**ticket** le billet; le ticket
*a single ticket* un aller simple
*a return ticket* un aller-retour
*book of tickets* le carnet de tickets
**ticket inspector** le contrôleur/
la contrôleuse
**ticket office** le guichet
**tide** la marée
*high tide* la marée haute
*low tide* la marée basse
**tidy** bien rangé(e)
**to tidy up** tout ranger
**tie** la cravate
**tight** (fitting) serré(e)
**tights** le collant
**tile** (on roof) la tuile
(on wall, floor) le carreau
**till** (cash desk) la caisse
(until) jusqu'à
*till 2 o'clock* jusqu'à deux heures
**time** le temps
(of day) l'heure *f*
*this time* cette fois
*what time is it?* quelle heure est-il?
**timer** le minuteur
**timetable** l'horaire *m*
**tin** (can) la boîte
**tinfoil** le papier alu(minium)
**tin-opener** l'ouvre-boîtes *m*
**tip** (to waiter, etc) le pourboire
**to tip** (waiter, etc) donner un pourboire à
**tired** fatigué(e)
**tissue** (Kleenex®) le kleenex®
**to** à
(with name of country) en/au
*to London* à Londres
*to the airport* à l'aéroport

*to Canada* au Canada
*to France* en France
**toadstool** le champignon vénéneux
**toast** (to eat) le pain grillé; le toast
**tobacco** le tabac
**tobacconist's** le bureau de tabac
**today** aujourd'hui
**toddler** le bambin
**toe** le doigt de pied
**together** ensemble
**toilet** les toilettes
*toilet for disabled* les toilettes
  pour handicapés
**toilet brush** la balayette pour les WC
**toilet paper** le papier hygiénique
**toiletries** les articles de toilette
**token** le jeton
**toll** (motorway) le péage
**tomato** la tomate
*tinned tomatoes* les tomates en boîte
*tomato soup* la soupe de tomates
**tomorrow** demain
*tomorrow morning* demain matin
*tomorrow afternoon* demain après-midi
*tomorrow evening* demain soir
**tongue** la langue
**tonic water** le tonic
**tonight** ce soir
**tonsillitis** l'angine *f*
**too** (also) aussi
*it's too big* c'est trop grand
*it's too hot* il fait trop chaud
*it's too noisy* il y a trop de bruit
**toolkit** la trousse à outils
**tools** les outils
**tooth** la dent
**toothache** le mal de dents
*I have toothache* j'ai mal aux dents
**toothbrush** la brosse à dents
**toothpaste** le dentifrice
**toothpick** le cure-dent
**top**: *the top floor* le dernier étage
**top** (of bottle) le bouchon
(of pen) le capuchon
(of pyjamas, bikini, etc) le haut
(of hill, mountain) le sommet
*on top of* sur

**topless**: *to go topless* enlever le haut
**torch** la lampe de poche
**torn** déchiré(e)
**total** (amount) le total
**to touch** toucher
**tough** (meat) dur(e)
**tour** l'excursion *f*
*guided tour* la visite guidée
**tour guide** le/la guide
**tour operator** le tour-opérateur;
  le voyagiste
**tourist** le/la touriste
**tourist (information) office**
  le syndicat d'initiative
**tourist route** l'itinéraire touristique *m*
**tourist ticket** le billet touristique
**to tow** remorquer
**towbar** (on car) la barre de remorquage
**tow rope** le câble de remorquage
**towel** la serviette
**tower** la tour
**town** la ville
**town centre** le centre-ville
**town hall** la mairie
**town plan** le plan de la ville
**toxic** toxique
**toy** le jouet
**toyshop** le magasin de jouets
**tracksuit** le survêtement
**traditional** traditionnel(-elle)
**traffic** la circulation
**traffic jam** l'embouteillage *m*
**traffic lights** les feux
**traffic warden** le/la contractuel(le)
**trailer** la remorque
**train** le train
*by train* par le train
*the first train* le premier train
*the last train* le dernier train
*the next train* le prochain train
**trainers** les baskets
**tram** le tramway
**tranquillizer** le tranquillisant
**to translate** traduire
**translation** la traduction
**to travel** voyager
**travel agent's** l'agence de voyages *f*

travel guide le guide
travel insurance l'assurance voyage f
travel pass la carte de transport
travel sickness le mal des transports
traveller's cheques les chèques de voyage
tray le plateau
tree l'arbre m
trekking poles les bâtons de randonnée m
trip l'excursion f
trolley le chariot
trouble les ennuis
to be in trouble avoir des ennuis
trousers le pantalon
truck le camion
true vrai(e)
trunk (luggage) la malle
trunks (swimming) le maillot (de bain)
to try essayer
to try on (clothes, shoes) essayer
t-shirt le tee-shirt
Tuesday mardi
tumble dryer le sèche-linge
tunnel le tunnel
to turn tourner
to turn round faire demi-tour
to turn off (light, etc) éteindre
(to turn off engine) couper le moteur
to turn on (light, etc) allumer
(engine) mettre en marche
turquoise (colour) turquoise
tweezers la pince à épiler
twice deux fois
twin-bedded room la chambre à deux lits
twins (male) les jumeaux
(female) les jumelles
to type taper à la machine
typical typique
tyre le pneu
tyre pressure la pression des pneus

## U

ugly laid(e)
ulcer l'ulcère m
mouth ulcer l'aphte m
umbrella le parapluie
(sunshade) le parasol

uncle l'oncle m
uncomfortable inconfortable
unconscious sans connaissance
under sous
undercooked pas assez cuit(e)
underground le métro
underpants (man's) le caleçon
underpass le passage souterrain
to understand comprendre
do you understand? vous comprenez?
I don't understand je ne comprends pas
underwear les sous-vêtements
to undress se déshabiller
unemployed au chômage
to unfasten (clothes, etc) défaire
(door) ouvrir
United Kingdom le Royaume-Uni
United States les États-Unis
university l'université f
unkind pas gentil(-ille)
unleaded petrol l'essence sans plomb f
unlikely peu probable
to unlock ouvrir
to unpack (suitcase) défaire
unpleasant désagréable
to unplug débrancher
to unscrew dévisser
up: to get up (out of bed) se lever
upside down à l'envers
upstairs en haut
urgent urgent(e)
urine l'urine f
us nous
USB flash drive la clé USB
USB port le port USB
to use utiliser
useful utile
username le nom d'utilisateur
usual habituel(-elle)
usually d'habitude
U-turn le demi-tour

## V

vacancy (in hotel) la chambre
vacant libre
vacation les vacances
vaccination le vaccin

**vacuum cleaner** l'aspirateur *m*
**vagina** le vagin
**valid** (ticket, driving licence, etc) valable
**valley** la vallée
**valuable** d'une grande valeur
**valuables** les objets de valeur
**value** la valeur
**valve** la soupape
**van** la camionnette
**vase** le vase
**VAT** la TVA
**vegan** végétalien(ne)
*I'm a vegan* je suis végétalien(ne)
**vegetables** les légumes
**vegetarian** végétarien(ne)
*I'm vegetarian* je suis végétarien(ne)
**vehicle** le véhicule
**vein** la veine
**velvet** le velours
**vending machine** le distributeur automatique
**venereal disease** la maladie vénérienne
**ventilator** le ventilateur
**very** très
**vest** le maillot de corps
**vet** le/la vétérinaire
**via** par
**to video** (from TV) enregistrer
**video** (machine) le magnétoscope
(cassette) la (cassette) vidéo
**video game** le jeu vidéo
**view** la vue
*a room with a sea view* une chambre avec vue sur la mer
**villa** la maison de campagne
**village** le village
**vinegar** le vinaigre
**vineyard** le vignoble
**viper** la vipère
**virus** le virus
**visa** le visa
**visit** le séjour; la visite
**to visit** visiter
**visiting hours** les heures de visite
**visitor** le/la visiteur(-euse)
**vitamin** la vitamine
**voice** la voix

**voicemail** la messagerie vocale
**volcano** le volcan
**volleyball** le volley-ball
**volts** les volts *mpl*
**voltage** le voltage
**to vomit** vomir
**voucher** le bon

## W

**wage** le salaire
**waist** la taille
**waistcoat** le gilet
**to wait for** attendre
**waiter** le/la serveur(-euse)
**waiting room** la salle d'attente
**waitress** la serveuse
**to wake up** se réveiller
**Wales** le pays de Galles
**walk** la promenade
*to go for a walk* faire une promenade
**to walk** aller à pied; marcher
**walking boots** les chaussures de marche
**walking stick** la canne
**wall** le mur
**wallet** le portefeuille
**to want** vouloir
*I want...* je veux...
*we want...* nous voulons...
**war** la guerre
**ward** (hospital) la salle
**wardrobe** l'armoire *f*
**warehouse** l'entrepôt *m*
**warm** chaud(e)
*it's warm* (weather) il fait bon
*it's too warm* il fait trop chaud
**to warm up** (milk, etc) faire chauffer
**warning triangle** le triangle de présignalisation
**to wash** laver
*to wash oneself* se laver
**washbasin** le lavabo
**washing machine** la machine à laver
**washing powder** la lessive
**washing-up bowl** la cuvette
**washing-up liquid** le produit pour la vaisselle
**wasp** la guêpe

**wasp sting** la piqûre de guêpe
**waste bin** la poubelle
**watch** la montre
**to watch** (look at) regarder
**watchstrap** le bracelet de montre
**water** l'eau *f*
*bottled water* l'eau en bouteille
*cold water* l'eau froide
*drinking water* (fit to drink) l'eau potable
*hot water* l'eau chaude
*sparkling mineral water* l'eau
  minérale gazeuse
*still mineral water* l'eau minérale plate
**waterfall** la cascade
**water heater** le chauffe-eau
**watermelon** la pastèque
**waterproof** imperméable
**water-skiing** le ski nautique
**water sports** les sports nautiques
**waterwings** les bracelets gonflables
**waves** (on sea) les vagues
**waxing** (hair removal) l'épilation à la cire *f*
**way** (manner) la manière
(route) le chemin
**way in** (entrance) l'entrée *f*
**way out** (exit) la sortie
**we** nous
**weak** faible
(coffee, etc) léger(-ère)
**to wear** porter
**weather** le temps
**weather forecast** la météo
**web** (internet) le Web
**website** le site web
**wedding** le mariage
**wedding anniversary** l'anniversaire
  de mariage *m*
**wedding present** le cadeau de mariage
**Wednesday** mercredi
**week** la semaine
*last week* la semaine dernière
*next week* la semaine prochaine
*per week* par semaine
*this week* cette semaine
**weekday** le jour de semaine
**weekend** le week-end
*next weekend* le week-end prochain

*this weekend* ce week-end
**weekly** par semaine; hebdomadaire
(pass, ticket) valable pendant une semaine
**to weigh** peser
**weight** le poids
**welcome!** bienvenu(e)!
**well** (for water) le puits
(healthy) en bonne santé
*he's not well* il est souffrant
*I'm very well* je vais très bien
**well done** (steak) bien cuit(e)
**wellingtons** les bottes en caoutchouc
**Welsh** gallois(e)
**west** l'ouest *m*
**wet** mouillé(e)
**wetsuit** la combinaison de plongée
**what** que; quel/quelle; quoi
*what is it?* qu'est-ce que c'est?
**wheel** la roue
**wheelchair** le fauteuil roulant
**wheel clamp** le sabot
**when** quand
(at what time?) à quelle heure?
*when is it?* c'est quand?; à quelle heure?
**where** où
*where is it?* c'est où?
*where is the hotel?* où est l'hôtel?
**which** quel/quelle
*which (one)?* lequel/laquelle?
*which (ones)?* lesquels/lesquelles?
**while** pendant que
*in a while* bientôt; tout à l'heure
**white** blanc (blanche)
**who** qui
*who is it?* qui c'est?
**whole** entier(-ière)
**wholemeal bread** le pain complet
**whose:** *whose is it?* c'est à qui?
**why** pourquoi
**wide** large
**widow** la veuve
**widower** le veuf
**width** la largeur
**wife** la femme
**wi-fi** le wi-fi
**wig** la perruque
**to win** gagner

**wind** le vent
**windbreak** (camping, etc) le pare-vent
**windmill** le moulin à vent
**window** la fenêtre
(shop) la vitrine
**windscreen** le pare-brise
**windscreen wipers** les essuie-glaces
**windsurfing** la planche à voile
*to go windsurfing* faire de la planche à voile
**windy:** *it's windy* il y a du vent
**wine** le vin
*dry wine* le vin sec
*house wine* le vin en pichet
*red wine* le vin rouge
*rosé wine* le rosé
*sparkling wine* le vin mousseux
*sweet wine* le vin doux
*white wine* le vin blanc
**wine list** la carte des vins
**wing** (bird, aircraft) l'aile *f*
**wing mirror** le rétroviseur latéral
**winter** l'hiver *m*
**wire** le fil
**164**
**wireless** sans fil
**wireless internet** l'internet sans fil
**with** avec
*with ice* avec des glaçons
*with milk/sugar* avec du lait/sucre
**without** sans
*without ice* sans glaçons
*without milk/sugar* sans lait/sucre
**witness** le témoin
**woman** la femme
**wonderful** merveilleux(-euse)
**wood** le bois
**wooden** en bois
**wool** la laine
**word** le mot
**work** le travail
**to work** (person) travailler
(machine, car) fonctionner; marcher
*it doesn't work* ça ne marche pas
**work permit** le permis de travail
**world** le monde
**worried** inquiet(-iète)
**worse** pire
**worth:** *it's worth...* ça vaut...

**to wrap (up)** emballer
**wrapping paper** le papier d'emballage
**wrinkles** les rides
**wrist** le poignet
**to write** écrire
*please write it down* vous me l'écrivez, s'il vous plaît?
**writing paper** le papier à lettres
**wrong** faux (fausse)
**wrought iron** le fer forgé

## X

**X-ray** la radiographie
**to x-ray** radiographier

## Y

**yacht** le yacht
**year** l'an *m*; l'année *f*
*last year* l'année dernière
*next year* l'année prochaine
*this year* cette année
**yearly** annuel(le)
**yellow** jaune
**Yellow Pages** les pages jaunes
**yes** oui
*yes please* oui, merci
**yesterday** hier
**yet:** *not yet* pas encore
**yoghurt** le yaourt
*plain yoghurt* le yaourt nature
**yolk** le jaune d'œuf
**you** (familiar) tu
(polite) vous
**young** jeune
**your** (familiar sing) ton/ta
(familiar plural) tes
(polite singular) votre
(polite plural) vos
**youth hostel** l'auberge de jeunesse *f*

## Z

**zebra crossing** le passage pour piétons
**zero** le zéro
**zip** la fermeture éclair
**zone** la zone
**zoo** le zoo
**zoom lens** le zoom

# Dictionary

## A

**à** to; at
**abbaye** f abbey
**abcès** m abscess
**abeille** f bee
**abîmer** to damage
**abonné(e)** m/f subscriber;
  season ticket holder
**abonnement** m subscription; season ticket
**abri** m shelter
**abrité(e)** sheltered
**accélérateur** m accelerator
**accepter** to accept
**accès** m access
*accès aux trains* to the trains
*accès aux quais* to the trains
*accès interdit* no entry
*accès internet* internet access
*accès réservé* authorized entry only
*avez-vous un accès internet?* do you
  have internet access?
**accident** m accident
**accompagner** to accompany
**accord** m agreement
**accotement** m verge
**accueil** m reception; information
**accueillir** to greet; to welcome
**ACF** m Automobile Club de France
**achat** m purchase
**acheter** to buy
**acier** m steel
**acte de naissance** m birth certificate
**activité** f activity
**adaptateur** m adaptor (electrical)
**addition** f bill
**adhérent(e)** m/f member
**adolescent(e)** m/f teenager
**adresse** f address
**adresse électronique** f e-mail address
**adresser** to address
*adressez-vous à* enquire at (office)
**adroit(e)** skilful
**adulte** m/f adult

**aérogare** f terminal
**aéroglisseur** m hovercraft
**aéroport** m airport
**affaires** fpl business; belongings
*bonne affaire* bargain
**affiche** f poster; notice
**affluence** f crowd
**affreux(-euse)** awful
**âge** m age
*d'un certain âge* middle-aged
*du troisième âge* senior citizen
**âgé(e)** elderly
*âgé de ... ans* aged ... years
**agence** f agency; branch
*agence de voyages* travel agency
*agence immobilière* estate agent's
**agenda** m diary
*agenda électronique* m personal
  organizer (electronic)
**agent** m agent
*agent de police* police officer
**agiter** to shake
*agiter avant emploi* shake before use
**agneau** m lamb
**agrandissement** m enlargement
**agréable** pleasant; nice
**agréé(e)** registered; authorized
**agression** f attack (mugging)
**aider** to help
**aigre** sour
**aiguille** f needle
**ail** m garlic
**aimer** to enjoy; to love (person)
**air**: *en plein air* in the open air
**aire**: *aire de jeux* play area
*aire de repos* rest area
*aire de service* service area
*aire de stationnement* layby
**airelles** fpl bilberries; cranberries
**alarme** f alarm
**alcool** m alcohol; fruit brandy
**alcoolisé(e)** alcoholic
**alentours** mpl surroundings

**algues** *fpl* seaweed
**alimentation** *f* food
**allée** *f* driveway; path
**allégé(e)** low-fat
**Allemagne** *f* Germany
**allemand(e)** German
**aller** to go
**aller (simple)** *m* single ticket
**aller-retour** *m* return ticket
**allergie** *f* allergy
**allô?** hello? *(on telephone)*
**allumage** *m* ignition
**allumé(e)** on *(light)*
**allume-feu** *m* fire lighter
**allumer** to turn on; to light
*allumez vos phares* switch on headlights
**allumette** *f* match
**alpinisme** *m* mountaineering
**alsacien(ne)** Alsatian
**ambassade** *f* embassy
**ambulance** *f* ambulance
**améliorer** to improve
**amende** *f* fine
**amer(-ère)** bitter
**américain(e)** American
**Amérique** *f* America
**ameublement** *m* furniture
**ami(e)** *m/f* friend
*petit(e) ami(e)* boyfriend/girlfriend
**amortisseur** *m* shock absorber
**amour** *m* love
*faire l'amour* to make love
**ampoule** *f* blister; light bulb
**amusant(e)** funny *(amusing)*
**amuser** to entertain
*(bien) s'amuser* to enjoy oneself
**an** *m* year
*Nouvel An* *m* New Year
**analgésique** *m* painkiller
**ananas** *m* pineapple
**ancien(ne)** old; former
**ancre** *f* anchor
**anesthésique** *m* anaesthetic
**ange** *m* angel
**angine** *f* tonsillitis
*angine de poitrine* angina
**Anglais** *m* Englishman

**anglais** *m* English *(language)*
**anglais(e)** English
**Angleterre** *f* England
**animal** *m* animal
*animal domestique* pet
**animalerie** *f* pet shop
**animations** *fpl* entertainment; activities
**anis** *m* aniseed
**anisette** *f* aniseed liqueur
**année** *f* year; vintage
*bonne année!* happy New Year!
**anniversaire** *m* anniversary; birthday
**annonce** *f* advertisement
**annuaire** *m* directory
**annulation** *f* cancellation
**annuler** to cancel
**antenne** *f* aerial
*antenne parabolique* *f* satellite dish
**anti-insecte** *m* insect repellent
**antibiotique** *m* antibiotic
**antigel** *m* antifreeze
**antihistaminique** *m* antihistamine
**antimoustique** *m* mosquito repellent
**antiquaire** *m/f* antique dealer
**antiquités** *fpl* antiques
**antiseptique** *m* antiseptic
**antivol** *m* bike lock; immobilizer *(on car)*
**août** August
**apéritif** *m* apéritif
**aphte** *m* mouth ulcer
**appareil** *m* appliance; camera
*appareil acoustique* hearing aid
*appareil photo* camera
*appareil photo numérique* digital camera
**appartement** *m* apartment; flat
**appât** *m* bait *(for fishing)*
**appel** *m* phone call
**appeler** to call *(speak, phone)*
*appeler en PCV* to reverse the charges
**appendicite** *f* appendicitis
**apporter** to bring
**apprendre** to learn
*il a des difficultés d'apprentissage*
  he/she has a learning disability
**appuyer** to press
**après** after
**après-midi** *m* afternoon

**après-rasage** *m* after-shave
**après-shampooing** *m* conditioner
**aquarium** *m* fish tank
**arachide** *f* groundnut
**araignée** *f* spider
**arbre** *m* tree
**arête** *f* fishbone
**argent** *m* money; silver *(metal)*
*argent de poche* pocket money
*argent liquide* cash
**argot** *m* slang
**armoire** *f* wardrobe
**arranger** to arrange
**arrêt** *m* stop
*arrêt d'autobus* bus stop
*arrêt facultatif* request stop
**arrêter** to arrest; to stop
*arrêter le moteur* to turn off the engine
**arrêtez!** stop!
**arrhes** *fpl* deposit *(part payment)*
**arrière** *m* rear; back
**arrivées** *fpl* arrivals
**arriver** to arrive; to happen
**arrobase** *f* @
**arrondissement** *m* district *(in large city)*
**art** *m* art
**arthrite** *f* arthritis
**article** *m* item; article
*articles de toilette* toiletries
**articulation** *f* joint *(body)*
**artisan(e)** *m/f* craftsman/woman
**artisanat** *m* arts and crafts
**artiste** *m/f* artist
**ascenseur** *m* lift
**aspirateur** *m* vacuum cleaner
**aspirine** *f* aspirin
**assaisonnement** *m* seasoning; dressing
**asseoir** to sit (someone) down
*s'asseoir* to sit down
**assez** enough; quite *(rather)*
**assiette** *f* plate
**associé(e)** *m/f* partner *(business)*
**assorti(e)** assorted; matching
**assurance** *f* insurance
**assuré(e)** insured
**assurer** to assure; to insure
**asthme** *m* asthma

**atelier** *m* workshop; artist's studio
**attacher** to fasten *(seatbelt)*
**attaque** *f* fit *(medical)*
*attaque (d'apoplexie)* stroke
**attendre** to wait *(for)*
**attention!** look out!
*attention au feu* danger of fire
*faire attention* to be careful
**atterrissage** *m* landing *(aircraft)*
**attestation** *f* certificate
*l'attestation d'assurance* green card
**attrayant(e)** attractive
**au-delà de** beyond
**au-dessus de** above; on top of
**au lieu de** instead of
**au revoir** goodbye
**au secours!** help!
**aube** *f* dawn
**auberge** *f* inn
*auberge de jeunesse* youth hostel
**aubergine** *f* aubergine
**aucun(e)** none; no; not any
**audiophone** *m* hearing aid
**augmenter** to increase
**aujourd'hui** today
**aussi** also
**aussitôt** immediately
*aussitôt que possible* as soon as possible
**Australie** *f* Australia
**australien(ne)** Australian
**autel** *m* altar
**auteur** *m* author
**auto-école** *f* driving school
**auto-stop** *m* hitch-hiking
**autobus** *m* bus
**autocar** *m* coach
**automatique** automatic
**automne** *m* autumn
**automobiliste** *m/f* motorist
**autoradio** *m* car radio
**autorisé(e)** permitted; authorized
**autoroute** *f* motorway
**autre** other
*autres directions* other routes
**auvent** *m* awning *(for caravan etc)*; car port
**avalanche** *f* avalanche
**avaler** to swallow

*ne pas avaler* not to be taken internally
**avance** *f* advance
*à l'avance* in advance
**avant** before; front
*à l'avant* at the front
*en avant* forward
**avec** with
**avenir** *m* future
**avenue** *f* avenue
**avertir** to inform; to warn
**avion** *m* aeroplane
**aviron** *m* oar; rowing *(sport)*
**avis** *m* notice; warning
**aviser** to advise
**avocat** *m* avocado; lawyer
**avoine** *f* oats
**avoir** to have
**avortement** *m* abortion
**avril** April

# B

**bacon** *m* bacon
**bagages** *mpl* luggage
*bagages à main* hand luggage
*faire les bagages* to pack
**bague** *f* ring *(on finger)*
**baguette** *f* stick of French bread
**baie** *f* bay *(along coast)*
**baignade** *f* bathing
*baignade interdite* no bathing
**baignoire** *f* bath *(tub)*
**bain** *m* bath
*bain de bouche* mouthwash
*bain moussant* bubble bath
**baiser** kiss
**baisser** to lower
**bal** *m* ball; dance
**balade** *f* walk; drive; trek
**balai** *m* broom *(brush)*
*balai à franges* mop *(for foor)*
**balance** *f* scales *(for weighing)*
**balançoire** *f* swing *(for children)*
**balcon** *m* circle *(theatre)*; balcony
**ball-trap** *m* clay pigeon shooting
**balle** *f* ball *(small: golf, tennis, etc)*
**ballet** *m* ballet
**ballon** *m* balloon; ball *(large)*; brandy glass

**bambin** *m* toddler
**banane** *f* banana; bumbag
**banc** *m* seat; bench
**banlieue** *f* suburbs
**banque** *f* bank
**bar** *m* bar
**barbe** *f* beard
*barbe à papa* candy floss
**barque** *f* rowing boat
**barrage** *m* dam
*barrage routier* road block
**barre** *f* bar; rod
*barre de remorquage* towbar
**barré**: *route barrée* road closed
**barrer** to cross out
**barrière** *f* barrier
**bas** *m* bottom *(of page, etc)*; stocking
*en bas* below; downstairs
**bas(se)** low
**baskets** *fpl* trainers
**bassin** *m* pond; washing-up bowl
**bateau** *m* boat; ship
*bateau à rames* rowing boat
*bateau-mouche* river boat
**bâtiment** *m* building
**bâton (de ski)** *m* ski pole
**bâton (de randonnée)** *m* trekking pole
**batte** *f* bat *(baseball, cricket)*
**batterie** *f* battery *(for car)*
*batterie à plat* flat battery
**baume pour les lèvres** *m* lip salve
**bavoir** *m* bib *(baby's)*
**beau (belle)** lovely; handsome; beautiful; nice *(enjoyable)*
**beau-frère** *m* brother-in-law
**beau-père** *m* father-in-law; stepfather
**beaucoup (de)** much/many; a lot of
**bébé** *m* baby
**beignet** *m* fritter; doughnut
**belge** Belgian
**Belgique** *f* Belgium
**belle-fille** *f* daughter-in-law
**belle-mère** *f* mother-in-law; step-mother
**béquilles** *fpl* crutches
**berger** *m* shepherd
**berlingots** *mpl* boiled sweets
**besoin**: *avoir besoin de* to need

**beurre** m butter
*beurre doux* unsalted butter
**biberon** m baby's bottle
**bibliothèque** f library
**bicross** m BMX
**bicyclette** f bicycle
**bien** well; right; good
*bien cuit(e)* well done (steak)
**bientôt** soon; shortly
**bienvenu(e)** welcome!
**bière** f beer
*bière (à la) pression* draught beer
*bière blonde* lager
*bière bouteille* bottled lager
*bière brune* bitter
**bifteck** m steak
**bijouterie** f jeweller's; jewellery
**bijoux** mpl jewellery
**bikini** m bikini
**billet** m note; ticket
*billet aller-retour* return ticket
*billet d'avion* plane ticket
*billet de banque* banknote
*billet simple* one-way ticket
**biologique** organic
**biscotte** f breakfast biscuit; rusk
**biscuit** m biscuit
**bisque** f thick seafood soup
**blanc (blanche)** white; blank
*en blanc* blank (on form)
**blanc d'œuf** m egg white
**blanchisserie** f laundry
**blé** m wheat
**blessé(e)** injured
**blesser** to injure
**bleu** m bruise
**bleu(e)** blue; very rare (steak)
*bleu marine* navy blue
**bloc-notes** m note pad
**blond(e)** fair (hair)
**bloqué(e)** stuck
**body** m body (clothing)
**bœuf** m beef
**boire** to drink
**bois** m wood
**boisson** f drink
*boisson non alcoolisée* soft drink

**boîte** f can; box
*boîte à fusibles* fuse box
*boîte à lettres* post box
*boîte de conserve* tin (of food)
*boîte de nuit* night club
*boîte de vitesses* gearbox
**bol** m bowl (for soup, etc)
**bombe** f aerosol; bomb
**bon** m token; voucher
**bon (bonne)** good; right; nice
*bon anniversaire* happy birthday
*bon marché* inexpensive
**bonbon** m sweet
**bondé(e)** crowded
**bonhomme** m chap
*bonhomme de neige* snowman
**bonjour** hello; good morning/afternoon
**bonnet** m hat
*bonnet de bain* bathing cap
**bonneterie** f hosiery
**bonsoir** good evening
**bord** m border; edge; verge
*à bord* on board
*au bord de la mer* at the seaside
**bosse** f lump (swelling)
**botte** f boot; bunch
**bottillons** mpl ankle boots
**bouche** f mouth
*bouche d'incendie* fire hydrant
**bouché(e)** blocked
**bouchée** f mouthful; chocolate
*bouchée à la reine* vol-au-vent
**boucherie** f butcher's shop
**bouchon** m cork; plug (for sink); top (of bottle)
**boucle d'oreille** f earring
**bouée de sauvetage** f life belt
**bougie** f candle; spark plug
**bouillabaisse** f rich fish soup/stew
**bouilli(e)** boiled
**bouillir** to boil
**bouilloire** f kettle
**bouillon** m stock
**bouillotte** f hot-water bottle
**boulangerie** f bakery
**boule** f ball
**boules** fpl game similar to bowls
**bouquet** m bunch (of flowers)

**Bourgogne** Burgundy
**boussole** *f* compass
**bout** *m* end
**bouteille** *f* bottle
**boutique** *f* shop
**bouton** *m* button; switch; spot
*bouton de fièvre* cold sore
*boutons de manchette* cufflinks
**boxe** *f* boxing
**bracelet** *m* bracelet
*bracelet de montre* watchstrap
**braisé(e)** braised
**bras** *m* arm
**brasserie** *f* café; brewery
**break** *m* estate car; station wagon
**Bretagne** *f* Brittany
**breton(ne)** from Brittany
**bricolage** *m* do-it-yourself
**briquet** *m* cigarette lighter
**briser** to break; to smash
**britannique** British
**brocante** *f* second-hand goods; flea market
**broche** *f* brooch; spit
**brochette** *f* skewer; kebab
**brocoli** *m* broccoli
**brodé main** hand-embroidered
**bronzage** *m* suntan
**bronze** *m* bronze
**brosse** *f* brush
*brosse à cheveux* hairbrush
*brosse à dents* toothbrush
*brosse à dents électrique* electric toothbrush
**brouillard** *m* fog
**bruit** *m* noise
**brûlé(e)** burnt
**brûler** to burn
**brûlerie** *f* coffee-shop
**brûlures d'estomac** *fpl* heartburn
**brun(e)** brown; dark
**brushing** *m* blow-dry
**brut(e)** gross; raw
**Bruxelles** Brussels
**bûche** *f* log *(for fire)*
*bûche de Noël* Yule log
**buisson** *m* bush
**bulletin de consigne** *m* left-luggage ticket

**bureau** *m* desk; office
*bureau de change* foreign exchange office
*bureau de location* booking office
*bureau de poste* post office
*bureau de renseignements* information office
*bureau des objets trouvés* lost property office
**bus** *m* bus
**butane** *m* camping gas

## C

**ça va** it's OK; I'm OK
*ça va?* are you OK?; how are you?
**cabaret** *m* cabaret
**cabine** *f* beach hut; cubicle; cabin
*cabine d'essayage* changing room
**cabinet** *m* office
**câble de frein** brake cable
**câble d'embrayage** gear cable
**câble de remorquage** *m* tow rope
**cacahuète** *f* peanut
**cacao** *m* cocoa
**cacher** to hide
**cadeau** *m* gift
**cadenas** *m* padlock
**cadre** *m* picture frame
**cafard** *m* cockroach
**café** *m* coffee; café
*café au lait* white coffee
*café crème* a strong white coffee
*café décaféiné* decaff coffee
*café instantané* instant coffee
*café noir* black coffee
**cafetière** *f* coffee pot
**cahier** *m* exercise book
**caisse** *f* cash desk; case
*caisse d'épargne* savings bank
**caissier(-ière)** *m/f* cashier; teller
**calculatrice** *f* calculator
**caleçon** *m* boxer shorts
**calendrier** *m* calendar; timetable
**calmant** *m* sedative
**cambriolage** *m* break-in
**cambrioleur(-euse)** *m/f* burglar
**caméscope** *m* camcorder
*caméscope numérique* digital camcorder

**camion** *m* lorry; truck
**camionnette** *f* van
**camomille** *f* camomile
**campagne** *f* countryside; campaign
**camper** to camp
**camping** *m* camping; camp-site
**camping-gaz**® camping stove
*camping sauvage* camping on unofficial sites
**Canada** *m* Canada
**canadien(ne)** Canadian
**canal** *m* canal
**canapé** *m* sofa; open sandwich
*canapé-lit* sofa bed
**canard** *m* duck
**canif** *m* penknife
**canne** *f* walking stick
*canne à pêche* fishing rod
**cannelle** *f* cinnamon
**canoë** *m* canoe
**canot** *m* boat
*canot de sauvetage* lifeboat
**canotage** *m* boating
**caoutchouc** *m* rubber *(material)*
**capable** efficient
**capitale** *f* capital *(city)*
**capot** *m* bonnet; hood *(of car)*
**cappuccino** *m* cappuccino
**câpres** *fpl* capers
**capuchon** *m* hood; top *(of pen)*
**car** *m* coach
**carabine de chasse** *f* hunting rifle
**carafe** *f* carafe; decanter
**caravane** *f* caravan
**carburateur** *m* carburettor
**Carême** *m* Lent
**carnet** *m* notebook; book
*carnet de billets* book of tickets
*carnet de chèques* cheque book
**carotte** *f* carrot
**carré** *m* square
**carreau** *m* tile *(on wall, floor)*
**carrefour** *m* crossroads
**carte** *f* map; card; menu; pass *(bus, train)*
**carte bleue** credit card
*carte d'abonnement* season ticket
*carte d'embarquement* boarding card/pass

*carte d'identité* identity card
*carte de crédit* credit card
*carte de paiement* charge card; debit card
*carte des vins* wine list
*carte grise* log book *(car)*
*carte magnétique* swipecard
*carte mémoire* memory stick
*carte orange* monthly or yearly season ticket *(for Paris transport system)*
*carte postale* postcard
*carte routière* road map
*carte SIM* SIM card
*carte vermeil* senior citizen's rail pass
*carte-clé électronique* keycard *(electronic key)*
**cartes (à jouer)** *fpl* playing cards
**carton** *m* cardboard; (large cardboard) box
**cartouche** *f* carton *(of cigarettes)*
**cas** *m* case
**cascade** *f* waterfall
**caserne** *f* barracks
**casher** kosher
**casier** *m* rack; locker
**casino** *m* casino
**casque** *m* helmet
*casque (à écouteurs)* headphones
**casquette** *f* cap *(hat)*
**cassé(e)** broken
**casse-croûte** *m* snacks
**casser** to break
*casser la croûte* to have a snack
**casserole** *f* saucepan
**cassette** *f* cassette
**catch** *m* wrestling
**cathédrale** *f* cathedral
**catholique** Catholic
**cause** *f* cause
*pour cause de* on account of
**caution** *f* security *(for loan)*; deposit
*caution à verser* deposit required
**cave** *f* cellar
**caveau** *m* cellar
**caviar** *m* caviar(e)
**CD** *m* CD
**CD-Rom** *m* CD ROM
**ceci** this
**cédez le passage** give way

**CE** *f* EC (European Community)
**ceinture** *f* belt
*ceinture de sécurité* seatbelt
*ceinture porte-monnaie* moneybelt
**cela** that
**célèbre** famous
**célibataire** single *(unmarried)*
**cendrier** *m* ashtray
**cent** *m* hundred
**centimètre** *m* centimetre
**central(e)** central
**centre** *m* centre
*centre commercial* shopping centre
*centre de loisirs* leisure centre
*centre d'affaires* business centre
*centre équestre* riding school
*centre-ville* city centre
**céramique** *f* ceramics
**cercle** *m* circle; ring
**céréales** *fpl* cereal *(for breakfast)*
**cerise** *f* cherry
**certain(e)** certain *(sure)*
**certificat** *m* certificate

**cerveau** *m* brain

**cervelle** *f* brains *(as food)*
**cesser** to stop
**cette** this; that
**ceux-ci/celles-ci** these ones
**ceux-là/celles-là** those ones
**CFF** *mpl* Swiss Railways
**chacun/chacune** each
**chaîne** *f* chain; channel; *(mountain)* range
*chaîne (stéréo)* stereo
*chaînes obligatoires* snow chains
  compulsory
**chair** *f* flesh
**chaise** *f* chair
*chaise de bébé* high chair
*chaise longue* deckchair
**châle** *m* shawl
**chalet** *m* chalet
**chambre** *f* bedroom; room
*chambre à air* inner tube
*chambre à coucher* bedroom
*chambre à deux lits* twin-bedded room
*chambre d'hôte* bed and breakfast
*chambre individuelle* single room

*chambre pour deux personnes*
  double room
**chambres** rooms to let
**champ** *m* field
*champ de courses* racecourse
**champagne** *m* champagne
**champignon** *m* mushroom
*champignon vénéneux* toadstool
**chance** *f* luck
**change** *m* exchange
**changement** *m* change
**changer** to change
*changer de l'argent* to change money
*changer de train* to change train
*se changer* to change clothes
**chanson** *f* song
**chanter** to sing
**chanterelle** *f* chanterelle
**chantier** *m* building site; roadworks
**chapeau** *m* hat
**chapelle** *f* chapel
**chaque** each; every
**charbon** *m* coal
*charbon de bois* charcoal
**charcuterie** *f* pork butcher's;
  delicatessen; cooked meat
**chargeur:** *le chargeur pour (téléphone)*
  *portable* mobile phone charger
**chariot** *m* trolley
**charter** *m* charter flight
**chasse** *f* hunting; shooting
*chasse gardée* private hunting
**chasse-neige** *m* snowplough
**chasser** to hunt
**chasseur** *m* hunter
**chat** *m* cat
**châtaigne** *f* chestnut
**château** *m* castle; mansion
**chaud(e)** hot
**chauffage** *m* heating
**chauffer** to heat up *(milk, water)*
**chauffeur** *m* driver
**chaussée** *f* carriageway
*chaussée déformée* uneven road surface
*chaussée rétrécie* road narrows
*chaussée verglacée* icy road
**chaussette** *f* sock

**chaussure** f shoe; boot
**chauve** bald *(person)*
**chauve-souris** f bat *(creature)*
**chef** m chef; chief; head; leader
**chef de train** guard *(on train)*
**chef-d'œuvre** m masterpiece
**chef-lieu** m county town
**chemin** m path; lane; track; way
**chemin de fer** railway
**cheminée** f chimney; fireplace
**chemise** f shirt
**chemise de nuit** nightdress
**chemisier** m blouse
**chèque** m cheque
**chèque de voyage** traveller's cheque
**cher (chère)** dear; expensive
**chercher** to look for
**aller chercher** to fetch; to collect
**cheval** m horse
**faire du cheval** to ride *(horse)*
**cheveux** mpl hair
**cheville** f ankle
**chèvre** f goat
**chevreau** m kid *(goat, leather)*
**chevreuil** m venison
**chez** at the house of
**chez moi** at my home
**chien** m dog
**chiffon** m duster; rag
**chili con carne** chilli *(dish)*
**chips** fpl crisps
**chirurgien** m surgeon
**chocolat** m chocolate
**chocolat à croquer** plain chocolate
**chocolat au lait** milk chocolate
**choisir** to choose
**choix** m range; choice; selection
**chômage: au chômage** unemployed
**chope** f tankard
**chorale** f choir
**chose** f thing
**chou** m cabbage
**chou-fleur** m cauliflower
**chute** f fall
**cidre** m cider
**ciel** m sky
**cigare** m cigar

**cigarette** f cigarette
**cil** m eyelash
**cimetière** m cemetery; graveyard
**cinéma** m cinema
**cintre** m coat hanger
**cirage** m shoe polish
**circuit** m round trip; circuit
**circulation** f traffic
**circuler** to operate *(train, bus, etc)*
**cire** f wax; polish
**cirque** m circus
**ciseaux** mpl scissors
**cité** f city; housing estate
**citron** m lemon
**citron vert** lime
**citronnade** f still lemonade; lemon squash
**citronnelle** lemongrass
**clair(e)** clear; light
**classe** f grade; class
**clavicule** f collar bone
**clavier** m keyboard
**clé** f key; spanner
**clé de contact** ignition key
**clé minute** keys cut while you wait
**clé USB** flash pen
**clef** f key
**client(e)** m/f client; customer
**clignotant** m indicator *(on car)*
**climatisation** f air-conditioning
**climatisé(e)** air-conditioned
**climatiseur** m air-conditioning unit
**clinique** f clinic *(private)*
**cloche** f bell *(church, school)*
**clocher** m steeple
**clou** m nail *(metal)*
**clou de girofle** clove
**cocher** to tick *(on form)*
**cochon** m pig
**cocktail** m cocktail
**cocktail-bar** cocktail bar
**cocotte** f casserole dish
**cocotte-minute** f pressure cooker
**code** m code
**code barres** barcode
**code confidentiel** pin number
**code postal** postcode
**cœur** m heart

**coffre-fort** *m* strongbox; safe
**cognac** *m* brandy
**coiffeur** *m* hairdresser; barber
**coiffeuse** *f* hairdresser
**coin** *m* corner
**coincé(e)** jammed; stuck
**col** *m* collar; pass *(in mountains)*
**colis** *m* parcel
**collant** *m* pair of tights
**colle** *f* glue
**collège** *m* secondary school
**collègue** *m/f* colleague
**coller** to stick; to glue
**collier** *m* necklace; dog collar
**colline** *f* hill
**collision** *f* crash *(car)*
**colonne** *f* column
**colonne vertébrale** *f* spine
**combien** how much/many
**combinaison de plongée** *f* wetsuit
**combinaison de ski** *f* ski suit
**combustible** *m* fuel
**comédie** *f* comedy
*comédie musicale* musical *(show)*
**commande** *f* order *(in restaurant)*
**commander** to order
**comme** like
*comme ça* like this; like that
**commencer** to begin
**comment?** pardon?; how?
**commerçant(e)** *m/f* trader
**commerce** *m* commerce; business; trade
**commissariat (de police)** *m* police
station
**commode** *f* chest of drawers
**commotion** *f* shock
*commotion (cérébrale)* concussion
**communication** *f* communication;
call *(on telephone)*
**communion** *f* communion
**compagne** *f* girlfriend
**compagnie** *f* firm; company
**compagnon** *m* boyfriend
**compartiment** *m* compartment *(train)*
**complet(-ète)** full (up)
**complètement** completely
**comporter** to consist of

*se comporter* to behave
**composer** to dial *(a number)*
**composter** to date-stamp/punch *(ticket)*
*composter votre billet* validate your ticket
**comprenant** including
**comprendre** to understand
**comprimé** *m* tablet
**compris(e)** included
*non compris* not included
**comptant** *m* cash
**compte** *m* number; account
*compte en banque* bank account
**compter** to count *(add up)*
**compteur** *m* speedometer; meter
**comptoir** *m* counter *(in shop, bar, etc)*
**comte** *m* count; earl
**concert** *m* concert
**concierge** *m/f* caretaker; janitor
**concours** *m* contest; aid
**concurrent(e)** *m/f* competitor
**conducteur(-trice)** *m/f* driver
**conduire** to drive
**conduite** *f* driving; behaviour
**conférence** *f* conference
**confession** *f* confession
**confirmer** to confirm
**confiserie** *f* sweetshop
**confiture** *f* jam; preserve
**congélateur** *m* freezer
**congelé(e)** frozen
**connaître** to know
**conseil** *m* advice; council
**conseiller** to advise
**conserver** to keep; to retain *(ticket, etc)*
**consigne** *f* deposit; left luggage
**consommation** *f* drink
**consommé** *m* clear soup
**constat** *m* report
**constipé(e)** constipated
**construire** to build
**consulat** *m* consulate
**contacter** to contact
**contenir** to contain
**content(e)** pleased
**contenu** *m* contents
**continuer** to continue
**contraceptif** *m* contraceptive

**contrat** m contract
*contrat de location* lease
**contravention** f fine *(penalty)*
**contre** against; versus
**contre-filet** m sirloin
**contrôle** m check
*contrôle des passeports* passport control
*contrôle radar* speed trap
**contrôler** to check
**contrôles de sécurité** mpl security check
**contrôleur(-euse)** m/f ticket inspector
**convenu(e)** agreed
**convoi exceptionnel** m large load
**coordonnées** fpl contact details
**copie** f copy *(duplicate)*
**copier** to copy
**coque** f shell; cockle; hull
**coquelicot** m poppy
**coquet(te)** pretty *(place, etc)*
**coquillages** mpl shellfish
**coquille** f shell
*coquille Saint-Jacques* scallop
**corail** m coral; type of train
**corde** f rope
*corde à linge* clothes line
**cordonnerie** f shoe repair shop
**cornet** m cone
**corniche** f coast road
**cornichon** m gherkin
**corps** m body
**correspondance** f connection *(transport)*
**correspondant(e)** m/f penfriend
**corrida** f bull-fight
**Corse** f Corsica
**costume** m suit *(man's)*
**côte** f coast; hill; rib
*Côte d'Azur* French Riviera
**côté** m side
*à côté de* beside; next to
**côtelette** f cutlet
**coton** m cotton
*coton hydrophile* cotton wool
*coton-tige*® cotton bud
**cou** m neck
**couche (de bébé)** f nappy
**coucher de soleil** m sunset
**couchette** f bunk; berth

**coude** m elbow
**coudre** to sew
**couette** f continental quilt; duvet
**couler** to run *(water)*
**couleur** f colour
**coulis** m purée
**couloir** m corridor; aisle
**coup** m stroke; shot; blow
*coup de pied* kick
*coup de soleil* sunburn
*coup de téléphone* phone call
**coupe** f goblet *(ice cream)*
*coupe (de cheveux)* haircut
**coupe-ongles** m nail clippers
**couper** to cut
**couple** m couple *(two people)*
**coupure** f cut
*coupure de courant* power cut
**cour** f court; courtyard
**courant** m power; current
**courant(e)** common; current
**courir** to run
**couronne** f crown
**courrier** m mail; post
*courrier électronique* e-mail
**courroie de ventilateur** f fan belt
**cours** m lesson; course; rate
**course** f race *(sport)*; errand
*course hippique* horse race
*faire des courses* to go shopping
**court de tennis** m tennis court
**court(e)** short
**cousin(e)** m/f cousin
**coussin** m cushion
**coût** m cost
**couteau** m knife
**coûter** to cost
**coûteux(-euse)** expensive
**couture** f sewing; seam
**couvent** m convent; monastery
**couvercle** m lid
**couvert** m cover charge; place setting
*couverts* cutlery
**couvert(e)** covered
**couverture** f blanket; cover
**crabe** m crab
**cranberry (jus de)** cranberry juice

**crapaud** *m* toad
**cravate** *f* tie
**crayon** *m* pencil
**crèche** *f* creche
**crème** *f* cream *(food, lotion)*
**crème à raser** shaving cream
**crème anglaise** custard
**crème Chantilly** whipped cream
**crème fermentée** soured cream
**crème hydratante** moisturizer
**crème pâtissière** confectioner's custard
**crème solaire** suncream
**crémerie** *f* dairy
**crêpe** *f* pancake
**crêperie** *f* pancake shop/restaurant
**cresson** *m* watercress
**crevaison** *f* puncture
**crevette** *f* shrimp; prawn
**cric** *m* jack *(for car)*
**crier** to shout
**crime** *m* crime; offence; murder
**crise** *f* crisis; attack *(medical)*
**crise cardiaque** heart attack
**cristal** *m* crystal
**croire** to believe
**croisement** *m* junction *(road)*
**croisière** *f* cruise
**croix** *f* cross
**croquant(e)** crisp; crunchy
**croque-madame** *m* toasted cheese sandwich with ham and fried egg
**croque-monsieur** *m* toasted ham and cheese sandwich
**croustade** *f* pastry shell with filling
**croûte** *f* crust
**cru(e)** raw
**crudités** *fpl* raw vegetables
**crue subite** *f* flash flood
**crustacés** *mpl* shellfish
**cube de bouillon** *m* stock cube
**cuiller** *f* spoon
**cuiller à café** teaspoon
**cuir** *m* leather
**cuisiné(e)** cooked
**cuisine** *f* cooking; cuisine; kitchen
**cuisine familiale** home cooking
**faire la cuisine** to cook

**cuisiner** to cook
**cuisinier** *m* cook
**cuisinière** *f* cook; cooker
**cuisse** *f* thigh
**cuisses de grenouille** frogs' legs
**cuit(e)** cooked
**bien cuit** well done *(steak)*
**cuivre** *m* copper
**cuivre jaune** brass
**culotte** *f* panties
**curieux(-euse)** strange
**curseur** *m* cursor *(computer)*
**cuvée** *f* vintage
**cuvette** *f* washing up bowl
**cyclisme** *m* cycling
**cystite** *f* cystitis

# D

**daltonien(ne)** colour-blind
**dame** *f* lady
**dames** ladies
**danger** *m* danger
**dangereux(-euse)** dangerous
**dans** into; in; on
**danser** to dance
**date** *f* date *(day)*
**date de naissance** date of birth
**date limite de vente** sell-by date
**daube** *f* stew
**de** from; of; some
**dé** *m* dice
**début** *m* beginning
**débutant(e)** *m/f* beginner
**décaféiné(e)** decaffeinated
**décembre** December
**décès** *m* death
**décharge** *f* electric shock
**décharge publique** rubbish dump
**déchargement** *m* unloading
**déchirer** to rip
**déclaration** *f* statement; report
**déclaration de douane** customs declaration
**décollage** *m* takeoff
**décoller** to take off *(plane)*
**décolleté** *m* low neck
**décongeler** to defrost
**découvrir** to discover

**décrire** to describe
**décrocher** to lift the receiver
**dedans** inside
**défaire** to unfasten; to unpack
**défaut** *m* fault; defect
**défectueux(-euse)** faulty
**défense de...** no.../... forbidden
*défense de fumer* no smoking
*défense de stationner* no parking
**dégâts** *mpl* damage
**dégeler** to thaw
**dégivrer** to de-ice *(windscreen)*
**dégustation** *f* tasting
*dégustation de vins* wine tasting
**dehors** outside; outdoors
**déjeuner** *m* lunch
**délicieux(-euse)** delicious
**délit** *m* offence
**deltaplane** *m* hang-glider
**demain** tomorrow
**demande** *f* application; request
*demandes d'emploi* situations wanted
**demander** to ask (for)
**demandeur d'emploi** *m* job seeker
**démaquillant** *m* make-up remover
**démarqué(e)** reduced *(goods)*
**démarreur** *m* starter *(in car)*
**demi(e)** half
**demi-pension** *f* half board
**demi-sec** medium-dry
**demi-tarif** *m* half fare
**demi-tour** *m* U-turn
**dent** *f* tooth
**dentelle** *f* lace
**dentier** *m* dentures
**dentifrice** *m* toothpaste
**dentiste** *m/f* dentist
**déodorant** *m* deodorant
**dépannage** *m* breakdown service
**dépanneuse** *f* breakdown van
**départ** *m* departure
**département** *m* county
**dépasser** to exceed; to overtake
**dépenses** *fpl* expenditure
**dépliant** *m* brochure
**dépôt** *m* deposit; depot
*dépôt d'ordures* rubbish dump

**dépression** *f* depression; nervous
  breakdown
**depuis** since
**déranger** to disturb
**dérapage** skid
*déraper* to skid
**dernier(-ère)** last; latest
**derrière** at the back; behind
**derrière** *m* bottom *(buttocks)*
**dès** from; since
*dès votre arrivée* as soon as you arrive
**désagréable** unpleasant
**descendre** to go down; to get off
**description** *f* description
**déshabiller** to undress
*se déshabiller* to get undressed
**désirer** to want
**désodorisant** *m* air freshener
**désolé(e)** sorry
**dessein** *m* design; plan
**desserré(e)** loose *(not fastened)*
**dessert** *m* pudding
**dessous (de)** underneath (of)
**dessus (de)** on top (of)
**destinataire** *m/f* addressee
**destination** *f* destination
*à destination de* bound for
**détail** *m* detail
*en détail* in detail
**détergent** *m* detergent
**détourner** to divert
**deux** two
*deux fois* twice
*les deux* both
**deuxième** second
**devant** in front (of)
**développer** to develop
**devenir** to become
**déviation** *f* diversion
**devis** *m* quotation *(price)*
**devises** *fpl* currency
**dévisser** to unscrew
**devoir** to have to; to owe
**diabète** *m* diabetes
**diabétique** diabetic
**diamant** *m* diamond
**diaphragme** *m* cap *(contraceptive)*

**diapositive** *f* slide *(photograph)*
**diarrhée** *f* diarrhoea
**dictionnaire** *m* dictionary
**diététique** *f* dietary; health foods
**différent(e)** different
**difficile** difficult
**digue** *f* dyke; jetty
**dimanche** *m* Sunday
**dinde** *f* turkey
**dîner** to have dinner
**dîner** *m* dinner
*dîner spectacle* cabaret dinner
**dire** to say; to tell
**direct**: *train direct* through train
**directeur** *m* manager; headmaster
**direction** *f* management; direction
**directrice** *f* manageress; headmistress
**discothèque** *f* disco; nightclub
**discussion** *f* argument
**disjoncteur** *m* circuit breaker
**disloquer** to dislocate
**disparaître** to disappear
**disparu(e)** missing *(disappeared)*
**disponible** available
**disque** *m* record; disk *(computer)*
*disque de stationnement* parking disk
*disque dur* hard disk
**disquette** *f* floppy disk
**dissolvant** *m* nail polish remover
**distractions** *fpl* entertainment
**distributeur** *m* dispenser
*distributeur automatique* vending machine; cash machine
**divers(e)** various
**divertissements** *mpl* entertainment
**divorcé(e)** divorced
**docteur** *m* doctor
**doigt** *m* finger
*doigt de pied* toe
**domestique** *m/f* servant; maid
**domicile** *m* home; address
**donner** to give; to give away
**doré(e)** golden
**dormir** to sleep
**dos** *m* back *(of body)*
**dossier** *m (computer)* folder; *(for papers)* file
**douane** *f* customs

**double** double
**doubler** to overtake
**douche** *f* shower
**douleur** *f* pain
**douloureux(-euse)** painful
**doux (douce)** mild; gentle; soft; sweet
**douzaine** *f* dozen
**dragée** *f* sugared almond
**drap** *m* sheet
**drapeau** *m* flag
**drogue** *f* drug
**droguerie** *f* hardware shop
**droit** *m* right *(entitlement)*
**droit(e)** right *(not left)*; straight
**droite** *f* right-hand side
*à droite* on/to the right
*tenez votre droite* keep to right
**dur(e)** hard; hard-boiled; tough
**durée** *f* duration
**DVD** DVD
**lecteur de DVD** DVD player

# E

**eau** *f* water
*eau de Javel* bleach
*eau douce* fresh water *(not salt)*
*eau du robinet* tap-water
*eau minérale* mineral water
*eau potable* drinking water
*eau salée* salt water
*eau-de-vie* brandy
**ébène** *f* ebony
**échanger** to exchange
**échantillon** *m* sample
**échapper** to escape
**écharpe** *f* scarf *(woollen)*
**échelle** *f* ladder
*échelle de secours* fire escape
**éclairage** *m* lighting
**éclairs** *mpl* lightning
**éclatement** *m* blowout *(of tyre)*
**écluse** *f* lock *(in canal)*
**école** *f* school
*école maternelle* nursery school
**écologique** ecological
**écossais(e)** Scottish
**Écosse** *f* Scotland

**écotourisme** *m* eco-tourism
**écouter** to listen to
**écran** *m* screen
**écran solaire** sunscreen *(lotion)*
**écran total** sunblock
**écrire** to write
**écrivain** *m* author
**écrou** *m* nut *(for bolt)*
**écurie** *f* stable
**édulcorant** *m* sweetener
**église** *f* church
**élastique** *m* elastic band
**électricien** *m* electrician
**électricité** *f* electricity
**électrique** electric
**électronique** electronic
**élément** *m* unit; element
**élevé(e) en plein air** free-range
**emballer** to wrap (up)
**embarcadère** *m* jetty *(landing pier)*
**embarquement** *m* boarding
**embouteillage** *m* traffic jam
**embrayage** *m* clutch *(in car)*
**émission** *f* programme; broadcast
**emplacement** *m* parking space; pitch
   *(place for tent/caravan)*
**emploi** *m* use; job
**emporter** to take away
**à emporter** take-away
**emprunter** to borrow
**en** some; any; in; to; made of
**en cas de** in case of
**en face de** opposite
**en gros** in bulk; wholesale
**en panne** out of order
**en retard** late
**en train/voiture** by train/car
**encaisser** to cash *(cheque)*
**enceinte** pregnant
**enchanté(e)!** pleased to meet you!
**encore** still; yet; again
**encre** *f* ink
**endommager** to damage
**endroit** *m* place; spot
**enfant** *m/f* child
**enfler** to swell *(bump, eye, etc)*
**enlever** to take away; to take off *(clothes)*

**enlever le haut** to go topless
**enneigé(e)** snowed up
**ennui** *m* boredom; nuisance; trouble
**ennuyeux** boring
**enregistrement** *m* check-in desk
**enregistrer** to record; to check in; to video
**enseignement** *m* education
**enseigner** to teach
**ensemble** together
**ensuite** next; after that
**entendre** to hear
**entier(-ière)** whole
**entorse** *f* sprain
**entracte** *m* interval
**entre** between
**entrecôte** *f* rib steak
**entrée** *f* entrance; admission; starter *(food)*
**entrée gratuite** admission free
**entrée interdite** no entry
**entreprise** *f* firm; company
**entrer** to come in; to go in
**entretien** *m* maintenance; interview
**entrez!** come in!
**enveloppe** *f* envelope
**enveloppe matelassée** padded envelope
**envers: l'envers** wrong side
**à l'envers** upside down; back to front
**environ** around; about
**environs** *mpl* surroundings
**envoyer** to send
**envoyer un SMS à** to text
**je t'enverrai un SMS** I'll text you
**épais(se)** thick
**épargner** to save *(money)*
**épaule** *f* shoulder
**épi** *m* ear (of corn)
**épi de maïs** corn-on-the-cob
**épice** *f* spice
**épicerie** *f* grocer's shop
**épicerie fine** delicatessen
**épilation** *f* hair removal
**épilation à la cire** *f* waxing
**épileptique** epileptic
**épinards** *mpl* spinach
**épine** *f* thorn
**épingle** *f* pin
**épingle à nourrice** safety pin**

**éponge** f sponge
**époque** f age
**d'époque** period (furniture)
**épuisé(e)** sold out; used up; tired out
**épuiser** to use up; to run out of
**équipage** m crew
**équipe** f team; shift
**équipement** m equipment
**équitation** f horse-riding
**erreur** f mistake
**escalade** f climbing
**escalator** m escalator
**escalier** m stairs
**escalier de secours** fire escape
**escalier mécanique** escalator
**escargot** m snail
**escarpement** m cliff (in mountains)
**Espagne** f Spain
**espagnol(e)** Spanish
**espèce** f sort
**espérer** to hope
**esquimau** m ice lolly
**essai** m trial; test
180 **essayer** to try; to try on
**essence** f petrol
**essence sans plomb** unleaded petrol
**essorer** to spin(-dry); to wring
**essoreuse** f spin dryer
**essuie-glace** m windscreen wipers
**essuie-tout** m kitchen paper
**esthéticienne** f beautician
**estivants** mpl summer holiday-makers
**estomac** m stomach
**estragon** m tarragon
**et** and
**étage** m storey
**le dernier étage** the top floor
**étain** m tin; pewter
**étang** m pond
**étape** f stage
**état** m state
**États-Unis** United States
**été** m summer
**éteindre** to turn off
**éteint(e)** out (light)
**étiquette** f label
**étiquette à bagages** luggage tag

**étoile** f star
**étranger(-ère)** m/f foreigner
**à l'étranger** overseas; abroad
**être** to be
**étroit(e)** narrow; tight
**étudiant(e)** m/f student
**étudier** to study
**étui** m case (camera, glasses)
**étuvée: à l'étuvée** braised
**eurochèque** m eurocheque
**Europe** f Europe
**européen(ne)** European
**eux** them
**évanoui(e)** fainted
**événement** m occasion; event
**éventail** m fan (handheld)
**éventé(e)** flat (beer)
**évêque** m bishop
**évier** m sink (washbasin)
**éviter** to avoid
**exact(e)** right (correct)
**examen** m examination
**excédent de bagages** m excess baggage
**excellent(e)** excellent
**excès de vitesse** m speeding
**exclu(e)** excluded
**exclure** to expel
**exclusif(-ive)** exclusive
**excursion** f trip; outing; excursion
**excuses** fpl apologies
**excusez-moi!** excuse me!
**exemplaire** m copy
**exercice** m exercise
**expéditeur** m sender
**expert(e)** m/f expert
**expirer** to expire (ticket, passport)
**expliquer** to explain
**exporter** to export
**exposition** f exhibition
**exprès** on purpose; deliberately
**en exprès** express (parcel, etc)
**extérieur(e)** outside
**extincteur** m fire extinguisher
**extra** top-quality; first-rate

# F
**fabrication** f manufacturing

**fabriquer** to manufacture
*fabriqué en...* made in...
**face: en face (de)** opposite
**fâché(e)** angry
**facile** easy
**façon** f way; manner
**facteur(-trice)** m/f postman
**facture** f invoice
*facture détaillée* itemized bill
**faible** weak
**faïence** f earthenware
**faim** f hunger
*avoir faim* to be hungry
**faire** to make; to do
*faire du stop* to hitchhike
**faisan** m pheasant
**fait main** handmade
**falaise** f cliff
**famille** f family
**farci(e)** stuffed
**fard à paupières** m eye shadow
**farine** f flour
**fatigue** f tiredness
**fatigué(e)** tired
**fausse couche** f miscarriage
**faute** f mistake; foul (of football)
**fauteuil** m armchair; seat
*fauteuil roulant* wheelchair
**faux (fausse)** fake; false; wrong
**fax** m fax
**faxer** to fax
**félicitations** fpl congratulations
**femme** f woman; wife
*femme au foyer* housewife
*femme d'affaires* businesswoman
*femme de chambre* chambermaid
*femme de ménage* cleaner
*femme policier* policewoman
**fenêtre** f window
**fenouil** m fennel
**fente** f crack; slot
**fer** m iron (material, golf club)
*fer à repasser* iron (for clothes)
**férié(e): jour férié** public holiday
**ferme** f farmhouse; farm
**fermé(e)** closed
**fermer** to close/shut; to turn off

*fermer à clé* to lock
**fermeture** f closing
*fermeture Éclair®* zip
**ferroviaire** railway; rail
**ferry** m car ferry
**fête** f holiday; fête; party
*fête des rois* Epiphany
*fête foraine* funfair
**feu** m fire; traffic lights
*feu (de joie)* bonfire (celebration)
*feu d'artifice* fireworks
*feu de position* sidelight
*feu rouge* red light
**feuille** f leaf; sheet (of paper)
**feuilleton** m soap opera
**feutre** m felt; felt-tip pen
**février** February
**fiancé(e)** engaged (to be married)
**ficelle** f string; thin French stick
**fiche** f token; form; slip (of paper)
**fichier** m file (computer)
*fichier joint* attachment
**fièvre** f fever
*avoir de la fièvre* to have a temperature    181
**figue** f fig
**fil** m thread; lead (electrical)
*fil dentaire* dental floss
**file** f lane; row
**filet** m net; fillet (of meat, fish)
*filet à bagages* luggage rack
**fille** f daughter; girl
**film** m film
*film étirable* cling film
**fils** m son
**filtre** m filter
*filtre à huile* oil filter
**fin** f end
**fin(e)** thin (material); fine (delicate)
**fini(e)** finished
**finir** to end; to finish
**fixe: le (téléphone) fixe** landline phone
**fixer** to fix
**flacon** m bottle (small)
**flamand(e)** Flemish
**flan** m custard tart
**flash** m flash (for camera)
**fleur** f flower

**fleuriste** *m/f* florist
**fleuve** *m* river
**flipper** *m* pinball
**flûte** *f* long, thin loaf
**foie** *m* liver
*foie gras* goose liver
**foire** *f* fair
*foire à/aux...* special offer on...
**fois** *f* time
*cette fois* this time
*une fois* once
**folle** mad
**foncé(e)** dark *(colour)*
**fonctionner** to work *(machine)*
**fond** *m* back *(of hall, room)*; bottom
**fondre** to melt
**force** *f* strength
**forêt** *f* forest
**forfait** *m* fixed price; ski pass
**forme** *f* shape; style
**formidable** great *(wonderful)*
**formulaire** *m* form *(document)*
**fort(e)** loud; strong
**182**
**forteresse** *f* fort
**fosse** *f* pit; grave
*fosse septique* septic tank
**fou (folle)** mad
**fouetté(e)** whipped *(cream, eggs)*
**foulard** *m* scarf *(headscarf)*
**foule** *f* crowd
**four** *m* oven
*four à micro-ondes* microwave
**fourchette** *f* fork
**fournir** to supply
**fourré(e)** filled; fur-lined
**fourrure** *f* fur
**fraîche** fresh; cool; wet *(paint)*
**frais** fresh; cool
**frais** *mpl* costs; expenses
**fraise** *f* strawberry
**framboise** *f* raspberry
**français(e)** French
**Français(e)** Frenchman/woman
**frapper** to hit; to knock *(on door)*
**frein** *m* brake
*frein à main* handbrake
**freiner** to brake

**fréquent(e)** frequent
**frère** *m* brother
**fret** *m* freight *(goods)*
**frigo** *m* fridge
**frit(e)** fried
**friterie** *f* chip shop
**frites** *fpl* french fries; chips
**friture** *f* small fried fish
**froid(e)** cold
**fromage** *m* cheese
**froment** *m* wheat
**front** *m* forehead
**frontière** *f* border; boundary
**frotter** to rub
**fruit** *m* fruit
*fruit de la passion* passionfruit
*fruits de mer* seafood
*fruits secs* dried fruit
**fuite** *f* leak
**fumé(e)** smoked
**fumée** *f* smoke
**fumer** to smoke
**fumeurs** smokers
**fumier** *m* manure
**funiculaire** *m* funicular railway
**fuseau** *m* ski pants
**fusible** *m* fuse
**fusil** *m* gun

## G

**gagner** to earn; to win
**galerie** *f* art gallery; arcade; roof-rack
**gallois(e)** Welsh
**gambas** *fpl* large prawns
**gant** *m* glove
*gant de toilette* face cloth
*gants de ménage* rubber gloves
**garage** *m* garage
**garantie** *f* guarantee
**garçon** *m* boy; waiter
**garde** *f* custody; guard
*garde-côte* coastguard
**garder** to keep; to look after
**garderie** *f* creche
**gardien(ne)** *m/f* caretaker; warden
**gare** *f* railway station
*gare routière* bus terminal

garer to park
garni(e) served with vegetables or chips
gas-oil *m* diesel fuel
gâteau *m* cake; gateau
gauche left
*à gauche* to/on the left
gâteau *m* cake
gaufre *f* waffle
gaz *m* gas
*gaz d'échappement* exhaust fumes
gaz-oil *m* diesel fuel
gazeux(-euse) fizzy
gel *m* frost
*gel pour cheveux* hair gel
gelé(e) frozen
gelée *f* jelly; aspic
gênant inconvenient
gendarme *m* policeman *(in rural areas)*
gendarmerie *f* police station
gendre *m* son-in-law
généreux(-euse) generous
genou *m* knee
gentil(-ille) kind *(person)*
gérant(e) *m/f* manager/manageress
gérer to manage *(be in charge of)*
gibier *m* game *(hunting)*
gigahertz *m* gigahertz
gigaoctet *m* gigabyte
gilet *m* waistcoat
*gilet de sauvetage* life jacket
gingembre *m* ginger
gîte *m* self-catering house/flat
glace *f* ice; ice cream; mirror
glacé(e) chilled; iced
glacier *m* glacier; ice-cream maker
glacière *f* cool-box *(for picnic)*
glaçon *m* ice cube
glissant(e) slippery
glisser to slip
gluten gluten
gomme *f* rubber *(eraser)*
gorge *f* throat; gorge
gosse *m/f* kid *(child)*
gothique Gothic
goût *m* flavour; taste
goûter to taste
goyave guava

GPS (système de navigation) GPS *(global positioning system)*
graine *f* seed
gramme *m* gram
grand(e) great; high *(speed, number)*; big; tall
grand-mère *f* grandmother
grand-père *m* grandfather
Grande-Bretagne *f* Great Britain
grands-parents *mpl* grandparents
grange *f* barn
granité *m* flavoured crushed ice
grappe *f* bunch *(of grapes)*
gras(se) fat; greasy
gratis for free
gratuit(e) free of charge
grave serious
gravure *f* print *(picture)*
grêle *f* hail
grenier *m* attic
grenouille *f* frog
grève *f* strike
grillé(e) grilled
grille-pain *m* toaster
Grèce *f* Greece
grippe *f* flu
gris(e) grey
gros(se) big; large; fat
gros lot *m* jackpot
grotte *f* cave
groupe *m* group; party; band
*groupe sanguin* blood group
guêpe *f* wasp
guerre *f* war
gueule de bois *f* hangover
guichet *m* ticket office; counter
guide *m* guide; guidebook
*guide de conversation* phrase book
guidon *m* handlebars
guitare *f* guitar
gynécologue gynaecologist

## H

habillé(e) dressed
habiller to dress
*s'habiller* to get dressed
habitant(e) *m/f* inhabitant

**habiter** to live (in)
**habituel(le)** usual; regular
**haché(e)** minced
*steak haché m* hamburger steak
**hachis** *m* minced meat
**halles** *fpl* central food market
**hamburger** *m* burger
**hameçon** *m* hook *(fishing)*
**hanche** *f* hip
**handicapé(e)** disabled *(person)*
**haricot** *m* bean
**haut** *m* top *(of ladder, bikini, etc)*
*en haut* upstairs
**haut débit** broadband
**haut(e)** high; tall
**hauteur** *f* height
**haut-parleur** loudspeaker
**hebdomadaire** weekly
**hébergement** *m* lodging
**hélicoptère médical** *m* air ambulance
**hépatite** *f* hepatitis
**herbe** *f* grass
*fines herbes* herbs
**hernie** *f* hernia
**heure** *f* hour; time of day
*à l'heure* on time
*heure de pointe* rush hour
**heureux(-euse)** happy
**hibou** *m* owl
**hier** yesterday
**hippisme** *m* horse riding
**hippodrome** *m* racecourse
**historique** historic
**hiver** *m* winter
**hollandais(e)** Dutch
**homard** *m* lobster
**homéopathie** *f* homeopathy
**homéopathique** homeopathic
 *(remedy etc)*
**homme** *m* man
*homme au foyer* house-husband
*homme d'affaires* businessman
*hommes* gents
**homo** *m/f* gay *(person)*
**honnête** honest
**honoraires** *mpl* fee
**hôpital** *m* hospital

**horaire** *m* timetable; schedule
**horloge** *f* clock
**hors:** *hors de* out of
*hors-saison* off-season
*hors service* out of order
*hors-taxe* duty-free
**hôte** *m* host; guest
**hôtel** *m* hotel
*hôtel de ville* town hall
**hôtesse** *f* stewardess
**huile** *f* oil
*huile d'arachide* peanut oil
*huile d'olive* olive oil
*huile de tournesol* sunflower oil
**huître** *f* oyster
**hypermarché** *m* hypermarket
**hypermétrope** long-sighted
**hypertension** *f* high blood pressure

# I

**ici** here
**idée** *f* idea
**il y a...** there is/are...
*il y a un défaut* there's a fault
*il y a une semaine* a week ago
**île** *f* island
**illimité(e)** unlimited
**immédiatement** immediately
**immeuble** *m* building *(offices, flats)*
**immunisation** *f* immunisation
**impair(e)** odd *(number)*
**impasse** *f* dead end
**imperméable** waterproof
**important(e)** important
**importer** to import
**impossible** impossible
**impôt** *m* tax
**imprimer** to print
**incendie** *m* fire
**inclus(e)** included; inclusive
**inconfortable** uncomfortable
**incorrect(e)** wrong
**indicateur** *m* guide; timetable
**indicatif** *m* dialling code
**indications** *fpl* instructions; directions
**indice UVA** *m* factor *(sunblock)*
*indice 25* factor 25

**indigestion** f indigestion
**indispensable** essential
**infectieux(-euse)** infectious
**infection** f infection
**inférieur(e)** inferior; lower
**infirmerie** f infirmary
**infirmier(-ière)** m/f nurse
**informations** fpl news; information
**infusion** f herbal tea
**ingénieur** m/f engineer
**ingrédient** m ingredient
**inhalateur** m inhaler
**inondation** f flood
**inquiet(-iète)** worried
**inscrire** to write (down); to enrol
**insecte** m insect
**insolation** f sunstroke
**installations** fpl facilities
**instant** m moment
*un instant!* just a minute!
**institut** m institute
*institut de beauté* beauty salon
**insuline** f insulin
**intelligent(e)** intelligent
**interdit** forbidden
**intéressant(e)** interesting
**intérieur: à l'intérieur** indoors
**international(e)** international
**interprète** m/f interpreter
**intervention** f operation (surgical)
**intoxication alimentaire** f food
poisoning
**introduire** to introduce; to insert
**inutile** useless; unnecessary
**invalide** m/f disabled person
**invité(e)** m/f guest (house guest)
**inviter** to invite
**iPod** m iPod®
**irlandais(e)** Irish
**Irlande** f Ireland
**Irlande du Nord** f Northern Ireland
**issue de secours** f emergency exit
**Italie** f Italy
**italien(ne)** Italian
**itinéraire** m route
*itinéraire touristique* scenic route
**ivoire** m ivory

**ivre** drunk

# J

**jaloux(-ouse)** jealous
**jamais** never
**jambe** f leg
**jambon** m ham
**janvier** January
**Japon** m Japan
**jardin** m garden
**jauge (de carburant)** f fuel gauge
**jauge (de niveau d'huile)** f dipstick
**jaune** yellow
**jaune d'œuf** m egg yolk
**jaunisse** f jaundice
**jetable** disposable
**jetée** f pier
**jeter** to throw
**jeton** m token
**jeu** m game; set (of tools, etc); gambling
*jeu en réseau* computer game
*jeu vidéo* video game
*jeu-concours* quiz
**jeudi** m Thursday
**jeune** young
**jeunesse** f youth
**joindre** to join; to enclose
**joli(e)** pretty
**jonquille** f daffodil
**joue** f cheek
**jouer** to play (games)
**jouet** m toy
**jour** m day
*jour férié* public holiday
**journal** m newspaper
**journaliste** m/f journalist
**journée** f day (length of time)
**juge** m/f judge
**juif (juive)** Jewish
**juillet** July
**juin** June
**jumeaux** mpl twins
**jumelles** fpl twins; binoculars
**jupe** f skirt
**jus** m juice
*jus de fruit* fruit juice
*jus d'orange* orange juice

*jus de viande* gravy
**jusqu'à (au)** until; till
**juste** fair; reasonable

## K

**kart** *m* go-cart
**kayak** *m* canoe
**kilo** *m* kilo
**kilométrage** *m* mileage
*kilométrage illimité* unlimited mileage
**kilomètre** *m* kilometre
**kiosque** *m* kiosk; newsstand
**kit mains-libres** hands-free kit *(for phone)*
**kiwi** kiwi fruit
**klaxonner** to sound one's horn
**kyste** *m* cyst

## L

**là** there
**lac** *m* lake
**lacets** *mpl* shoelaces
**laid(e)** ugly
**laine** *f* wool
*laine polaire* fleece *(top/jacket)*
**laisse** *f* leash
**laisser** to leave
*laissez en blanc* leave blank
**lait** *m* milk
*lait cru* unpasteurised milk
*lait démaquillant* cleansing milk
*lait demi-écrémé* semi-skimmed milk
*lait écrémé* skim(med) milk
*lait entier* full-cream milk
*lait longue conservation* long-life milk
*lait maternisé* baby milk *(formula)*
*lait solaire* suntan lotion
**laiterie** *f* dairy
**laitue** *f* lettuce
**lame** *f* blade
*lames de rasoir* razor blades
**lampe** *f* light; lamp
*lampe de poche* torch
**landau** *m* pram; baby carriage
**langue** *f* tongue; language
**lapin** *m* rabbit
**laque** *f* hair spray
**lard** *m* fat; *(streaky)* bacon

**lardons** *mpl* diced bacon
**large** wide; broad
**largeur** *f* width
**laurier** *m* sweet bay; bay leaves
**lavable** washable
**lavabo** *m* washbasin
*lavabos* toilets
**lavage** *m* washing
**lavande** *f* lavender
**lave-auto** *m* car wash
**lave-glace** *m* screen wash
**lave-linge** *m* washing machine
**laver** to wash
*se laver* to wash oneself
**laverie automatique** *f* launderette
**lave-vaisselle** *m* dishwasher
**laxatif** *m* laxative
**layette** *f* baby clothes
**leçon** *f* lesson
*leçons particulières* private lessons
**lecture** *f* reading
**légal(e)** legal
**léger(-ère)** light; weak *(tea, etc)*
**légume** *m* vegetable
**lendemain** *m* next day
**lent(e)** slow
**lentement** slowly
**lentille** *f* lentil; lens *(of glasses)*
*lentille de contact* contact lens
**lesbienne** *f* lesbian
**lessive** *f* soap powder; washing
**lettre** *f* letter
*lettre recommandée* registered letter
**leur(s)** their
**levée** *f* collection *(of mail)*
**lever** to lift
*se lever* to get up *(out of bed)*
**lever de soleil** *m* sunrise
**levier:** *levier de vitesse* *m* gear lever
**lèvre** *f* lip
**levure** *f* yeast
**libellule** *f* dragonfly
**librairie** *f* bookshop
**libre** free; vacant
**libre-service** self-service
**lieu** *m* place *(location)*
**lièvre** *m* hare

**ligne** *f* line; service; route
**lime à ongles** *f* nail file
**limitation de vitesse** *f* speed limit
**limonade** *f* lemonade
**lin** *m* linen *(cloth)*
**linge** *m* linen *(bed, table)*; laundry
**lingerie** *f* lingerie
**lingettes** *fpl* baby wipes
**lion** *m* lion
**liquide** *f* liquid
*liquide de freins* brake fluid
*liquide d'embrayage* clutch fluid
**lire** to read
**liste** *f* list
**lit** *m* bed
*grand lit* double bed
*lit d'enfant* cot
*lit simple* single bed
*lits jumeaux* twin beds
**litre** *m* litre
**livraison** *f* delivery *(of goods)*
*livraison des bagages* baggage reclaim
**livre** *f* pound
**livre** *m* book
**local(e)** local
**locataire** *m/f* tenant; lodger
**location** *f* hiring (out); letting
**logement** *m* accommodation
**loger** to stay *(reside for while)*
**logiciel** *m* computer software
**loi** *f* law
**loin** far
**lointain(e)** distant
**loisir** *m* leisure
**Londres** London
**long(ue)** long
*le long de* along
**longe** *f* loin *(of meat)*
**longtemps** for a long time
**longueur** *f* length
**lot** *m* prize; lot *(at auction)*
**loterie** *f* lottery
**lotion** *f* lotion
**loto** *m* numerical lottery
**lotte** *f* monkfish; angler fish
**louer** to let; to hire; to rent
*à louer* for hire/to rent

**loup** *m* wolf; sea perch
**loupe** *f* magnifying glass
**lourd(e)** heavy
**loyer** *m* rent
**luge** *f* sledge; toboggan
**lumière** *f* light
**lundi** *m* Monday
**lune** *f* moon
*lune de miel* honeymoon
**lunettes** *fpl* glasses
*lunettes de soleil* sunglasses
*lunettes protectrices* goggles
**luxe** *m* luxury
**lycée** *m* secondary school

## M
**M** sign for the Paris metro
**machine** *f* machine
*machine à laver* washing machine
**mâchoire** *f* jaw
**Madame** *f* Mrs; Ms; Madam
**madeleine** *f* small sponge cake
**Mademoiselle** *f* Miss
**madère** *m* Madeira *(wine)*
**magasin** *m* shop
*grand magasin* department store
**magnétoscope** *m* video recorder
**magret de canard** *m* breast fillet of duck
**mai** May
**maigre** lean *(meat)*
**maigrir** to slim
**maillet** *m* mallet
**maillot** *m* vest
*maillot de bain* swimsuit
**main** *f* hand
**maintenant** now
**maire** *m* mayor
**mairie** *f* town hall
**mais** but
**maison** *f* house; home
*maison de campagne* villa
**maître d'hôtel** *m* head waiter
**maître-nageur
 (sauveteur)/maître nageuse
 (sauveteuse)** *m/f* lifeguard
**majuscule** *f* capital letter
**mal** badly

mal *m* harm; pain
*mal de dents* toothache
*mal de mer* seasickness
*mal de tête* headache
*faire du mal à quelqu'un* to harm
 someone
malade sick *(ill)*
malade *m/f* sick person; patient
maladie *f* disease
malentendu *m* misunderstanding
malle *f* trunk *(luggage)*
maman *f* mummy
manche *f* sleeve
mangue *f* mango
Manche *f* the Channel
mandat *m* money order
manger to eat
manicure *f* manicure
manière *f* way *(manner)*
manifestation *f* demonstration
manque *m* shortage; lack
manteau *m* coat
maquereau *m* mackerel
maquillage *m* make-up
marais *m* marsh
marbre *m* marble (material)
marc *m* white grape spirit
marchand *m* dealer; merchant
*marchand de poisson* fishmonger
*marchand de vin* wine merchant
marche *f* step; march; walking
*marche arrière* reverse gear
marché *m* market
*marché aux puces* flea market
*marché d'artisanat* craft fair
*marché fermier* farmers' market
marcher to walk; to work *(machine, car)*
*en marche* on *(machine)*
mardi *m* Tuesday
*mardi gras* Shrove Tuesday
marée *f* tide
*marée basse* low tide
*marée haute* high tide
margarine *f* margarine
mari *m* husband
mariage *m* wedding
marié *m* bridegroom

marié(e) married
mariée *f* bride
marier to marry
*se marier* to get married
mariné(e) marinated
marionnette *f* puppet
marque *f* make; brand *(name)*
marquer to score *(goal, point)*
marron brown
marron *m* chestnut
mars March
marteau *m* hammer
masculin male *(person, on forms)*
massage *m* massage
mât *m* mast
match de football *m* football match
match en nocturne *m* floodlit fixture
matelas *m* mattress
*matelas pneumatique* lilo®
*matelas mousse* sleeping mat
matériel *m* equipment; kit
matin *m* morning
mauvais(e) bad; wrong; off *(food)*
maximum *m* maximum
mazout *m* oil *(for heating)*
mécanicien *m* mechanic
méchant(e) naughty; wicked
médecin *m* doctor
médicament *m* medicine; drug;
 medication
médiéval(e) medieval
Méditerranée *f* Mediterranean Sea
méduse *f* jellyfish
mégahertz *m* megahertz
mégaoctet *m* megabyte
*512 mégaoctets* 512 megabytes
meilleur(e) best; better
*meilleurs vœux* best wishes
mél *m* e-mail address
membre *m* member *(of club, etc)*
même same
mémoire *f* memory
ménage *m* housework
méningite *f* meningitis
mensuel(le) monthly
menthe *f* mint; mint tea
menu *m* menu *(set)*

*menu à prix fixe* set price menu
*menu du jour* today's menu
**mer** *f* sea
*mer du Nord* North Sea
**mercerie** *f* haberdasher's
**merci** thank you
**mercredi** *m* Wednesday
**mère** *f* mother
**merlan** *m* whiting
**merlu** *m* hake
**mérou** *m* grouper
**merveilleux(-euse)** wonderful
**message** *m* message
**messagerie vocale** voicemail
**messe** *f* mass *(church)*
**messieurs** *mpl* men; gents
*Messieurs* gentlemen
**messieurs** gents
**mesure** *f* measurement
**mesurer** to measure
**métal** *m* metal
**météo** *f* weather forecast
**métier** *m* trade; occupation; craft
**mètre** *m* metre
*mètre à ruban* tape measure
**métro** *m* underground railway
**mettre** to put; to put on
*mettre au point* focus *(camera)*
*mettre en marche* to turn on
**meublé(e)** furnished
**meubles** *mpl* furniture
*meubles de style* period furniture
**mi-bas** *mpl* pop-socks; knee-highs
**micro** *m* microphone
**midi** *m* midday; noon
**Midi** *m* the south of France
**miel** *m* honey
**mieux** better; best
**migraine** *f* headache; migraine
**milieu** *m* middle
**mille** *m* thousand
**millimètre** *m* millimetre
**million** *m* million
**mince** slim; thin
**mine** *f* expression; mine *(coal, etc)*
**mineur** *m* miner
**mineur(e)** under age; minor

**mini-brasserie** micro-brewery
**minimum** *m* minimum
**minuit** *m* midnight
**minuscule** tiny
**minute** *f* minute
**minuteur** *m* timer
**mirabelle** *f* plum; plum brandy
**miroir** *m* mirror
**mise en plis** *f* set *(for hair)*
**mistral** *m* strong cold dry wind
**mite** *f* moth *(clothes)*
**mixte** mixed
**Mo** Mb *(megabyte)*
**mobile (portable)** mobile *(phone)*
**mobilier** *m* furniture
**mode** *f* fashion
*à la mode* fashionable
*mode d'emploi* instructions for use
**modem** *m* modem
**moderne** modern
**moelle** *f* marrow *(beef, etc)*
**moi** me
**moineau** *m* sparrow
**moins** less; minus
*moins (de)* less (than)
*moins cher* cheaper
**moins** *m* the least
**mois** *m* month
**moississure** *f* mould *(fungus)*
**moitié** *f* half
*à moitié prix* half-price
**moka** *m* coffee cream cake; mocha coffee
**molle** soft
**moment** *m* moment
*en ce moment* at the moment
**mon/ma/mes** my
**monastère** *m* monastery
**monde** *m* world
*il y a du monde* there's a lot of people
**moniteur** *m* instructor; coach
**monitrice** *f* instructress; coach
**monnaie** *f* currency; change
**monnayeur** *m* automatic change machine
**monospace** *m* people carrier
**monsieur** *m* gentleman
**Monsieur** *m* Mr; Sir
**montagne** *f* mountain

**montant** *m* amount *(total)*
**monter** to take up; to go up; to rise; to get in *(car)*
*monter à cheval* to horse-ride
**montre** *f* watch
**montrer** to show
**monument** *m* monument
**moquette** *f* fitted carpet
**morceau** *m* piece; bit; cut *(of meat)*
**mordu(e)** bitten
**morsure** *f* bite
*morsure de serpent* snake bite
**mort(e)** dead
**mosquée** *f* mosque
**mot** *m* word; note *(letter)*
*mot de passe* password
*mots croisés* crossword puzzle
**motel** *m* motel
**moteur** *m* engine; motor
**motif** *m* pattern
**moto** *f* motorbike
**mou (molle)** soft
**mouche** *f* fly
**moucheron** *m* midge
**mouchoir** *m* handkerchief
**mouette** *f* seagull
**mouillé(e)** wet
**moule** *f* mussel
**moulin** *m* mill
*moulin à vent* windmill
**moulinet** *m* reel *(fishing)*
**mourir** to die
**mousse** *f* foam; mousse
*mousse à raser* shaving foam
*mousse coiffante* hair mousse
**mousseux(-euse)** sparkling *(wine)*
**moustache** *f* moustache
**moustique** *m* mosquito
**moutarde** *f* mustard
**mouton** *m* sheep; lamb; mutton
**moyen(ne)** *adj* average
**moyenne** *f* average
**MP3 (lecteur de)** MP3 player
**muguet** *m* lily of the valley; thrush *(candida)*
**muni(e) de** supplied with; in possession of
**mur** *m* wall
**mûr(e)** mature; ripe

**mûre** *f* blackberry
**muscade** *f* nutmeg
**musée** *m* museum
*musée d'art* art gallery
**musique** *f* music
**Musulman(e)** Muslim
**myope** short-sighted

# N

**nager** to swim
**naissance** *f* birth
**nappe** *f* tablecloth
**nappé(e)** coated *(with chocolate, etc)*
**natation** *f* swimming
**national(e)** national
**nationalité** *f* nationality
**natte** *f* plait
**nature** *f* wildlife
**naturel(le)** natural
**nautique** nautical; water
**navette** *f* shuttle *(bus service)*
**navigation** *f* sailing
**navire** *m* ship
**né(e)** born
**négatif** *m* negative *(photography)*
**neige** *f* snow
**neiger** to snow
**nettoyage** *m* cleaning
*nettoyage à sec* dry-cleaning
**nettoyer** to clean
**neuf (neuve)** new
**neveu** *m* nephew
**névralgie** *f* headache
**nez** *m* nose
**niche** *f* kennel
**nid** *m* nest
*nid de poule* pothole
**nièce** *f* niece
**niveau** *m* level; standard
**noce** *f* wedding
**nocturne** *m* late opening
**Noël** *m* Christmas
*joyeux Noël!* merry Christmas!
**noir(e)** black
**noisette** *f* hazelnut
**noix** *f* nut; walnut
**nom** *m* name; noun

**nom de famille** family name
**nom de jeune fille** maiden name
**nom d'utilisateur** username
**nombre** *m* number
**nombreux(-euse)** numerous
**non** no; not
**non alcoolisé(e)** non-alcoholic
**non-fumeur** non-smoking
**nord** *m* north
**normal(e)** normal; standard *(size)*
**nos** our
**notaire** *m* solicitor
**note** *f* note; bill; memo
**notre** our
**nœud** *m* knot
**nourrir** to feed
**nourriture** *f* food
**nouveau (nouvelle)** new
*de nouveau* again
**nouvelles** *fpl* news
**novembre** November
**nu(e)** naked; bare
**nuage** *m* cloud
**nuageux(-euse)** cloudy
**nucléaire** nuclear
**nuit** *f* night
*bonne nuit* good night
**numérique** digital
**numéro** *m* number; act; issue
*numéro de mobile/de portable*
mobile number

## O

**objectif** *m* objective; lens *(of camera)*
**objet** *m* object
*objets de valeur* valuable items
*objets trouvés* lost property
**obligatoire** compulsory
**oblitérer** to stamp *(ticket, stamp)*
**obsèques** *fpl* funeral
**obtenir** to get; to obtain
**occasion** *f* occasion; bargain
*d'occasion* second-hand
**occupé(e)** busy; hired *(taxi)*
**occupé(e)** engaged
**océan** *m* ocean
**octobre** October

**odeur** *f* smell
**œuf** *m* egg
*œuf de Pâques* Easter egg
**office** *m* service *(church)*; office
*office du tourisme* tourist office
**offre** *f* offer
**oie** *f* goose
**oignon** *m* onion
**œil** *m* eye
**œillet** *m* carnation
**oiseau** *m* bird
**olive** *f* olive
**ombre** *f* shade/shadow
*à l'ombre* in the shade
**oncle** *m* uncle
**onde** *f* wave
**ongle** *m* nail *(finger)*
**opéra** *m* opera
**or** *m* gold
**orage** *m* storm
**orange** orange; amber *(traffic light)*
**orange** *f* orange
**orangeade** *f* orange squash
**orchestre** *m* orchestra; stalls *(in theatre)*
**ordinaire** ordinary
**ordinateur** *m* computer
*l'ordinateur de poche* palmtop computer
**ordonnance** *f* prescription
**ordre** *m* order
*à l'ordre de* payable to
**ordures** *fpl* litter *(rubbish)*
**oreille** *f* ear
**oreiller** *m* pillow
**oreillons** *mpl* mumps
**organiser** to organize
**organiseur** *m* PDA
**orge** *f* barley
**origan** *m* oregano
**os** *m* bone
**oseille** *f* sorrel
**osier** *m* wicker
**ou** or
**où** where
**oublier** to forget
**ouest** *m* west
**oui** yes
**ours(e)** *m/f* bear *(animal)*

**oursin** m sea urchin
**outils** mpl tools
**ouvert(e)** open; on (tap, gas, etc)
**ouvert(e)** open
*ouvert(e) 24 heures sur 24* 24-hour
**ouverture** f overture; opening
**ouvrable** working (day)
**ouvre-boîtes** m tin-opener
**ouvre-bouteilles** m bottle-opener
**ouvrir** to open

# P

**page** f page
*pages jaunes* Yellow Pages
**paiement** m payment
**paille** f straw
**pain** m bread; loaf of bread
*pain bis* brown bread
*pain complet* wholemeal bread
*pain grillé* toast
**pair(e)** even
**paire** f pair
**paix** f peace

192

**palais** m palace
**pâle** pale
**palmes** fpl flippers
**palourde** f clam
**pamplemousse** m grapefruit
**panaché** m shandy
**pané(e)** in breadcrumbs
**panier** m basket
*panier repas* packed lunch
**panne** f breakdown
**panneau** m sign
**pansement** m bandage
**pantalon** m trousers
**pantoufles** fpl slippers
**pape** m pope
**papeterie** f stationer's shop
**papier** m paper
*papier à lettres* writing paper
*papier alu(minium)* foil
*papier cadeau* gift-wrap
*papier hygiénique* toilet paper
*papiers* identity papers; driving licence
**papillon** m butterfly
**pâquerette** f daisy

**Pâques** m Easter
**paquet** m package; pack; packet
**par** by; through; per
*par example* for example
*par jour* per day
*par téléphone* by phone
*par voie orale* take by mouth (medicine)
**paradis** m heaven
**paralysé(e)** paralysed
**parapluie** m umbrella
**parasol** m sunshade
**parc** m park
*parc d'attractions* funfair
**parce que** because
**parcmètre** m parking meter
**parcours** m route
**pardon!** sorry!; excuse me!
**parer** to ward off
**pare-brise** m windscreen
**pare-chocs** m bumper
**parent(e)** m/f relative
**parents** mpl parents
**paresseux(-euse)** lazy
**parfait(e)** perfect
**parfum** m perfume; flavour
**parfumerie** f perfume shop
**pari** m bet
**parier sur** to bet on
**parking** m car park
*parking assuré* parking facilities
*parking souterrain* underground car park
*parking surveillé* attended car park
**parler (à)** to speak (to) ; to talk (to)
**paroisse** f parish
**partager** to share
**parterre** m flowerbed
**parti** m political party
**partie** f part; match (game)
**partir** to leave; to go
*à partir de* from
**partout** everywhere
**pas** not
*pas encore* not yet
**pas** m step; pace
**passage** m passage
*passage à niveau* level crossing
*passage clouté* pedestrian crossing

*passage interdit* no through way
*passage souterrain* underpass
**passager(-ère)** *m/f* passenger
**passé(e)** past
**passe-temps** *m* hobby
**passeport** *m* passport
**passer** to pass; to spend *(time)*
**se passer** to happen
**passerelle** *f* gangway *(bridge)*
**passionnant(e)** exciting
**passoire** *f* sieve; colander
**pastèque** *f* watermelon
**pasteur** *m* minister *(of religion)*
**pastille** *f* lozenge
**pastis** *m* aniseed-flavoured apéritif
**pataugeoire** *f* paddling pool
**pâte** *f* pastry; dough; paste
**pâté** *m* pâté
**pâtes** *fpl* pasta
**patient(e)** *m/f* patient *(in hospital)*
**patin** *m* skate
*patins à glace* ice skates
*patins à roulettes* roller skates
**patinoire** *f* skating rink
**pâtisserie** *f* cake shop; little cake
**patron** *m* boss; pattern *(knitting, dress, etc)*
**patronne** *f* boss
**pauvre** poor
**payer** to pay (for)
*payé(e)* paid
*payé(e) d'avance* prepaid
**pays** *m* land; country
*du pays* local
**Pays-Bas** *mpl* Netherlands
**paysage** countryside; scenery
**PDA** *m* PDA
**péage** *m* toll *(motorway, etc)*
**peau** *f* hide *(leather)*; skin
**pêche** *f* peach; fishing
**pêcher** to fish
**pêcheur** *m* angler
**pédale** *f* pedal
**pédalo** *m* pedal boat/pedalo
**pédicure** *m/f* chiropodist
**peigne** *m* comb
**peignoir** *m* dressing gown; bath-robe
**peindre** to paint; to decorate

**peinture** *f* painting; paintwork
**peler** to peel *(fruit)*
**pèlerinage** *m* pilgrimage
**pelle** *f* spade
*pelle à poussière* dustpan
**pellicule** *f* film *(for camera)*
*pellicule couleur* colour film
*pellicule noir et blanc* black and white film
**pelote** *f* ball *(of string, wool)*
*pelote basque* pelota *(ball game for 2 players)*
**pelouse** *f* lawn
**pencher** to lean
**pendant** during
**pendant que** while
**pénicilline** *f* penicillin
**péninsule** *f* peninsula
**pénis** *m* penis
**penser** to think
**pension** *f* guesthouse
*pension complète* full board
**pente** *f* slope
**Pentecôte** *f* Whitsun
**pépin** *m* pip
**perceuse électrique** *f* electric drill
**perdre** to lose
**perdu(e)** lost *(object)*
**père** *m* father
**périmé(e)** out of date
**périphérique** *m* ring road
**perle** *f* bead; pearl
**permanente** *f* perm
**permettre** to permit
**permis** *m* permit; licence
*permis de chasse* hunting permit
*permis de conduire* driving licence
*permis de pêche* fishing permit
**perruque** *f* wig
**persil** *m* parsley
**personne** *f* person
**peser** to weigh
**pétanque** *f* type of bowls
**pétillant(e)** fizzy
**petit(e)** small; slight
*petit déjeuner* breakfast
*petit pain* roll
**petit-fils** *m* grandson

**petite-fille** *f* granddaughter
**pétrole** *m* oil *(petroleum)*; paraffin
**peu** little; few
*à peu près* approximately
*un peu (de)* a bit (of)
**peur** *f* fear
*avoir peur (de)* to be afraid (of)
**peut-être** perhaps
**phare** *m* headlight; lighthouse
**pharmacie** *f* chemist's; pharmacy
**pharmacien(ne)** pharmacist
**phoque** *m* seal *(animal)*
**photo** *f* photograph
**photocopie** *f* photocopy
**photocopier** to photocopy
**photocopieuse** photocopier
**piano** *m* piano
**pichet** *m* jug; carafe
**pie** *f* magpie
**pièce** *f* room *(in house)*; play *(theatre)*; coin
*pièce d'identité* means of identification
*pièce de rechange* spare part
*pièce jointe* attachment

194

**pied** *m* foot
*à pied* on foot
**pierre** *f* stone
**piéton** *m* pedestrian
**pignon** *m* pine kernel
**pile** *f* pile; battery *(for radio, etc)*
**pilon** *m* drumstick *(of chicken)*
**pilote** *m/f* pilot
**pilule** *f* pill
*pilule du lendemain* morning-after pill
**piment** *m* chilli *(fruit)*
**pin** *m* pine
**pince** *f* pliers
*pince à cheveux* hairgrip
*pince à épiler* tweezers
*pince à linge* clothes peg
**pipe** *f* pipe *(smoking)*
**piquant(e)** spicy; hot
**pique-nique** *m* picnic
**piquer** to sting
**piquet** *m* peg *(for tent)*
**piqûre** *f* insect bite; injection; sting
**pire** worse
**piscine** *f* swimming pool

**pissenlit** *m* dandelion
**pistache** *f* pistachio *(nut)*
**piste** *f* ski-run; runway *(airport)*
*piste cyclable* cycle track
*piste de luge* toboggan run
*piste pour débutants* nursery slope
*pistes tous niveaux* slopes for all levels
 of skiers
**pistolet** *m* pistol
**placard** *m* cupboard
**place** *f* square *(in town)*; seat; space *(room)*
*places debout* standing room
**plafond** *m* ceiling
**plage** *f* beach
*plage seins nus* topless beach
**plainte** *f* complaint
**plaisanterie** *f* joke
**plaisir** *m* enjoyment; pleasure
**plaît: s'il vous/te plaît** please
**plan** *m* map *(of town)*
*plan de la ville* street map
**planche** *f* plank
*planche à découper* chopping board
*planche à repasser* ironing board
*planche à voile* sailboard; wind-surfing
*planche de surf* surfboard
**plancher** *m* floor *(of room)*
**plante** *f* plant; sole *(of foot, shoe)*
**plaque** *f* sheet; plate
*plaque d'immatriculation* *f* numberplate
**plat** *m* dish; course *(of meal)*
*plat à emporter* take-away meal
*plat de résistance* main course
*plat principal* main course
**plat(e)** level *(surface)*; flat
*à plat* flat *(battery)*
**platane** *m* plane tree
**plateau** *m* tray
**plâtre** *m* plaster
**plein(e) (de)** full (of)
*le plein!* fill it up! *(car)*
*plein sud* facing south
*plein tarif* peak rate
**pleurer** to cry *(weep)*
**pleuvoir** to rain
*il pleut* it's raining
**plier** to fold

**plomb** m lead; fuse
**plombage** m filling (in tooth)
**plombier** m plumber
**plongée (avec masque et tuba)** f
snorkelling
**plonger** to dive
**pluie** f rain
**plume** f feather
**plus** more; most
*plus grand(e) (que)* bigger (than)
*plus tard* later
**plusieurs** several
**pneu** m tyre
*pneu dégonflé* flat tyre
*pneu de rechange* spare tyre
*pneus cloutés* snow tyres
**poche** f pocket
**poché(e)** poached
**poêle** f frying-pan
**poème** m poem
**poids** m weight
*poids lourd* heavy goods vehicle
**poignée** f handle
**poignet** m wrist
**poil** m hair; coat (of animal)
**poinçonner** to punch (ticket, etc)
**point** m place; point; stitch; dot
*à point* medium rare (meat)
**point mort** neutral (car)
*au point mort* in neutral (car)
**pointure** f size (of shoes)
**poire** f pear; pear brandy
**poireau** m leek
**pois** m pea; spot (dot)
*petits pois* peas
**poison** m poison
**poisson** m fish
**poissonnerie** f fishmonger's shop
**poitrine** f breast; chest
**poivre** m pepper
**poivron** m pepper (capsicum)
**polaire** f fleece
**police** f policy (insurance); police
**policier** m policeman; detective
film/novel
**pollué(e)** polluted
**pommade** f ointment

**pomme** f apple; potato
**pomme de terre** f potato
**pompe** f pump
*pompe à vélo* bicycle pump
**pompes funèbres** fpl undertaker's
**pompier** m fireman
**pompiers** fire brigade
**poney** m pony
**pont** m bridge; deck (of ship)
*faire le pont* to have a long weekend
**populaire** popular
**porc** m pork; pig
**port** m harbour; port
**port USB** USB port
**portable** m mobile phone; laptop
**portatif** portable
**porte** f door; gate
**portefeuille** m wallet
**porter** to wear; to carry
**porte-bagages** m luggage rack
**porte-clefs** m keyring
**porte-monnaie** m purse
**porteur** m porter
**portier** m doorman
**portion** f helping; portion
**porto** m port (wine)
**poser** to put; to lay down
**posologie** f dosage
**posséder** to own
**poste** f post; post office
*poste de contrôle* checkpoint
*poste de secours* first-aid post
**poste** m radio/television set; extension
(phone)
**poster** m poster (decorative)
**poster** to post
**pot** m pot; carton (yoghurt, etc)
*pot d'échappement* exhaust pipe
*pot catalytique* catalytic converter
**potable** ok to drink
**potage** m soup
**poteau** m post (pole)
*poteau indicateur* signpost
**poterie** f pottery
**poubelle** f dustbin
**pouce** m thumb
**poudre** f powder

**poule** f hen
**poulet** m chicken
**poumon** m lung
**poupée** f doll
**pour** for
**pourboire** m tip
**pourquoi** why
**pourri(e)** rotten *(fruit, etc)*
**pousser** to push
**poussette** f push chair
**pousser** to push
**poussière** f dust
**pouvoir** to be able to
**pré** m meadow
**préfecture de police** f police headquarters
**préféré(e)** favourite
**préférer** to prefer
**premier(-ière)** first
*premier cru* first-class wine
*premiers secours* first aid
**prendre** to take; to get; to catch
**prénom** m first name
**préparer** to prepare; to cook
**près de** near (to)
**présenter** to present; to introduce
**préservatif** m condom
**pressé(e)** squeezed; pressed
**pressing** m dry cleaner's
**pression** f pressure
*pression des pneus* tyre pressure
**prêt(e)** ready
*prêt à cuire* ready to cook
**prêt-à-porter** m ready-to-wear
**prêter** to lend
**prêtre** m priest
**prévision** f forecast
**prier** to pray
**prière de...** please...
**prince** m prince
**princesse** f princess
**principal(e)** main
**printemps** m spring
**priorité** f right of way
*priorité à droite* give way to traffic from right
**prise** f plug; socket
**privé(e)** private

**prix** m price; prize
*à prix réduit* cut-price
*prix d'entrée* admission fee
*prix de détail* retail price
**probablement** probably
**problème** m problem
**prochain(e)** next
**proche** close *(near)*
**produits** mpl produce; product
**professeur** m teacher
**profiter de** to take advantage of
**profond(e)** deep
**programme** m schedule; programme *(list of performers, etc)*
*programme informatique* computer program
**promenade** f walk; promenade; ride *(in vehicle)*
*faire une promenade* to go for a walk
**promettre** to promise
**promotionnel(le)** special low-price
**prononcer** to pronounce
**propre** clean; own
**propriétaire** m/f owner
**propriété** f property
**protège-slip** m panty-liner
**protestant(e)** Protestant
**provenance** f origin; source
**provisions** fpl groceries
**province** f province
**provisoire** temporary
**provisoirement** for the time being
**proximité: à proximité** nearby
**prune** f plum; plum brandy
**pruneau** m prune
**public** m audience
**public(-ique)** public
**publicité** f advertisement *(on TV)*
**puce** f flea; microchip
**puce: marché aux puces** flea market
**puissance** f power
**puits** m well *(for water)*
**pull** m sweater
**pullover** m sweater
**purée** f purée; mashed
**PV** m parking ticket
**pyjama** m pyjamas

## Q

**quai** *m* platform
**qualifié(e)** skilled
**qualité** *f* quality
**quand** when
**quantité** *f* quantity
**quarantaine** *f* quarantine
**quart** *m* quarter
**quartier** *m* neighbourhood; district
**quatre** *m* four
**que** that; than; whom; what
*qu'est-ce que c'est?* what is it?
**quel(le)** which; what
**quelqu'un** someone
**quelque** some
**quelque chose** something
**quelquefois** sometimes
**question** *f* question
**queue** *f* queue; tail
*faire la queue* to queue (up)
**qui** who; which
**quincaillerie** *f* hardware; hardware shop
**quinzaine** *f* fortnight
**quitter** to leave a place
**quoi** what
**quotidien(ne)** daily

## R

**rabais** *m* reduction
**raccourci** *m* short cut
**raccrocher** to hang up (phone)
**race** *f* race (people)
**racine** *f* root
**radeau** *m* raft
**radiateur** *m* radiator; heater
**radio** *f* radio
**radiographie** *f* X-ray
**radis** *m* radish
**rafraîchissements** *mpl* refreshments
**rafting** *m* raft
**rage** *f* rabies
**ragoût** *m* stew; casserole
**raide** steep
**raie** *f* skate (fish)
**raifort** *m* horseradish
**raisin** *m* grapes
*raisin blanc* green grapes

*raisin noir* black grapes
*raisins secs* sultanas; raisins; currants
**raison** *f* reason
**ralentir** to slow down
**ralentissement** *m* tailback
**rallonge** *f* extension (electrical)
**randonnée** *f* hike
*randonnée à cheval* pony-trekking
**râpe** *f* grater
**râpé(e)** grated
**rappel** *m* reminder (on signs)
**rappeler** to remind
*se rappeler* to remember
**rapide** quick; fast
**rapide** *m* express train
**raquette** *f* racket; bat; snowshoe
**rare** rare; unusual
**raser** to shave off
*se raser* to shave
**rasoir** *m* razor
*rasoir électrique* shaver
**rater** to miss (train, flight etc)
**RATP** *f* Paris transport authority
**rayé(e)** striped
**rayon** *m* shelf; department (in store); spoke (of wheel)
*rayon hommes* menswear
**RC** ground floor
**reboucher** to recork
**récemment** recently
**récepteur** *m* receiver (of phone)
**réception** *f* reception; check-in
**réceptionniste** *m/f* receptionist
**recette** *f* recipe
**recharge** *f* refill
**rechargeable** refillable (lighter, pen)
**recharger** to recharge (battery, etc)
**réchaud de camping** *m* camping stove
**réclamation** *f* complaint
**réclame** *f* advertisement
**recommandé(e)** registered (mail)
**recommander** to recommend
**récompense** *f* reward
**reconnaître** to recognize
**reçu** *m* receipt
**réduction** *f* reduction; discount; concession
**réduire** to reduce

**refuge** *m* mountain hut
**refuser** to reject; to refuse
**regarder** to look at
**régime** *m* diet *(slimming)*
**région** *f* region
**règle** *f* rule; ruler *(for measuring)*
**règles** *fpl* period *(menstruation)*
**règles douloureuses** cramps
**règlement** *m* regulation; payment
**régler** to pay; to settle
**réglisse** *f* liquorice
**réhausseur** *m* booster seat
**reine** *f* queen
**relais routier** *m* roadside restaurant
**rembourser** to refund
**remède** *m* remedy
**remercier** to thank
**remettre** to put back
**remettre à plus tard** to postpone
**se remettre** to recover *(from illness)*
**remonte-pente** *m* ski tow
**remorque** *f* trailer
**remorquer** to tow

198

**remplir** to fill; to fill in/out/up
**renard** *m* fox
**rencontrer** to meet
**rendez-vous** *m* date; appointment
**rendre** to give back
**renouveler** to renew
**renseignements** *mpl* information
**les renseignements** directory inquiries
**rentrée** *f* return to work after break
**rentrée (des classes)** start of the new
  school year
**renverser** to knock down *(in car)*
**réparations** *fpl* repairs
**réparer** to fix *(repair)*
**repas** *m* meal
**repasser** to iron
**répondeur** *m* answer-phone
**répondre (à)** to reply; to answer
**réponse** *f* answer; reply
**repos** *m* rest
**se reposer** to rest
**représentation** *f* performance
**requis(e)** required
**RER** *m* Paris high-speed commuter train

**réseau** *m* network
**il n'y a pas de réseau** there's no signal
**réservation** *f* reservation; booking
**réserve naturelle** *f* nature reserve
**réservé(e)** reserved
**réserver** to book *(reserve)*
**réservoir** *m* tank
**réservoir de carburant** fuel tank
**respirer** to breathe
**ressort** *m* spring *(metal)*
**restaurant** *m* restaurant
**reste** *m* rest *(remainder)*
**rester** to remain; to stay
**restoroute** *m* roadside or motorway
  restaurant
**retard** *m* delay
**retirer** to withdraw; to collect *(tickets)*
**retour** *m* return
**retourner** to go back
**retrait** *m* withdrawal; collection
**retrait d'espèces** cash withdrawal
**retraité(e)** retired
**retraité(e)** *m/f* old-age pensioner
**rétrécir** to shrink *(clothes)*
**rétroviseur** *m* rearview mirror
**rétroviseur latéral** wing mirror
**réunion** *f* meeting
**réussir (à)** to succeed
**réussite** *f* success; patience *(game)*
**réveil** *m* alarm clock
**réveiller** to wake *(someone)*
**se réveiller** to wake up
**réveillon** *m* Christmas/New Year's Eve
**revenir** to come back
**réverbère** *m* lamppost
**revue** *f* review; magazine
**rez-de-chaussée** *m* ground floor
**rhum** *m* rum
**rhumatisme** *m* rheumatism
**rhume** *m* cold *(illness)*
**rhume des foins** hay fever
**riche** rich
**rideau** *m* curtain
**rides** *fpl* wrinkles
**rien** nothing; anything
**rien à déclarer** nothing to declare
**rire** to laugh

rivage *m* shore
rive *f* river bank
rivière *f* river
riz *m* rice
RN trunk road
robe *f* gown; dress
robinet *m* tap
rocade *f* ringroad
rocher *m* rock *(boulder)*
rognon *m* kidney *(to eat)*
roi *m* king
roman *m* novel
roman(e) Romanesque
romantique romantic
romarin *m* rosemary
rond(e) round
rond-point *m* roundabout
rose pink
rose *f* rose
rossignol *m* nightingale
rôti(e) roast
rôtisserie *f* steakhouse; roast meat counter
roue *f* wheel
roue de secours spare wheel
rouge red
rouge à lèvres *m* lipstick
rouge-gorge *m* robin
rougeole *f* measles
rougeur *f* rash *(skin)*
rouillé(e) rusty
rouleau à pâtisserie *m* rolling pin
rouler to roll; to go *(by car)*
route *f* road; route
route barrée road closed
route nationale trunk road
route principale major road
route secondaire minor road
routier *m* lorry driver
Royaume-Uni *m* United Kingdom
ruban *m* ribbon; tape
rubéole *f* rubella
rue *f* street
rue sans issue no through road
ruelle *f* lane; alley
ruisseau *m* stream
russe Russian

S
SA Ltd; plc
sable *m* sand
sables mouvants quicksand
sabot *m* wheel clamp
sac *m* sack; bag
sac à dos backpack
sac à main handbag
sac de couchage sleeping bag
sac poubelle bin liner
sachet de thé *m* tea bag
sacoche *f* panniers *(for bike)*
sacoche d'ordinateur portable laptop bag
safran *m* saffron
sage good *(well-behaved)*; wise
sage-femme *f* midwife
saignant(e) rare *(steak)*
saigner to bleed
saint(e) *m/f* saint
Saint-Sylvestre *f* New Year's Eve
saisir to seize
saison *f* season
basse saison low season
de saison in season
haute saison high season
saisonnier seasonal
salade *f* lettuce; salad
salade de fruits fruit salad
salaire *m* salary; wage
sale dirty
salé(e) salty; savoury
salle *f* lounge *(airport)*; hall; ward *(hospital)*
salle à manger dining room
salle d'attente waiting room
salle de bains bathroom
salon *m* sitting room; lounge
salon de beauté beauty salon
salut! hi!
samedi *m* Saturday
SAMU *m* emergency services
sandales *fpl* sandals
sandwich *m* sandwich
sang *m* blood
sanglier *m* wild boar
sans without
sans alcool alcohol-free
sans connaissance unconscious

*sans fil* wireless
*sans issue* no through road
*sans OGM* GM-free
**santé** *f* health
*santé!* cheers!
*en bonne santé* well *(healthy)*
**sapeurs-pompiers** *mpl* fire brigade
**SARL** *f* Ltd; plc
**sauce** *f* sauce
**sauf** except (for)
**saumon** *m* salmon
**sauter** to jump
**sauvegarder** to back up *(computer)*
**sauver** to rescue
**savoir** to know *(be aware of)*
*savoir faire quelque chose* to know
  how to do sth
**savon** *m* soap
**scène** *f* stage
**scie** *f* saw
**score** *m* score *(of match)*
**scotch** *m* whisky
**séance** *f* meeting; performance
**200** **seau** bucket
**sec (sèche)** dried *(fruit, beans)*
**sèche-cheveux** *m* hairdryer
**sèche-linge** *m* tumble dryer
**sécher** to dry
**seconde** *f* second *(in time)*
*en seconde* second class
**secouer** to shake
**secours** *m* help
**secrétaire** *m/f* secretary
**secrétariat** *m* office
**secteur** *m* sector; mains
**sécurité** *f* security; safety
**séjour** *m* stay; visit
**sel** *m* salt
**self** *m* self-service restaurant
**selle** *f* saddle
**semaine** *f* week
**sens** *m* meaning; direction
*sens interdit* no entry
*sens unique* one-way street
**sentier** *m* footpath
*sentier écologique* nature trail
**sentir** to feel

**septembre** September
**séparément** separately
**série** *f* series; set
**seringue** *f* syringe
**serré(e)** tight *(fitting)*
**serrer** to grip; to squeeze
*serrez à droite* keep to the right
**serrure** *f* lock
**serrurerie** *f* locksmith's
**serveur** *m* waiter
**serveuse** *f* waitress
*servez-vous* help yourself
**service** *m* service; service charge; favour
*service compris* service included
*service d'urgences* A & E
**serviette** *f* towel; briefcase
*serviette hygiénique* sanitary towel
**servir** to dish up; to serve
**seul(e)** alone; lonely
**seulement** only
**sexe** *m* sex
**shampooing** *m* shampoo
*shampooing antipelliculaire* anti-
  dandruff shampoo
**short** *m* shorts
**si** if; yes *(to negative question)*
**SIDA** *m* AIDS
**siècle** *m* century
**siège** *m* seat; head office
*siège pour bébés/enfants* car seat
  *(for children)*
**signaler** to report
**signer** to sign
**simple** simple; single; plain
**site** *m* site
*site internet* site (website)
*site web* website
**situé(e)** located
**ski** *m* ski; skiing
*ski de randonnée/fond* cross-country
  skiing
*ski hors-piste* off-piste skiing
*ski nautique* water-skiing
**slip** *m* underpants; panties
*slip (de bain)* trunks *(swimming)*
**SMS** *m* text message
**snack** *m* snack bar

**SNCB** *f* Belgian Railways
**SNCF** *f* French Railways
**société** *f* company; society
**sœur** *f* sister
**soie** *f* silk
**soif** *f* thirst
*avoir soif* to be thirsty
**soin** *m* care
*soins du visage* facial
**soir** *m* evening
**soirée** *f* evening; party
**soja** *m* soya; soya bean
**sol** *m* ground; soil
**soldat** *m* soldier
**solde** *m* balance (remainder owed)
**soldes** *mpl* sales
**soldes permanents** sale prices all year round
**sole** *f* sole (fish)
**soleil** *m* sun; sunshine
**somme** *f* sum
**sommelier** *m* wine waiter
**sommet** *m* top (of hill, mountain)
**somnifère** *m* sleeping pill
**sonner** to ring; to strike
**sonnette** *f* doorbell
**sonner** to ring bell
**sorbet** *m* water ice
**sorte** *f* kind (sort, type)
**sortie** *f* exit
*sortie de secours* emergency exit
*sortie interdite* no exit
**sortir** to go out (leave)
**soucoupe** *f* saucer
**soudain** suddenly
**souhaiter** to wish
**soûl(e)** drunk
**soulever** to lift
**soupape** *f* valve
**soupe** *f* soup
**souper** *m* supper
**sourcils** *mpl* eyebrows
**sourd(e)** deaf
**sourire** to smile
**souris** *f* mouse (also for computer)
**sous** underneath; under
**sous-sol** *m* basement

**sous-titres** *mpl* subtitles
**sous-vêtements** *mpl* underwear
**souterrain(e)** underground
**soutien-gorge** *m* bra
**souvenir** *m* memory; souvenir
**souvent** often
**spam** spam (email)
**sparadrap** *m* sticking plaster
**spécial(e)** special
**spécialité** *f* speciality
**spectacle** *m* show (in theatre); entertainment
**spectateurs** *mpl* audience
**spiritueux** *mpl* spirits
**sport** *m* sport
*sports nautiques* water sports
**sportif(-ive)** sports; athletic
**stade** *m* stadium
**stage** *m* course (period of training)
**standard** *m* switchboard
**station** *f* station (metro); resort
*station balnéaire* seaside resort
*station de taxis* taxi rank
*station thermale* spa
**station-service** service station
**stationnement** *m* parking
**stérilet** *m* coil (IUD)
**stimulateur (cardiaque)** *m* pacemaker
**store** *m* blind; awning
**stylo** *m* pen
**sucette** *f* lollipop; dummy
**sucre** *m* sugar
**sucré(e)** sweet
**sud** *m* south
**suisse** Swiss
**Suisse** *f* Switzerland
**suite** *f* series; continuation; sequel
**suivant(e)** following
**suivre** to follow
*faire suivre* please forward
**super** *m* four-star petrol
**supermarché** *m* supermarket
**supplément** *m* extra charge
**supplémentaire** extra
**sur** on; onto; on top of; upon
*sur place* on the spot
**sûr** safe; sure

**surcharger** to overload
**surchauffer** to overheat
**surf** *m* surfing
*faire du surf* to surf
*snowboard m* snowboard
**surgelés** *mpl* frozen foods
**surveillé(e)** supervised
**survêtement** *m* tracksuit
**suspension** *f* suspension *(of car)*
**sympa(thique)** nice; pleasant
**synagogue** *f* synagogue
**syndicat d'initiative** *m* tourist office
**système de navigation satellite**
  satnav *(satellite navigation system, for car)*

# T

**tabac** *m* tobacco; tobacconist's
**table** *f* table
**tableau** *m* painting; picture; board
*tableau de bord* dashboard
**tablier** *m* apron
**tache** *f* stain
**taie d'oreiller** *f* pillowcase
**taille** *f* size *(of clothes)*; waist
*grande taille* outsize (clothes)
*taille unique* one size
**tailleur** *m* tailor; suit *(women's)*
**talc** *m* talc
**talon** *m* heel; stub *(counterfoil)*
*talon minute* shoes reheeled while you wait
**tampon** *m* tampon
*tampon Jex*® scouring pad
**tante** *f* aunt
**taper** to strike; to type
**tapis** *m* carpet
*tapis de sol* groundsheet
**tard** late
*au plus tard* at the latest
**tarif** *m* price-list; rate; tarif
**tarte** *f* flan; tart
**tartine** *f* slice of bread and butter (or jam)
**tartiner:** *à tartiner* for spreading
**tasse** *f* cup; mug
**taureau** *m* bull
**tauromachie** *f* bull-fighting
**taux** *m* rate
*taux de change* exchange rate

*taux fixe* flat rate
**taxe** *f* duty; tax *(on goods)*
**taxi** *m* cab *(taxi)*
**TCF** *m* Touring Club de France *(AA)*
**teinture** *f* dye
**teinturerie** *f* dry cleaner's
**télé** *f* TV
**télébenne** *f* gondola lift
**télécabine** *f* gondola lift
**télécarte** *f* phonecard
**télécommande** *f* remote control
**téléphérique** *m* cable-car
**téléphone** *m* telephone
*téléphone portable* mobile phone
*téléphone portable-appareil photo*
  camera phone
*téléphone sans fil* cordless phone
**téléphoner (à)** to phone
**téléphoniste** *m/f* operator
**télésiège** *m* chair-lift
**téléviseur** *m* television (set)
**télévision** *f* television
**température** *f* temperature
**tempête** *f* storm
**temple** *m* temple; synagogue;
  protestant church
**temps** *m* weather; time
**tendon** *m* tendon
**tenir** to hold; to keep
**tennis** *m* tennis
**tension** *f* voltage; blood pressure
**tente** *f* tent
**tenue** *f* clothes; dress
*tenue de soirée* evening dress
**terrain** *m* ground; land; pitch; course
**terrasse** *f* terrace
**terre** *f* land; earth; ground
*terre cuite* terracotta
**tête** *f* head
**tétine** *f* dummy *(for baby)*; teat *(for bottle)*
**TGV** *m* high-speed train
**thé** *m* tea
*thé au lait* tea with milk
*thé nature* tea without milk
**théâtre** *m* theatre
**théière** *f* teapot
**thermomètre** *m* thermometer

**ticket** *m* ticket *(bus, cinema, museum)*
**ticket de caisse** receipt
**tiède** lukewarm
**tiers** *m* third; third party
**timbre** *m* stamp
**tirage** *m* printing; print *(photo)*
**tirage le mercredi** lottery draw on Wednesdays
**tire-bouchon** *m* corkscrew
**tire-fesses** *m* ski tow
**tirer** to pull
**tirez** pull
**tiroir** *m* drawer
**tisane** *f* herbal tea
**tissu** *m* material; fabric
**titre** *m* title
*à titre indicatif* for info only
*à titre provisoire* provisionally
**titulaire** *m/f* holder of *(card, etc)*
**toile** *f* canvas; web *(spider)*
*Toile* World Wide Web
**toilettes** *fpl* toilet; powder room
**toit** *m* roof
**toit ouvrant** sunroof
**tomate** *f* tomato
**tomber** to fall
**tonalité** *f* dialling tone
**tongs** *fpl* flip flops
**tonneau** *m* barrel *(wine/beer)*
**tonnerre** *m* thunder
**torchon** *m* tea towel
**tordre** to twist
**tôt** early
**total** *m* total *(amount)*
**toucher** to touch
**toujours** always; still; forever
**tour** *f* tower
**tour** *m* trip; walk; ride
**tourisme** *m* sightseeing
**touriste** *m/f* tourist
**touristique** tourist *(route, resort, etc)*
**tourner** to turn
**tournesol** *m* sunflower
**tournevis** *m* screwdriver
*tournevis cruciforme* phillips screwdriver
**tourte** *f* pie
**tous** all *pl*

*tous les jours* daily *(each day)*
**Toussaint** *f* All Saints' Day
**tousser** to cough
**tout(e)** all; everything
*tout à l'heure* in a while
*tout compris* all inclusive
*tout de suite* straight away
*tout droit* straight ahead
**tout le monde** everyone
**toutes** all *pl*
*toutes directions* all routes
**toux** *f* cough
**tradition** *f* custom *(tradition)*
**traditionnel(-elle)** traditional
**traduction** *f* translation
**traduire** to translate
**train** *m* train
**trajet** *m* journey
**tramway** *m* tram
**tranchant** sharp *(razor, knife)*
**tranche** *f* slice
**tranquille** quiet *(place)*
**transférer** to transfer
**transpirer** to sweat
**travail** *m* work
**travailler** to work *(person)*
*travailler à son compte* to be self employed
**travaux** *mpl* road works; alterations
**travers: à travers** through
**traversée** *f* crossing *(voyage)*
**traverser** to cross *(road, sea, etc)*
**tremplin** *m* diving-board
*tremplin de ski* ski jump
**très** very; much
**triangle de présignalisation** *m* warning triangle
**tricot** *m* knitting; sweater
**tricoter** to knit
**trimestre** *m* term
**trisomie** Down's syndrome
*il/elle est trisomique* he/she has Down's syndrome
**triste** sad
**trop** too; too much
**trottoir** *m* pavement; sidewalk
**trou** *m* hole

trousse *f* pencil case
*trousse de premiers secours* first aid kit
trouver to find
*se trouver* to be (situated)
tuer kill
tunnel *m* tunnel
tuyau *m* pipe *(for water, gas)*
*tuyau d'arrosage* hosepipe
TVA *f* VAT
typique typical

## U

UE *f* EU
ulcère *m* ulcer
ultérieur(e) later *(date, etc)*
un(e) one; a; an
*l'un ou l'autre* either one
uni(e) plain *(not patterned)*
Union européenne *f* European Union
unité *fpl* credit *(on mobile phone)*
université *f* university
urgence *f* urgency; emergency
*Urgences* A & E

urgentiste *m/f* paramedic
urine *f* urine
usage *m* use
usine *f* factory
utile useful
utiliser to use

## V

vacances *fpl* holiday(s)
*en vacances* on holiday
*grandes vacances* summer holiday
vaccin *m* vaccination
vache *f* cow
vagin *m* vagina
vague *f* wave *(on sea)*
vaisselle *f* crockery
valable valid *(ticket, licence, etc)*
valeur *f* value
valider to validate
valise *f* suitcase
vallée *f* valley
valoir to be worth
*ça vaut...* it's worth...
vanille *f* vanilla

vapeur *f* steam
varicelle *f* chickenpox
varié(e) varied; various
vase *m* vase
veau *m* calf; veal
vedette *f* speedboat; star *(film)*
végétal(e) vegetable
végétarien(ne) vegetarian
véhicule *m* vehicle
*véhicules lents* slow-moving vehicles
veille *f* the day before; eve
*veille de Noël* Christmas Eve
veine *f* vein
vélo *m* bike
*vélo tout terrain (VTT)* mountain bike;
  mountain biking (activity)
velours *m* velvet
venaison *f* venison
vendange(s) *fpl* harvest *(of grapes)*
vendeur(-euse) *m/f* sales assistant
vendre to sell
*à vendre* for sale
vendredi *m* Friday
*vendredi saint* Good Friday
vénéneux poisonous
venir to come
vent *m* wind
vente *f* sale
*vente aux enchères* auction
ventilateur *m* ventilator; fan
verglas *m* black ice
vérifier to check; to audit
vernis *m* varnish
*vernis à ongles* nail varnish
verre *m* glass
*verres de contact* contact lenses
verrouillage central *m* central locking
vers toward(s); about
versement *m* payment; instalment
verser to pour; to pay
vert(e) green
veste *f* jacket
vestiaire *m* cloakroom
vêtements *mpl* clothes
vétérinaire *m/f* vet
veuf *m* widower
veuillez... please...

**veuve** *f* widow
**via** by *(via)*
**viande** *f* meat
*viande hachée* mince *(meat)*
**vidange** *f* oil change (car)
**vide** empty
**videoclub** *m* video shop
**vie** *f* life
**vieux (vieille)** old
**vierge** blank *(disk, tape)*
**vigile** *m* security guard
**vigne** *f* vine; vineyard
**vignoble** *m* vineyard
**VIH** *m* HIV
**village** *m* village
**ville** *f* town; city
**vin** *m* wine
*vin en pichet* house wine
*vin pétillant* sparkling wine
**vinaigre** *m* vinegar
**violer** to rape
**violet(-ette)** purple
**vipère** *f* adder; viper
**virage** *m* bend; curve; corner
**vis** *f* screw
*vis platinées* points *(in car)*
**visage** *m* face
**visite** *f* visit; consultation *(of doctor)*
*visite guidée* guided tour
**visiter** to visit *(a place)*
**visiteur(-euse)** *m/f* visitor
**visser** to screw on
**vite** quickly; fast
**vitesse** *f* gear *(of car)*; speed
*vitesse limitée à...* speed limit...
**vitrail** *m* stained-glass window
**vitrine** *f* shop window
**vivre** to live
**VO: en VO** with subtitles *(film)*
**vœu** *m* wish
**voici** here is/are
**voie** *f* lane (of road); line; track
**voilà** there is/are
**voile** *f* sail; sailing
**voilier** *m* sailing boat
**voir** to see
**voisin(e)** *m/f* neighbour

**voiture** *f* car; coach (of train)
**vol** *m* flight; theft
*vol intérieur* domestic flight
**volaille** *f* poultry
**volant** *m* steering wheel
**voler** to fly *(bird)*; to steal
**volet** *m* shutter *(on window)*
**voleur(-euse)** *m/f* thief
**volonté** *f* will
*à volonté* as much as you like
**volts** *mpl* volts
**vomir** to vomit
**v.o.s.t.** original version with subtitles *(film)*
**vouloir** to want
**voyage** *m* journey
*voyage d'affaires* business trip
*voyage organisé* package holiday
**voyager** to travel
**voyageur(-euse)** *m/f* traveller
**vrai(e)** real; true
**VTT** *m* mountain bike
**vue** *f* view; sight

# W

**WC** *mpl* toilet
**wagon** *m* carriage; waggon
**wagon-couchettes** *m* sleeping car
**wagon-restaurant** *m* dining car
**web** *m* internet
**wifi** *m* wi-fi

# X

**xérès** *m* sherry

# Y

**yacht** *m* yacht
**yaourt** *m* yoghurt
*yaourt nature* plain yoghurt
**yeux** *mpl* eyes
**youyou** *m* dinghy

# Z

**zéro** *m* zero
**zona** *m* shingles *(illness)*
**zone** *f* zone
*zone piétonne* pedestrian area
**zoo** *m* zoo